GENDERED INNOVATIONS
IN SCIENCE
AND ENGINEERING

GENDERED INNOVATIONS IN SCIENCE AND ENGINEERING

Edited by Londa Schiebinger

Stanford University Press
Stanford, California

Stanford University Press
Stanford, California

Printed in the United States of America on acid-free, archival-quality paper

Library of Congress Cataloging-in-Publication Data

Gendered innovations in science and engineering / edited by Londa Schiebinger.
    p. cm.
  Includes bibliographical references and index.
  ISBN 978-0-8047-5814-7 (cloth : alk. paper) — ISBN 978-0-8047-5815-4 (pbk. : alk. paper)
  1. Women in science. 2. Women in engineering. 3. Sex discrimination in science. I. Schiebinger, Londa L.
Q130.G467 2008
305.43'5—dc22

                              2007029375

Typeset by Bruce Lundquist in 10/14 Minion

Assistance for the publication was provided by the Clayman Institute of Stanford University.

Contents

Preface

THE PROMINENT SCHOLARS featured in this volume explore gendered innovations in science and engineering; that is to say, they document how gender analysis, when turned to science and engineering, can profoundly enhance human knowledge. This is where the action is today. This volume provides, where possible, concrete examples of how taking gender into account has yielded new research results and sparked creativity by opening new questions for future research. Several government granting agencies, such as the National Institutes of Health and the European Commission, now require that requests for funding address whether, and in what sense, sex and gender are relevant to the objectives and methodologies of the research proposed. Few research scientists or engineers, however, know how to do gender analysis. The purpose of this book is to shed light on the how and why.

This volume emerged from an international workshop held at Stanford University's Michelle R. Clayman Institute for Gender Research in 2005. We are grateful to the National Science Foundation (SES-0114706) and the Gabilan Provost's Discretionary Fund, Stanford University, for funding for this project. Thanks, too, to Shannon Gilmartin, Michelle Cale, Jane Gruba-Chevalier, Andrea Henderson, Haley Minick, and Jeanette Jenkins, who supported the workshop and volume.

Contributors

HEIDI BALLARD is currently Assistant Professor of Environmental Science Education at University of California, Davis. Her work focuses on integrating local ecological knowledge with conventional science, participatory research approaches, and ecological monitoring in the context of community-based natural resource management.

MARGARET W. CONKEY is the Class of 1960 Professor of Anthropology at the University of California, Berkeley, and director of the Archaeological Research Facility. She has served as president of the Association for Feminist Anthropology and of the Archaeology Division of the American Anthropological Association. She has been active in feminist archaeology for more than twenty years. Her publications include, with Janet Spector, "Archaeology and the Study of Gender" (1984), with Joan Gero, *Engendering Archaeology: Women and Prehistory* (1991), and, most recently, "Dwelling at the Margins, Action at the Intersection? Feminist and Indigenous Archaeologies," *Ärchaeologies, Journal of the World Archaeological Congress* (2005).

FRANCE A. CÓRDOVA is president, and professor of physics, at Purdue University. She served as chancellor and distinguished professor of physics and astronomy at the University of California, Riverside, between 2002 and 2007. She has published more than 150 scientific papers. She was formerly the Chief Scientist of NASA and is the winner of NASA's highest honor, the Distinguished Service Medal. In 2000, she was recognized as a Kilby Laureate, for contributions to society through science, technology, innovation, invention, and education. Córdova has a BA in English from Stanford University, a PhD in physics from the California Institute of Technology, and an honorary doctorate from Loyola Marymount University.

LOUISE FORTMANN is a professor of natural resource sociology and the Rudy Grah Chair in Forestry and Sustainable Development in the Department of Environmental Science, Policy and Management at the University of California, Berkeley. She has published widely on tree tenure, gender, rural poverty, and community management of natural resources in east and southern Africa and northern California. Her most recent work is on the democratization of science. She cannot milk a cow.

LORI D. HAGER is a bioarchaeologist currently involved in the long-term excavation and analysis of human skeletons at the Neolithic site of Çatalhöyük, Turkey. She also studies burial practices in Native California and Guatemala. Her dissertation considered the evolution of sex differences in the human pelvis, and later she edited *Women in Human Evolution*. She is an associate at the Archaeological Research Facility, University of California, Berkeley, and teaches at Foothill College in Los Altos Hills, California.

MEI-PO KWAN is Distinguished Professor of Social and Behavioral Sciences and Dr. Martha L. Corry Faculty Fellow at the Ohio State University. She is an editor of the *Annals of the Association of American Geographers* and on the editorial board of the *Professional Geographer*. Kwan has made ground-breaking contributions to feminist perspectives on geospatial technologies. Her best known publications include "Feminist Visualization: Re-envisioning GIS as a Method in Feminist Geographic Research" (*Annals of the Association of American Geographers*, 2002) and "Affecting Geospatial Technologies: Toward a Feminist Politics of Emotion" (*The Professional Geographer*, 2007).

DANIELLE LAVAQUE-MANTY is a former program manager for the University of Michigan's ADVANCE project. She has a PhD in political science from the University of Michigan and an MFA in creative writing from the Ohio State University.

SARAH S. RICHARDSON is a doctoral candidate in the Program in Modern Thought and Literature at Stanford University, working in the fields of history and philosophy of biology, gender studies, and social studies of scientific knowledge. Her dissertation, "Gendering the Genome," analyzes gender in the models and metaphors of human sex chromosome genetics. Richardson co-edited the forthcoming volume *Revisiting Race in a Genomic Age.*

SUE V. ROSSER received her PhD in zoology from the University of Wisconsin–Madison in 1973. Since July 1999, she has served as dean of Ivan Allen College, the liberal arts college at Georgia Institute of Technology, where she is also professor of history, technology, and society and holds the Ivan Allen Dean's Chair in Liberal Arts and Technology. She has edited collections and written approximately 120 journal articles on the theoretical and applied problems of women and science and women's health. Author of ten books, her latest single-authored book is *The Science Glass Ceiling: Academic Women Scientists and their Struggle to Succeed* (2004) from Routledge. She served as co-PI on a $3.7 million ADVANCE grant from NSF from 2001 to 2006 and currently serves as PI on a $900,000 NSF grant to integrate gender into the statics course in engineering.

LONDA SCHIEBINGER is the John L. Hinds Professor of History of Science and the Barbara D. Finberg Director of the Michelle R. Clayman Institute for Gender Research at Stanford University. She an international expert on gender and science. Her books include *The Mind Has No Sex? Women in the Origins of Modern Science, Nature's Body: Gender in the Making of Science, Has Feminism Changed Science?* and, most recently, the prize-winning *Plants and Empire: Colonial Bioprospecting in the Atlantic World.* Schiebinger is the recipient of numerous prizes and awards, including the prestigious Alexander von Humboldt Research Prize.

LOUISE SPERLING is a senior scientist at the International Center for Tropical Agriculture. She has worked in the field of participatory plant breeding and seed system issues for twenty years, particularly in east, central, and southern Africa, and has facilitated a global network of participatory plant breeding practitioners, via the Consultative Group on International Agricultural Research Systemwide Programme on Participatory Research and Gender Analysis. Her work has been conducted in close collaboration with national agricultural research organizations, nongovernmental organizations, and the Pan-African Bean Research Alliance.

ABIGAIL J. STEWART is Sandra Schwartz Tangri Professor of Psychology and Women's Studies, and director of the ADVANCE program at the University of Michigan. Her current research examines educated women's lives and personalities; race, gender, and generation among graduates of a midwest high school; and gender, science, and technology among middle-school-age girls, undergraduate students, and faculty.

TATIANA BUTOVITSCH TEMM was formerly Corporate Communications Manager at the Volvo Car Corporation in Gothenburg, Sweden. She is the founder of Swedish-based Temm Communications. Temm has a degree in journalism from the Gothenburg University and has been working in the media sector ever since. She was responsible for developing and carrying out the communications around the concept car made by an all-women team. Today her work focuses on PR and brand development for gender-smart companies, spreading the knowledge from the Volvo Your Concept Car project to other industries.

CHARIS THOMPSON is Associate Professor of Rhetoric and Gender and Women's Studies, and director of the Science, Technology, and Society Center, University of California, Berkeley. She is author of *Making Parents: The Ontological Choreography of Reproductive Technologies* (2005) and *Charismatic Megafauna and Miracle Babies: Essays in Selective Pronatalism* (forthcoming) and is the winner of the 2007 Rachel Carson Book Prize. She serves on and participates in a number of stem cell–related committees and activities and is at work on a book entitled *Stem Cell Nations.*

C. MEGAN URRY is the Israel Munson Professor of Physics and Astronomy at Yale, Director of the Yale Center for Astronomy and Astrophysics, and Chair of the Physics Department at Yale. Her scientific research focuses on supermassive black holes in galaxies, and she has published over 145 refereed articles in scientific journals. A graduate of Tufts University and the Johns Hopkins University, Urry has worked to increase the number of women in science, most recently editing a newsletter on women in science (http://www.aas.org/cswa/STATUS.html).

1 Introduction:

Getting More Women into Science and Engineering—
Knowledge Issues

Londa Schiebinger

INNOVATIONS SURROUNDING WOMEN and gender have rocked science and technology in the past three decades. Who, for example, could have predicted that the chief scientist at NASA would be a woman (France A. Córdova, now president of Purdue University, and an author in this volume)? Or who would have thought that geneticists would dethrone the "master gene" model—that conceptualized mammalian sex as determined by a single master gene on the Y chromosome—and put in its place an account that emphasizes interactions between the testis and ovary factors (see Richardson this volume)? Or who would have imagined that an artificial knee would be designed with nineteen unique aspects to meet the distinctive skeletal and load-bearing needs of females?

In my lifetime, the situation for intellectual women in the United States has improved dramatically. We can measure these changes partially through images. Anyone growing up in American consumer culture understands the power of images. Images project messages about hopes and dreams, mien and demeanor, about who should be a scientist and what science is all about. We have seen some interesting changes in who is imagined to be a scientist in our society. Historically, when prompted to "draw a scientist," 98 percent of the students drew males (Kahle 1987, see Figure 1.1). By the 1990s, that had declined to 70 percent with some 16 percent of the scientists drawn being

Parts of this chapter appeared in the *Harvard Journal of Law and Gender*.

clearly female and another 14 percent ambiguous with respect to sex (Figure 1.2). In the 1990s, a remarkable 96 percent of the scientists continued to be depicted as Caucasian despite the prominence of Asians in science (Rahm and Charbonneau 1997).

We can also see gendered innovations in the content of science, in this case, in understandings of human evolution. Most of us grew up with an image of human evolution as the "evolution of man" (Figure 1.3). Evolutionary theory presented males as actively and aggressively driving forward human evolution. As Charles Darwin stated, only something he called the "equal transmission of characters" allowed traits selected for in males to be transmitted to females (Hrdy 1999).

In 1993, a much-heralded new image was produced to correct this picture. In that year the American Museum of Natural History in New York opened

FIGURE 1.1 Results of "Draw-a-Scientist" Test. Most school-aged children draw a male. Source: Jane Butler Kahle in *Gender Issues in Science Education* (Curtin University of Technology, 1987).

FIGURE 1.2 A woman naturalist working outdoors with glasses but without a lab coat. Source: Rahm and Charbonneau, *American Journal of Physics* (August 1997, 65(8), pp. 774–778), "Woman scientist," on p. 776 (Fig.1 (E)).

FIGURE 1.3 The evolution of man.

its new "Human Biology and Evolution" exhibit featuring this reconstruction of early humans from the 3.5 million-year-old footprints preserved in volcanic ash near Laetoli (Figure 1.4). This diorama clearly gives woman a place in human evolution, and although the assumptions captured in this image have changed dramatically since the 1960s, the process is still incomplete. The humans embodying the footprints are portrayed as a robust male towering over his smaller female consort, his arm positioned to protect and reassure her. We simply do not know, however, the sex or relationship of the two individuals who made these impressions—footprints cannot be sexed. These early humans might have been a large male and his much smaller mate, but

FIGURE 1.4 Reconstruction of the early humans presumed to have made the Laetoli footprints, as shown at the American Museum of Natural History in New York—fact or fantasy? Source: Image # 2A19270 © American Museum of Natural History.

they might also have been a parent comforting his or her adolescent offspring, or just two friends fleeing the volcano together.

The purpose of this volume is to analyze changes of this sort—gendered innovations—in science and engineering. By gendered innovations I mean transformations in the personnel, cultures, and content of science and engineering brought about by efforts to remove gender bias from these fields. As documented in this volume, understanding and removing gender bias has brought new insights to specific sciences and fields of engineering. I want to emphasize from the beginning that gender analysis is not attached to the X or Y chromosome—that, if properly trained, most researchers successfully master its theory and practice. Gender analysis, when applied rigorously and creatively, has the potential to enhance human knowledge and technical systems by opening them to new perspectives, new questions, and new missions.

To understand better how this works, I set out three distinct levels of analysis (see also Schiebinger 1999 and 2003):

1. Fix the Number of Women: Participation of *Women* in Science and Engineering. The first level focuses on increasing the participation of women in science and engineering. This level of analysis treats the history and sociology of women's engagement in scientific institutions. Who are the great women scientists? What are their achievements? What is the experience of women in university, industrial, and governmental laboratories? Programs aimed at increasing the number of women in science and engineering (rightly or wrongly) attempt to "fix the women"—that is, to make them more competitive—by increasing funding to women's research, teaching them how to negotiate for salary, or, more generally, how to succeed in a man's world.

2. Fix the Institutions: Gender in the *Cultures* of Science and Engineering. A culture is more than institutions, legal regulations, or a series of degrees or certifications. It consists in the unspoken assumptions and values of its members. Despite claims to objectivity and value neutrality, the sciences have identifiable cultures whose customs and folkways have developed over time. Many of these customs developed historically in the absence of women and, as I have argued elsewhere, also in opposition to their participation (Schiebinger 1989). How have the cultures of science and engineering, where success requires at least some mastery of the rituals of day-to-day conformity, codes governing language, styles of interactions, modes of dress, hierarchies of values and practices, been formed by their predominantly male practitioners? Programs that attempt to increase women's participation taking this approach work to "fix the institutions." The National Science Foundation's (NSF) current ADVANCE grants, for example, attempt to transform university cultures. These efforts range from understanding subtle gender biases in hiring practices, for example, to restructuring the academic work/life balance by offering parental leave, stopping the tenure clock, and the like.

3. Fix the Knowledge: Gender in the *Results* of Science and Engineering. Scholars have emphasized the consequences of exclusion for women, but what have been the consequences of this exclusion for human knowledge more generally? At this third level, authors focus on "fixing the knowledge." A number of chapters in this volume explore how gender analysis, when turned to science and engineering, profoundly enhances human knowledge. This is a vital issue to address today, and here we provide examples of how gender analysis has sparked creativity by opening new questions for future research. This work is crucial to our efforts to recruit and retain women. Importantly, programs, such as those at the National Institutes of Health (NIH—see below) have linked the project of increasing the number of women in the medical profession to that of reconceptualizing medical research.

WHILE IT IS USEFUL to distinguish issues at three analytical levels, these perspectives are obviously closely tied to one another. Emerging evidence reveals that women will *not* become equal participants in science and engineering until we have fully investigated and solved the knowledge problem. Disciplines are somewhat arbitrary ways of cutting knowledge. We need to be open to the possibility that human knowledge—what we know, what we value, what we consider important—may change dramatically as women become full partners. Science is about critical thinking, exploration, and travel into unknown worlds. We have much to gain by embarking on this voyage.

To set the stage for what follows, let me place the chapters within the analytics I distinguish.

Participation of Women in Science and Engineering

Many people believe in progress. They believe that things are gradually getting better for women. How many times have I been patted on the head and told, "Just wait, dear, and women will move to the top." One point I want to make is that progress for women is not a fact of nature but the result of careful interventions on the part of individuals, institutions, and governmental agencies.

Let me offer just three quick examples of how we cannot just sit back and wait for things to right themselves. Opportunities for women result from larger social and economic restructurings in a society in addition to changes in university cultures. As is widely known, women were excluded from modern universities from their founding in the twelfth century until the end of the nineteenth century. In this sense, women are real newcomers to university research labs. Women embarked on modern careers in science after the women's movements of the 1870s and 1880s propelled them into universities. As women gradually gained admittance to graduate schools—by the twentieth century a prerequisite for serious work in science—they began flooding into PhD programs in all fields. By the 1920s their numbers were at a historic high in the United States, with women earning 14 percent of doctorates in the physical and biological sciences. Between 1930 and 1960, however, the proportion of women PhDs plunged as a result of the rise of fascism in Europe, the Cold War, and McCarthyism in the United States. Shockingly, women did not regain their 1920s levels of participation in academic science until the 1970s (Rossiter 1982; Zuckerman et al. 1991).

A second example shows even more clearly how social structures influence women's opportunities in science and engineering. In the seventeenth century in Germany, 14 percent of all astronomers were women. Today the percentage of women astronomers in Germany is around 5 percent (counting all lecturers and professors at German universities). How was this possible? The very different economic and social structure of life in early modern Germany gave women an opportunity to participate in ways not available to them today. As I have argued elsewhere, astronomy in this period was organized along guild lines. Guilds were social and economic organizations through which most goods were produced and services provided. Guild production took place in the household. In astronomical families, the labor of husband and wife did not divide along modern lines: he was not fully professional, working in an observatory outside the home; she was not fully a housewife, confined to hearth and home. Nor were they independent professionals, each holding a chair of astronomy. Instead, they worked as a team and on common problems. Many took turns observing so that their observations, often made in their own attics, followed night after night without interruption. At other times they observed together, dividing the work so that they could make observations that a single person could not make accurately. Guild traditions within science allowed women, such as Maria Margaretha Winkelmann, to strengthen the empirical base of science (Schiebinger 1989).

A final example from the Massachusetts Institute of Technology (MIT) reveals that traditional departmental hiring processes do not always identify exceptional female candidates. MIT was successful at increasing its women faculty when its president and provost collaborated with department heads and women faculty committees to implement novel hiring procedures. These successes in both the Schools of Science and Engineering were pushed forward as a response to the disastrous 1996 reports on women faculty at MIT. Forward-looking deans, Robert Birgeneau in Science and Thomas Magnanti in Engineering, were able to help hiring committees find qualified women when encouraged to. These women hired in the School of Science achieved tenure at the same rate as their male colleagues and a slightly higher level of professional success than the men as measured by election to the prestigious National Academy of Sciences and the like (Hopkins 2006).

I am not arguing that we adopt any particular social order or university policy. My point is that the overall organization of society—the way we organize households, child care, economic production, roads, social services, universities, schools, and governments—all have an impact on women's opportunities in science. Foundational questioning and reorganization of society and science will be required to make women truly equal. Studies show that professional women currently do more domestic labor than professional men. At the same time these women are expected to compete on an equal footing with men (some of whom have stay-at-home partners) for jobs and salaries (Williams 2000). We need to end the social welfare state in the home for men (especially those with professional partners). Men need to assume their fair share of the pleasures and pains of organizing and caring for domestic spaces.

Since the Sputnik years, the United States and Western European countries have attempted to increase the participation of their populations in science—women as well as men. In the United States, this led to foundational legislation, including the Equal Pay Act of 1963, Equal Employment Opportunity Act, and Title IX of 1972, designed to foster equality for women. In her chapter in this volume, Sue Rosser documents how the NSF, beginning in the 1980s, has attempted to improve the numbers of women in science and engineering by jump-starting their careers with extra research monies and the like. In a later chapter, France Córdova summarizes similar efforts undertaken by the National Academies (the National Academy of Sciences, National Academy of Engineering, and the Institute of Medicine). Founded in 1991, the Academies' Committee on Women in Science and Engineering (CWSE) has worked with Congress and universities to develop policy aimed at assisting women's careers. (I should note that I attempted to include a chapter on innovations in Europe in this volume but European Union lawyers would not approve its publication.)

These initiatives—both on the part of the government and universities—have focused narrowly on getting more women in the door. As important as these measures are, they alone are not enough. In recent years, the NSF, CWSE, and numerous universities have moved to the second level in my stepped analysis and begun working toward understanding and helping to correct the underlying causes of inequality.

Gender in the Cultures of Science and Engineering

There have been two fundamental approaches in efforts nationwide to gain equality for women in the academy: liberal feminism and difference feminism. Oddly enough, many people in the United States and elsewhere practice feminist virtues, while at the same time shying away from calling themselves "feminists." I would venture to say that the vast majority of Americans are feminists, at least liberal feminists—that is to say that they support equality and professional opportunities for women—though most would not call themselves feminists. It is important to recognize that what is "feminist" in one time and place becomes business as usual in another. It is a curious phenomenon that when feminist practices or points of view become widely accepted in science and engineering, or in the culture more generally, they are no longer seen as "feminist," but as "just" or simply "true." The result is that the term *feminist* continues to refer to people and policies on the radical cutting edge. In her chapter on genetic models of sex determination, Sarah Richardson presents a classic example of how feminism disappears when its principles are mainstreamed into science. The fact that researchers may be unaware of the sources of new insights does not make those sources any less real—but it does serve to keep feminism on the sidelines.

Authors in this volume will use the term *feminist* to refer to efforts to bring about institutional and social change leading to greater equality for women because one needs to discuss this process and this is the appropriate English term for it. One thing to emphasize is that there are many feminisms. Sue Rosser (2005) has distinguished at least ten different feminist approaches to science and technology. Here I want to emphasize only two fundamental feminist perspectives: liberal and difference feminism. Although these two approaches differ, they are not mutually exclusive, nor does the one supersede the other. In some instances liberal feminism is the best approach—it is certainly the best understood in the United States. At other times the insights offered by what I call *difference feminism* lead best to reform.

Liberal feminism has been the major form of feminism in the United States and much of Western Europe since the English feminist Mary Wollstonecraft's vigorous call for equality in her 1792 *Vindication of the Rights of Woman*.

Liberal feminism has supported well the participation of women in the professions. It has informed major legislation guaranteeing women's rights, as well as equal education, pay, and opportunity. It is the theory underlying government and university interventions seeking greater equality for women at level one in my analysis. Liberal feminism has made such inroads that most people think of these issues in terms of "fairness" rather than of "feminism" (Rosser and Córdova, this volume).

While liberal feminism has supported reforms for women in the professions, it has also led to problems. Liberals generally see women as the in-principle equals of men and strive to provide women the skills and opportunities to make it in a man's world; they attempt to "fix the women" by making them more competitive. In the attempt to extend the rights of "man" to women, liberals have tended to ignore *sexual* and *gender* differences, or to deny them altogether. Liberal feminists tend to see sameness and assimilation as the only grounds for equality, and this often requires that women be like men. Only women have babies, but birthing is supposed to take place exclusively on weekends and holidays, not to disrupt the rhythm of working life. Consequently, women have tended to hide pregnancy, or even to "schedule" babies. One biologist, for example, had labor induced on a three-day weekend so she could attend a student's thesis defense the following Monday. Within a liberal frame of mind, women feel that they must compete with men on men's terms.

In the early 1980s, feminists began developing what is broadly called "difference feminism," embracing three basic tenets. First and foremost, difference feminism diverged from liberalism in emphasizing difference, not sameness, between men and women. This strand of feminism argued secondly that in order for women to become equal in science or engineering, changes are needed not just in women but, more importantly, in the culture of classrooms, research labs, and science and engineering departments. The value of difference feminism has been to bring to light cultural differences between men and women and to show how these have worked against women in the professions, including the professions of science and engineering. Culture is about communities' unspoken rules. It is about unwritten codes governing behavior, language, styles of interactions, modes of dress, hierarchies of values, and practices.

Discrimination against women is no longer overt—it's not the 1960s when jobs for professors of chemistry, for example, could read "no women need apply." Discrimination against women now is more often invisible and subtle. Even though it is subtle, unconscious cultural biases can work against women. Most people these days would tell you that they are all for women becoming equal and taking positions of leadership. Yet many professors, deans, provosts, and presidents, while well-meaning, are also often unaware of how unconscious cultural biases work against women and their success in academic culture. These gender biases are not intentional—these are not planned discriminations against women—but they are nonetheless very real and make it more difficult for women than for men to succeed within universities and laboratories as they exist today (Valian 1998; Committee on Maximizing the Potential of Women in Academic Science and Engineering et al. 2006).

Let me enumerate several examples to illustrate this point. Women are often held to different standards than are men. Research has shown that women needed 2.5 more publications than men to be awarded postdoctoral fellowships by the Medical Research Council in Sweden (Wennerås and Wold 1997). In the United States, evaluators also tend to score men higher simply because they are men. In a now well-known experiment, a group of social psychologists gave the *very same* article to evaluators with a variety of fictitious names: John T. McKay (a man), Joan T. McKay (a woman), J. T. McKay (supposedly sex-neutral), and Chris T. McKay (ambiguous with regard to sex). The articles were identical in all ways except for the name of the supposed author. Evaluators—both men and women—rated the article attributed to John superior to the article attributed to Joan. They preferred the ambiguous "J. T." to Joan, but ranked John higher than J. T. Readers scored the article significantly lower when they thought "Chris" was a woman (Goldberg 1968; Paludi and Strayer 1985).

This preference for males carries over into hiring decisions. Another study showed that faculty members—again both men and women—are more likely to evaluate a dossier more positively when that dossier was attributed to a man rather than to a woman (Steinpreis et al. 1999). These practices are reinforced by letters of recommendation that differ significantly with respect to sex. Letters for male applicants tend to be longer and more substantial; they also more often portray men as researchers and professionals and women as students and teachers (Trix and Psenka 2003). Gender bias follows women up the ladder. In our culture women are expected to exude politeness in both speech and manner; they are expected to nod and smile to express attentiveness (Hochschild 1989). Professional women who cannot always engage in these behaviors may be viewed as hostile or unfriendly. Consequently women are often "damned if they do" and "damned if they don't" when entering the ranks of leaders (Eagly and Karau 2002).

In addition to fine-tuning academic culture, we need to fundamentally restructure aspects of it, which is a more complex proposition. Historically, universities—like professional life in general—have been organized around the assumption that professors are male heads of households. Now that women are professionals too nothing systematic has been done to reform the professions to allow for the reproduction of life. This has direct consequences for professional women who remain largely in charge of domestic labor and child care. Women who wish to succeed in science and engineering often remain single and childless. In the United States, tenured women scientists are twice as likely to be single as their male counterparts. In addition, many women simply drop out of science and engineering when they decide to marry or have a family. Many professional women who also take charge of domestic life *do* compete successfully with men who have stay-at-home wives—but at a price to themselves and often their health (Schiebinger 1999; Mason and Goulden 2002). Here is where the example I provided above from guild life becomes interesting. It indicates the level of social restructuring that will be required if the United States is serious about increasing the numbers of women in science and engineering. Hours will need to be shortened, quality child and elder care need to be available and affordable, along with flextime even for high-powered careers and reentry programs for people who have taken time off for personal reasons.

Another asymmetry in professional culture that affects women's careers more than men's is the growing phenomenon of the dual-career academic couple. It is an interesting fact that women more often than men are partnered with professionals. Among heterosexual couples in the United States (and we don't have equivalent studies of same-sex couples), women tend to practice "hypergamy," that is to say, they tend to marry men of higher (or at least not lower) status than their own. This is due partly to the fact that women's social status was determined historically through marriage, while men's was more often determined by inheritance or success in a profession. Consequently, professional women today are disproportionately partnered with professionals compared to men. To make matters worse, academics tend to couple within the same discipline. While only 7 percent of the members of the American Physical Society are women, for example, an astonishing 44 percent of them are married to other physicists. An additional 24 percent are married to some other type of scientist. A remarkable 70 percent of women mathematicians and 46 percent of women chemists are married to men in their own fields. Although universities have begun to reform hiring practices to accommodate some, usually outstanding, dual-career couples, being a partner in such a couple makes it difficult to follow the logic of a career and seize oppor-tunities as they arise (Blondin 1990; McNeil and Sher 1998; Wolf-Wendel et al. 2003; Clayman Institute 2006).

Solutions to the problems of gender asymmetries in the cultures of science and engineering are not simple. Cultural change cannot be legislated; aca-demic culture must be understood and altered through the same consensual process that gave it rise. In recent years, the NSF has launched its ADVANCE program recognizing that the "lack of women's participation at the senior level of academe is often a systemic consequence of academic culture" (as re-ported by Rosser, this volume). Since 2001 NSF has made five-year grants of up to $3.75 million each to nineteen leading universities across the country to study and transform their ways of doing business. Several of these universi-ties have been particularly successful and two are highlighted in this volume. Sue Rosser reports on initiatives at Georgia Tech to remove subtle gender and racial biases in promotion and tenure decisions. Danielle LaVaque-Manty and Abigail Stewart report on the University of Michigan's successful Strategies and Tactics for Recruiting to Improve Diversity and Excellence (STRIDE) program aimed at reforming hiring practices. Michigan increased its hires in the natural sciences and engineering from women averaging 14 percent of the hires pre-STRIDE to around 35 percent post-STRIDE. In this program distin-guished senior science and engineering faculty (five men and four women) were "taught" the specifics of gender bias in hiring practices. This STRIDE committee, whose members were compensated by the university for their time, then prepared a handbook that they used to teach members of hiring committees about evaluating bias and other barriers women face in academia. The brilliance of this program is that these senior faculty are all regular mem-bers of departments (they are not consultants who come, often create a back-lash, and then disappear). By virtue of the fact that these newly trained gender experts are permanent and respected members of science and engineering faculties, knowledge concerning subtle gender bias cascades through those departments. The academic climate of opinion changes gradually as these fac-ulty go about their day-to-day work at the university.

Other initiatives are also under way. In spring 2005, the Government Accounting Office issued a report prepared for Senators Ron Wyden and Bar-bara Boxer on how Title IX of the United States Education Amendments of 1972 can be harnessed to increase the number of women and minorities in sci-ence (U.S. Government Accountability Office 2004). In spring 2006, Stanford's

Clayman Institute for Gender Research held a meeting to strategize how universities might collaborate nationally to move forward programs in this area. Stanford's Clayman Institute has also launched a multiyear study of dual-career academic couples at leading United States research universities. The goal of this and other studies is to transform the way universities do business and grow academic cultures where women, too, can flourish.

Much is being done at the level of gender in the cultures of science and engineering. Much remains to be accomplished. The recent joint statement on gender equity by the presidents of the nine leading United States universities is welcome in this regard ("University Leaders" 2005). These prestigious institutions continue to work together, sharing best practices and specific initiatives, to remove barriers that limit women's full participation in academic life. Their goal is to create conditions in which all faculty are allowed to achieve at the highest level. These types of efforts are crucial, but they will not be successful unless changes come also at a third level: gender in human knowledge and technology.

Gender in the Results of Science and Engineering

Many people may be willing to concede that women have not been given a fair shake, that social attitudes and scientific institutions need to be reformed. They may also be willing to concede that women are excluded in subtle and often invisible ways. They stop short, however, of analyzing how gendered practices and ideologies have structured knowledge. Does the exclusion of women from the sciences and engineering have consequences that go beyond the issues discussed above? Is the question of gender in science and engineering merely one of institutions and opportunities for women, or does it impact the content of these disciplines as well?

Since the Enlightenment, science has stirred hearts and minds with its promise of a "neutral" and privileged vantage point, above and beyond the rough and tumble of political life. Men and women alike have responded to the lure of science: "the promise of touching the world at its innermost being, a touching made possible by the power of pure thought" (Keller 1992). The power of Western science—its methods, techniques, and epistemologies—is celebrated for producing objective and universal knowledge, transcending cultural restraints. With respect to gender, race, and much else, however, science is not value neutral. Scholars have begun to document how gender inequalities, built into the institutions of science, have influenced the knowledge issuing from those institutions (Gero and Conkey 1991; Harding 1991; Schiebinger 1993, 1999, 2003, 2004; Rosser 1994; Spanier 1995; Hager 1997).

A number of chapters in this volume provide exemplary case studies of how removing gender bias can open science and engineering to new theoretical perspectives and research questions. Before we turn to these examples, let me say a word first about difference feminism in this regard. Difference feminism can be helpful in aiding our understanding of how the cultures of institutions must change in order to accommodate women. But difference feminism can be especially *unhelpful* when applied to knowledge. In the 1980s much difference feminism promoted the notion that women had a lot to contribute to science and engineering because, it was said, women hold different values and think differently. It is important to understand, however, that gender characteristics often attributed to women—cooperation, caring, cultivating a feeling for the organism, or whatever it may be—date back to the eighteenth century and were produced in efforts to keep women out of science and the public sphere (Schiebinger 1989). In romanticizing traditional femininity, difference feminism does little to overturn conventional stereotypes of men and women. Women's historically wrought gender differences cannot serve as an epistemological base for new theories and practices in the sciences. There is no "female style" or "women's ways of knowing" ready to be plugged in at the laboratory bench or clinical bedside. Women—as females of the species—do not do science differently; science should not necessarily be "for women, by women, about women." Difference feminism or standpoint theory, as it is sometimes called, can tend to exclude men from understanding how gender operates. Everyone—men and women—must contribute to reforming knowledge.

But this is not to say that gender bias has not had a huge impact on science and engineering: ignoring these biases is to ignore possible sources of error in the past and also the future. It must be emphasized that gender analysis requires rigorous training; there is no recipe that can simply be plugged into the design of a research project. It must also be emphasized that the tools for gender analysis are as diverse as the variants of feminism and of science or engineering. As with any set of tools, new ones will be fashioned and others discarded as circumstances change. Some transfer easily from science to science, others do not. The brilliance of their implementation depends, as with other research methods, on the creativity of the research team. Training in gender analysis is something that must become part of undergraduate and graduate education in the sciences and engineering. Gender analysis acts as yet another experimental control to heighten critical rigor.

Perhaps the best way to understand how gender analysis works is to study examples where this type of analysis has brought important critiques of bias and developed new perspectives or insights in particular areas.

The best example of how gender analysis has changed science comes from the biomedical sciences where a revolution in women's health research has taken place in the United States since the 1960s. As is now well known, before 1993 drugs were typically tested on men and the results generalized to women. As a result, adverse reactions to drugs occur twice as often in women as in men. Until recently, for example, little was known about the effects of aspirin on heart disease in women, yet women of an appropriate age were encouraged to take an aspirin each day (Rosser 1994; Ruzek et al. 1997).

Importantly, these biases were not redressed through the promised self-correcting mechanisms of scientific research. It seems fairly evident that studying drugs in nonrepresentative populations is simply bad science. Yet correction in this case required political intervention at the highest levels of government. In the 1990s, the NIH founded the Office of Research on Women's Health. This office has two missions: (1) to increase the number of women in the medical profession and, importantly, (2) to reconceptualize medical research. In addition, NIH launched the Women's Health Initiative, the largest single study ever undertaken by NIH (Haseltine and Jacobson 1997). As Bernadine Healy, former head of NIH who oversaw these innovations, put it: "let's face it, the way to get scientists to move into a certain area is to fund that area" (Gura 1995). In 1993 a federal law was passed that women must be included in clinical drug trials, and that cost could not be used as a justification for excluding them.

Second to medicine, biology has been a field much transformed by gender analysis. These transformations have not been driven by government policies or granting agencies but by a growing awareness that removing gender bias can improve the science. Because biology deals with sex and gender, and because biology has been open to women (45 percent of PhDs are currently women), biologists have moved more swiftly than others to remove glaring cultural bias. In addition, textbooks have been revised to include the contributions of women scientists and to remove outmoded and sexist metaphors (of heroic sperm capturing demure and passive eggs, for example).

In this volume, Sarah Richardson tells the powerful story of how gender analysis contributed to an overhaul of theories of sex determinism that guide research in reproductive biology. In the 1980s, geneticists championed a "master gene" model of sex determination (the notion that a single gene controls the development of an entire organ system). Further, they saw the Y chromosome as a trigger that (in tandem with sex hormones) explained sexual dimorphism. In this model, males determine sex; females develop by default. Richardson documents how the development of gender analysis in the 1990s along with an active women's movement in both society and science dethroned the master gene and put in its place a model of sex determination that takes into account the interactions of testis and ovarian factors in the co-production of sexual dimorphism. Today biologists see both male and female pathways as highly complex and interactive.

Richardson goes on to make the important point that although geneticists gradually became sensitive to gender issues, they did not credit feminism for the many insights it provided. It is a common phenomenon that when gender criticism becomes one among many tools of analysis in a research program, its feminist roots are ignored. As noted above, what is feminist in one time and place becomes business as usual, simply "good science," when it enters the mainstream.

Archaeologists, by contrast, tend to employ gender analysis more consciously, and Margaret Conkey opens her chapter with a taxonomy of feminist approaches to the study of prehistory. To discuss these approaches in concrete terms she analyzes Olga Soffer's work with Venus figurines of the Upper Paleolithic found in the modern-day Czech Republic. These Venus figurines point up certain difficulties confronting students of prehistoric societies. First, nature has a preservation bias: Durable goods (stone tools, metals, and the like) preserve well, but fiber-based technologies (weaving or plaiting) succumb quickly to the ravages of time. Second, archaeologists often shoehorn material evidence from prehistoric societies into modern-day assumptions about sexual divisions of labor and the like. Conkey shows that because Soffer was willing to question basic background assumptions and go at her finds with new questions and perspectives, she discovered new forms of evidence for the existence of textiles.

What Soffer uncovered, with the assistance of her colleague James Adovasio, was that these Venus figures contained evidence of lost technologies: coiling, plaiting, twining, and the like. In short, Soffer revealed the earliest evidence of weaving in human history. The significance of this work for gendered innovations in science is two-fold. First, Soffer lifted these Venus figurines out of the realm of biology (their heavy breasts and hips are often seen as fertility symbols). Further, she provided evidence of fiber technologies that archaeologists have previously undervalued because today these technologies are associated with females. Soffer's work significantly expands and corrects our view of prehistoric people and their cultures.

Paleoanthropologist Lori Hager finds that similar unexamined assumptions have contributed to "sexism in sexing" skeletons—the prized "finds" for human origins research. When viewed uncritically, fossils tend to tell us more about the assumptions of modern-day researchers than about our human ancestors. Working with partial and fragmented skeletons, paleoanthropologists have in the past tended to sex large and robust individuals male and diminutive specimens female. This bias is itself so robust that a whopping 90 percent of Australian Aboriginal skeletal remains have been sexed male—well over the 50 percent expected sex ratio. Hager discusses how gender analysis has helped researchers better recognize that the small and large fossils from the same era can represent either female and male members of one highly sexually dimorphic species, or individuals belonging to two different species, one robust and the other small.

Louise Fortmann, Heidi Ballard, and Louise Sperling's work on the environmental sciences again underlines the point that gender analysis is not something carried out in isolation but combines with and strengthens other methodologies. Their emphasis on "participatory research methods" is broader than, but consistent with, feminism. As they show, broadening notions of what counts as "science" often brings to light women's contributions and, more importantly, leads to reconceptualizing the environmental sciences. Fortmann, Ballard, and Sperling's several examples come from the realms of farming and forestry. First-world research on agrarian production systems proceeded for decades on the assumption that men were farmers and foresters while women were housewives. Women in various parts of the world, however, often do most of the subsistence farming and forestry and consequently possess specialized knowledge of plants and seeds. Broadening participation in research—that is, incorporating the knowledge of less-educated but skilled planters, harvesters, and seed selectors—can improve crop yields, better preserve biodiversity, and allow for sustainable harvesting. As Fortmann, Ballard, and Sperling argue, recognizing women's contributions has, in some instances, led to methodological innovation in management practices and policies in the environmental sciences.

In her chapter on geographic information systems (GIS) Mei-Po Kwan takes a slightly different approach, emphasizing how GIS, which has traditionally been seen as encompassing purely technical methods for managing and mapping geographic data, can serve as a tool for enhancing our understanding of women's lives. Kwan offers three highly interesting examples. Of particular note are the ways in which GIS has been deployed to understand gendered use of space. Employing GIS to map the daily paths of African American women in sample households in Portland, Oregon, Kwan is able to quantify how their lives are restricted spatially, not simply economically and socially. Understanding this dimension of urban design can assist governments in planning more equitable cities.

Taking women into account can also improve engineering designs. Several years ago, historian Rachel Weber explored how airplane cockpits had to be redesigned when women were admitted into the United States Air Force in the 1990s. As is often the case, changes made with women in mind improved the situation for men. The new cockpits not only accommodated the sitting height of the average woman but also of shorter men—who had previously also been excluded from careers as pilots (Weber 1997). In this volume, Tatiana Temm describes how an all-women design team at Volvo Car Corporation created a concept car designed especially for women. She emphasizes, however, that many of the innovations—greater visibility for shorter people, extra ease in opening doors, and the like—although designed for women, also improve the driving experience for men.

While researchers have produced a rich literature on a host of topics ranging from women in science to gender bias in scientific knowledge and the like, Charis Thompson argues in her chapter that policy in this area is often theoretically and empirically "anemic." She finds that researchers in the field of gender policy treat almost exclusively the (under)representation of women and minorities in science, often leaving aside more complex issues. Her contribution here on stem cell research begins to unravel some of the tangle in thinking about women, eggs, and embryos. The time has come, she notes, to begin in earnest the historical and contemporary study of the politics of gender and science, and to develop a clearer understanding of the different consequences that different approaches to stem cell research hold for women of different races and classes.

Moving Forward

It is abundantly clear that sexual divisions in physical and intellectual labor do structure institutions, knowledge, and everyday objects in our society. But it is also clear that gender analysis has not yielded results uniformly across the various fields of science and engineering. While examples of how gender has brought new insights abound in biomedicine, the life sciences, archaeology, primatology, and elsewhere, similar examples are not available for physics, chemistry, or electrical engineering, for example. Meg Urry argues in her chapter that photons have no gender, that gender bias, and hence the possibility for gender innovations, does not exist in physics—that is to say, in the knowledge created by physicists. It is true that the physical sciences have by and large resisted gender analysis (although, as Urry emphasizes, the culture of physics is highly gendered). There are several possible reasons why this is so. First, we observe that in disciplines such as biomedicine and biology that enjoy a good number of women practitioners, more progress has been made in knowledge issues. But which came first—the openness of the discipline to new intellectual insights or the greater numbers of women in those disciplines—is a topic open for research. One thing that is true is that the number of people trained in both physics (or chemistry) and gender studies is extremely small and something that should be remedied. Second, the lack of interest in gender analysis in the physical sciences may also be due to the fact that objects and processes of the physical sciences are less obviously gendered, if at all. That no gender dimensions exist in physics or chemistry, however, is currently a well-formulated hypothesis. We need to run the research.

Once we have made some headway developing gender analysis useful to the natural sciences, how do we mainstream this type of analysis in the day-to-day work of science and engineering? There are two next steps. First, we need to train students—undergraduate and graduate—along with faculty in how to integrate gender analysis into their research. While most people agree that students require advanced training in molecular biology or particle physics in order to excel in those fields, many believe that they can just "pick up" an understanding of gender along the way. Understanding gender, however, requires research, development, and training, as in any other field of intellectual endeavor. The NIH programs I described earlier work, for example, because a solid body of gender research on medical issues was available from a number of leading institutions across the United States.

Second, this is where policy kicks in. One of the goals of this volume is to move the NSF toward requiring that federally funded science integrate gender analysis into research design, where appropriate. The NSF is lagging behind other federal and international agencies in this regard. At the NIH, as noted above, the Office of Research on Women's Health requires proper consideration of sexual differences in medical research. At the European Commission also, the Directorate General for Research requires that project design address "systematically whether, and in what sense, sex and gender are relevant in the objectives and methodology of projects" (European Commission 2006; removing this requirement has been discussed. While using gender analysis in research is retained in the 7th Programme, compliance is not enforced; http://ec.europa.eu/research/science-society/index .cfm?fuseaction=public .topic&id=142 retrieved August 20, 2007). Moreover, a number of European countries, such as Sweden, have made increasing the number of women along with integrating gender analysis into research design part of their national science policy. Even where this is the case, however, more training in how to incorporate gender analysis into science and engineering research is needed. On a recent visit to Sweden I heard that although this is national policy, few researchers know what exactly to do.

Let me conclude by suggesting that much work remains to be done. One of the many tasks at hand is to continue to collect empirical examples of how gender analysis has enhanced theory or practice in specific subfields of science and engineering (see also Schiebinger 1999 and 2003). We also need to continue to develop frameworks of gender analysis that address these issues for sciences, such as physics and chemistry, where gender appears not to play as large a role in knowledge.

Let me emphasize again that this work is crucial to our efforts to recruit and retain women—we will not solve that problem until we solve the knowledge problem. It is intriguing that sciences, such as biomedicine, primatology, archaeology, and biology, where gender analysis has flourished, have relatively high numbers of women. In these fields and in many fields in the humanities, employing gender analysis has added spark and creativity by asking new questions and opening new areas to research. Can we afford to ignore such opportunities?

2 When Gender Criticism Becomes Standard Scientific Practice

The Case of Sex Determination Genetics

Sarah S. Richardson

THIS CHAPTER DOCUMENTS the contribution of gender analysis to the field of sex determination genetics. The cloning of the *SRY* (sex-determining region of the Y chromosome) gene in 1990 appeared to confirm a long-standing model of genetic sex determination—that of a single "master gene" on the Y chromosome that directs the development of the male gonads and thereby determines sex. By the late 1990s, however, this model fell as a result of challenges from all sides, including gender criticism. Today, the *SRY* gene is understood as one among many essential mammalian sex-determining factors involved in the genetic pathways of both testicular and ovarian determination. Mammals require cascades of gene product in proper dosages and at precise times to produce functioning male and female gonads, and researchers recognize a variety of healthy sexual phenotypes and sex determination pathways in humans.

What part did gender analysis play in this remarkable transformation in models of sex determination? In what follows, I document how gender criticism became a cognitive resource in the field of sex determination genetics during the 1990s and contributed to the development of a significantly revised genetic theory of sex determination. It contributed in at least three ways. First, feminist biologists and science analysts anticipated the revised model earlier than others. Second, feminist theories of sex and gender lent intellectual resources to the model reconstruction effort. Third, gender criticism sharpened the epistemic tools of the field of sex determination genetics. It improved the level of critical discourse about the assumptions, language, and interpretive models of the field, and provided an analytical framework for articulating and making visible previously unattended gaps in knowledge.

Developments both internal and external to the field facilitated the acceptance of gender criticism in the standard critical practices of sex determination research, a process I call "normalization of gender criticism."[1] I identify three stages in the progressive incorporation of gender criticism into sex determination genetics. First, cultural change in and around the field of sex determination genetics created the conditions for receptivity to gender criticism, including early feminist criticism from outside the field. Second, a respected female scientist in the field, Jennifer Graves, began to employ an explicitly feminist framework in her work. Graves introduced feminist criticism to the field and developed a formidable gender-critical alternative model of sex determination genetics. Third, over time, members of the larger sex determination research community came to see gender criticism as useful to their own thinking, incorporating feminist insights even while often not explicitly articulating them as such. In this way, gender criticism became a part of the mainstream critical practices of the field.

SRY, the Sex-Determining Gene

In 1959, analysis of human intersex individuals demonstrated that the genetic switch for male sex determination is located on the Y chromosome. It was not until the mid-1980s, however, when technologies for cloning, sequencing, and analyzing the human genome became cheaper, faster, and more ubiquitous, that a serious gene discovery program was undertaken for the "sex-determining gene." At this time, research groups at Massachusetts Institute of Technology in the United States, the National Institute for Medical Research, Medical Research Council, and Imperial Cancer Research Fund in London, and La Trobe University in Australia began competing to analyze the Y chromosome and clone the sex-determining gene.

The sex-determining gene became a high priority target in the early days of human genetic sequencing for several reasons. First, sex determination appeared to present a model system in which a single "master gene" controlled the development of an entire organ system. As geneticist Edward Southern wrote in 1987, "Sex determination, as a model for the developmental process in mammals, is undoubtedly the principal reason for the intense activity of research on the Y chromosome" (Goodfellow et al. 1987, 75).

The sex-determining gene was also a low-hanging fruit. The Y chromosome is many times smaller than the other twenty-three chromosomes and houses only a few genes; it is a comparatively tractable target for genetic analysis. Through recombinant technology and deletion analysis in the 1970s, researchers had already isolated the sex-determining gene to a small region of the Y chromosome. Rapid sequencing technologies and straightforward micro-level deletion analysis of the Y chromosome of intersexed mice and humans promised to reveal the location of the crucial switch. As leading geneticist Peter Goodfellow of the Imperial Cancer Research Fund in Britain wrote in 1987, "the stage is set for cloning the mammalian sex-determining gene" (Goodfellow et al. 1987, 1).

Finally, the male sex-determining gene represented a holy grail of sex difference research. Prevailing theory held that two factors control sex difference: a gene triggers gonad differentiation and sex hormones direct the development of the gonads and secondary sex characteristics. Sex hormones having been well characterized by the 1970s, the sex-determining switch would complete the account of the biology of human sex differences. Thus, the male sex-determining gene was a prestigious prize, a long-sought theoretical breakthrough that promised to answer persistent questions about male and female sex difference and found a new field of research.[2]

The genetic search for the male "sex-determining factor" began in earnest in 1986 (Wilkie 1991). Researchers used mouse models to probe a sex-determining region of the Y chromosome isolated from intersex patient karyotypes. In 1987, David Page, a researcher at MIT and the Whitehead Institute in Boston, announced that a gene called *ZFY* satisfied the criteria for the sex-determining gene (Page et al. 1987). Within a year, Australian researchers Jennifer Graves and Andrew Sinclair overturned the finding. Sinclair went on to identify the *SRY* gene for male gonad formation in 1990 (Berta et al. 1990). In 1991, accompanied by a *Nature* cover with the "star mouse, swinging on a stick and sporting enormous testicles to prove the point," Goodfellow, Peter Koopman, and Robin Lovell-Badge confirmed the sex-determining role of *SRY* by showing that a transgenic XX mouse would develop as a male if *SRY* is appended to one of the X chromosomes (Koopman et al. 1991; Sykes 2003, 71). Following on the heels of this work, in 1992 Page published the first genetic map of the Y chromosome (Vollrath et al. 1992).

The *SRY* model of sex determination confirmed the anticipated model of sex determination controlled by a single "master gene" on the Y chromosome. Media coverage of the discovery of the *SRY* added to the hype: "scientists now think they know what makes a male masculine," trumpeted the *New York Times*; "scientists believe that they have at last unraveled the secret of what makes a man," announced the *Guardian* (Angier 1990; Williams 1990). The scientific community celebrated *SRY* as an example of "the astonishing power of modern molecular techniques to resolve long-standing and difficult questions in genetics with consequences that extend far across biology" (Williams 1990). Textbooks immediately incorporated the *SRY* gene into accounts of sex determination. In 1992, the International Olympic Committee added a test for the *SRY* gene to its "gender verification" program for female athletes.

A Changing Public Discourse
About Gender and Science

The 1980s initiated a period of intense public debate about gender and science. The NIH Office of Research on Women's Health opened its doors in the early 1990s, raising the profile of women's and gender issues in American science. This period also witnessed significant expansion of feminist science studies pedagogy and scholarship in the academy. In research biology, particularly genetics and developmental biology, women entered the profession in numbers that for the first time approached parity.

In large part as a result of these developments, the 1990s saw increasing challenges to dominant biological models of sex and gender. Biological claims about intersexuality and homosexuality came under particular scrutiny. Feminist science analysts retheorized these phenomena as part of the normal spectrum of human sex and gender. Over the course of the decade this work found its way into sex determination genetics through a variety of channels. The mid-1990s controversy over sex chromosome testing for "gender verification" of female Olympians, ultimately leading to the termination of this practice, provided sex chromosome researchers, whose expertise was sought, with a public crash course in the social impact of scientific definitions of sex and gender (Puffer 2002). The intersex movement also became increasingly visible during the 1990s, emblemized by the founding of the Intersex Society of North America in 1993. Sex chromosome researchers who studied and provided care for intersex and gender dysphoric patients gained exposure to gender-critical perspectives and were drawn into political and medical advocacy in this community. The "gay nineties" also changed the discursive context and conditions of sex and gender research in biology. The 1990s, for instance, saw the burgeoning of diversity-affirming science writing highlighting the rich variety of sexual life in the natural world, in part a response to dominant assumptions that homosexuality is "unnatural" (see, for example, Bagemihl 1999 and Roughgarden 2004).

An Androcentric "Master Gene" Model of Sex Determination

Sex determination genetics in the 1980s inherited an "androcentric" theory of sex determination from endocrinology. First articulated in 1953 by Alfred Jost, the theory held that humans are bipotential until six weeks after conception, at which time two biological switches initiate sexual dimorphism. First, a gene on the Y chromosome triggers the development of the testes. Second, the testes begin producing two hormones, MIS (Müllerian Inhibiting Substance) and testosterone, which "masculinize" the fetus and initiate hormonal control of sexual development. Jost's 1950s research showed that errors in the development of a genetic male, either at the hormonal or the genetic level, cause mice to "revert" to a female developmental pathway. On this evidence, he hypothesized that the development of female gonads and secondary sexual characteristics is the body's "default" plan. In the absence of the two switches, a fetus will develop ovaries and become a phenotypic female. In 1959, cytogenetic studies of intersex patients by Charles Ford corroborated and extended Jost's view of sexual development. Ford's research established that no matter the number of X's, the presence of a single Y causes male gonads to develop, confirming that the sex-determining switch is located on the Y chromosome.

From Jost and Ford, then, the field of sex determination genetics inherited an androcentric framework for sex determination research: a gene on the Y chromosome initiates testis formation; testis formation is the crucial sex-determining event; and female sexual development proceeds as a "default" in the absence of this gene. This theory led researchers in the early 1980s to focus on isolating the "male-determining gene" on the Y chromosome and to see the question of *sex* determination as the question of the genetics of *male testis* determination.

"Master gene" theories in developmental genetics were the second principal source for 1980s models of sex determination. The search for the sex-determining gene in the 1980s was not, as one might suppose, directed toward medical or "gender verification" applications. Rather, its prospects for validating an emerging approach to general questions in developmental genetics drove much of the early interest in the sex-determining gene. As conference chair Peter Goodfellow wrote in the introduction to a symposium volume on sex determination genetics, researchers' interest in *SRY* at this time was primarily "as a model for genetic control of development in mammals" (Goodfellow et al. 1987, 1).

Sex determination research in the 1980s found kinship with a particular school of developmental biology that modeled developmental processes as genetic hierarchies controlled by "master switches" in the genome. The then prevailing paradigm for genetic control of development, as Goodfellow wrote, "assumes a hierarchy of regulatory genes," "an archetypical regulatory network." "In the simplest case, a master control gene directly regulates secondary genes which, in turn, regulate the expression of other genes" (Goodfellow et al. 1987, 1). Once the "master gene" that triggers this hierarchy is discovered, the identification of other genes involved in the hierarchy should be relatively simple. Assuming that the genes involved in testis determination must be an *important* and fundamental developmental process, such that all mammals would share a single, highly conserved genetic pathway, researchers saw the *SRY* as a perfect "archetype" of this hierarchical system. The aim of this research program was to clone *SRY* in order to build a simple model system for the elaboration of general theories in developmental genetics.

Master gene theories of genetic development, then, formed potent background expectations for sex determination researchers. Researchers showed strong disciplinary allegiance to these theories and were invested in the *SRY* model as proof in principle for their emergent field and research program.

Early Gender Criticism of Sex Determination Models

Anne Fausto-Sterling's "Life in the XY Corral" (1989) is a representative feminist critique of sex determination genetics in the 1980s. In the paper, Fausto-Sterling, a biologist, feminist science critic, and intersex patient activist, analyzed gender beliefs in theories of sex determination and argued that researchers had ignored explanatory gaps in their theories and failed to consider viable alternative models for sex determination. Her charge was three-fold. First, by equating the genetics of testis determination with the genetics of sex determination, researchers had neglected parallel investigation into the genetics of ovarian development. Second, researchers had privileged male over female processes by accepting a highly resonant metaphor of "male as presence and female as absence." Male processes of sexual development were deemed a more interesting, complex, and dynamic object of investigation than female processes. Third, researchers had assumed that sex organizes into a "clearcut" binary such that it can be unambiguously determined by genetic assay. Fausto-Sterling contrasted these conceptions of sex with feminist and social science concepts of sex and gender. An uncritical commitment to a binary concept of sex, she argued, "led researchers to ignore data which are better accounted for in approaches which accept the existence of intermediate states of sexuality" (326–327, 330).

Fausto-Sterling concluded that these assumptions about gender had "prevented the articulation of a coherent theory" of sex determination. She urged an alternative model of sex determination that includes both male and female developmental pathways and "permits the existence of intermediate states" (329). Fausto-Sterling cited a neglected model of sex determination proposed by Eva Eicher and Linda Washburn that included ovarian development and posited that many genes must interact along complex and overlapping pathways to create male and female gonads (1986). Not a sex determination geneticist, Fausto-Sterling's critique registered little response from specialists. Nevertheless, her alternative model and that of Eicher and Washburn represent an early gender-critical model of sex determination.

The 1990s: Mounting Difficulties with the *SRY* Model of Sex Determination

During the 1990s, the *SRY* model of sex determination encountered serious conceptual and empirical challenges. Jennifer Graves and Roger Short anticipated these challenges in a strong critique issued immediately after the announcement of the identification of *SRY*: "Will all mysteries of sex determination now be revealed? We think not," predicted Graves and Short (1990, 731).

Graves and Short raised several challenges to the *SRY* model of sex determination. First, *SRY* was insufficient to produce a fully sex-reversed, fertile transgenic mouse, and an X-linked gene was known to override the effect of *SRY* on testis determination (among other empirical anomalies to the *SRY* paradigm). Many more genes, perhaps in distinct pathways, must interact to successfully decide sexual fate. Graves and Short suggested that preference for a Y-chromosomal sex-determining mechanism neglected the role of the X chromosome in sex determination and hypothesized that an X-dosage mechanism may interact with the *SRY* pathway to determine sex.

Second, there was no evidence of a gene target for *SRY* in the early stages of testis formation, suggesting a more circumscribed role for *SRY* in sex determination than the "master gene" and "gene hierarchy" theories presumed. *SRY* need not, as was widely assumed, be a direct, active inducer of testis formation. A more complex and interactive model of sex determination would better account for the lack of a gene target for *SRY*. Graves and Short held that, contrary to expectation, the evidence implicated *SRY* in a double-inhibition pathway. Rather than functioning as an activating switch, *SRY* stops other genes that would inhibit still other genes causing testis development.

Third, Graves and Short challenged the developmental biologists' expectation that sex determination should be well conserved, universal, and nonredundant. They admonished sex determination geneticists to appreciate the diversity of sex determination processes, even among mammals.

In the early 1990s, scientists struggled to interpret research findings inconsistent with the *SRY* model of sex determination. The 1992 Boden Conference on Sex Chromosomes and Sex-Determining Genes, chaired by Jennifer Graves, offers a window into a field in transition as these questions came to a head. In the introduction to the conference volume and transcripts, Reed and Graves (1993) write:

> [W]e are gradually getting *an uneasy feeling* that [the portrait of sexual determination given by Jost] is flawed. The history of studies of sexual differentiation exemplifies the truism to "seek simplicity, then distrust it." . . . *[W]e were not prepared* for the ambiguities and difficulties that would follow in trying to interpret the role of *SRY* in aberrant phenotypes and to ascribe downstream function to its gene product. (1993, x, emphasis added)

Research on *SRY* also confounded researchers' expectations about the biological phenomenon of sex dimorphism in several ways. One was the role of *SRY* in the direct induction of the testis. The conference transcript reveals researchers encountering a lack of fit between the *SRY* model of sex determination and the data, throwing into turmoil their model-theoretic assumptions and description and interpretation of data:

CHAIRMAN: But do the transgenic mice tell us that *SRY* is the *only* gene involved in testis determination?

GOODFELLOW: The hoary old question of whether *SRY* can be the sex-determining gene because we know there must be other genes in the cascade, so it can't be the only gene! . . . I find it very compelling that all of the genetic information that you need to make a male is present in that 14kb [of the Y chromosome].

MONK: It *sometimes* makes a male.

BURGOYNE: It only sometimes makes a male, even when it's expressed!

GOODFELLOW: I give up!

(375, identity of "Chairman" (sic) unknown)

Researchers also expected that the sex-determining gene would be well-conserved in mammals such that the sex determination process in mice could then be easily generalized to humans and other species. This expectation (a common assumption when working with model organisms in molecular biology) proved unsustainable in this case.

CHAIRMAN: [O]ne of the big surprises is how poorly conserved *SRY* is between humans and marsupials.

FOSTER: Yes. We expected *SRY* to be well conserved. . . . We were expecting then—and right up until now—that [*SRY*], being a much more important gene and having a lot more selective pressure on it than any of the average house-keeping genes, would pop straight out and we'd find it on the marsupial Y chromosome. (384)

These and other inconsistencies between expectation and observation reveal, in 1992, a growing frustration with the received model of sex determination. Conference contributors, however, were unprepared at this early stage to formulate an alternative model of sex determination or examine the broader assumptions that structured research in the field.

During the mid-1990s, researchers accumulated more anomalies to the *SRY* model and identified several other important genes in the sex determination pathway. In an early contribution, Ken McElreavey, Eric Vilain, and coworkers at the Pasteur Institute in France reviewed more than a hundred cases of human intersex subjects for whom *SRY* did not offer a sufficient explanation of the phenotype (McElreavey et al. 1993). They hypothesized from these cases that there must be another major factor in sex determination, an "anti-testis" factor, which *SRY* acts to suppress. Opposing a "genetic hierarchy" concept of sex determination, they proposed a "regulatory gene cascade" hypothesis, in which many factors participate in pushing the balance of sex determination in favor of male or female, explaining the observed spectrum of intersex phenotypes.

While articulating a nonbinary vision of the biology of sex and gender, McElreavey and Vilain's hypothesis also picked up on broader conceptual shifts in biology in the 1990s. Simple notions of genetic determinism and gene action increasingly fell short of providing adequate explanations of molecular-level phenomena. By the late 1990s, biologists would move away from metaphors of "master genes" and "genetic programs" and toward nonreductionist, complex regulatory network approaches to biological explanation (see Podolsky and Tauber 1997, Keller 2000, Sarkar 2006).

In another significant mid-1990s finding, researchers identified two species of voles that lacked *SRY* but still reliably produced a fertile male phenotype (Just et al. 1995). This confirmed that *SRY* was neither necessary nor sufficient to produce a male phenotype in all mammals. Comparative genomic evidence that *SRY* is poorly conserved, or highly variable in sequence and target, even between mice, chimpanzees, and humans, and that *SRY* is a relatively recently evolved gene, corroborated this view. These findings suggested that *SRY* may function differently from species to species and also may interact with other sex-determining mechanisms in the genome.

The characterization of the genes *DAX1*, *SOX9*, *DMRT1*, and *WNT4*, all non-Y chromosomal genes that can override *SRY* to cause sex reversal, contributed further to pressures in the late 1990s for a revised model of sex determination. These and others in the expanding docket of genes involved in sex determination increasingly challenged the "master gene" model of *SRY* gene action. A consensus began to emerge that *SRY* was far more "average" than expected, pointing toward a sex determination model of a "cascade" or several cascades of genes working in complex regulatory relation to one another.

Jennifer Graves' "Feminist View" of Sex Determination

Jennifer Graves is a leading scientist and a public figure in Australia, recently tapped to direct Australia's high-profile effort to sequence the kangaroo genome. A member of the Australian Academy of Science, she has been described as a "National Treasure" (White 2001). Graves is also a rare woman principal investigator in a male-dominated field, as well as a marsupial researcher in a world of mouse models and an Australian with comparatively little public funding in a research environment driven by lavishly endowed American and British labs. As a result, for much of her career Graves was somewhat of an outsider in the field of sex determination genetics.

Graves's specialty is comparative genomics of mammals and marsupials and the genetics of sex chromosomes and sex determination. She is best known for her lab's 1988 work disproving David Page's candidate sex determination gene as the mammalian sex-determining gene (Sinclair et al. 1988). Her critiques of Y chromosome-centric models of sex determination and her "Y chromosome degeneration theory" have made her a figure of some controversy and colorful media attention (Jones 2002; Sykes 2003).[3] As a result, as she said in an interview, "I unexpectedly became a ball-breaking feminist Y chromosome knocker" (White 2001).

Graves did not publicly self-identify as a feminist until her appointment to the Australian Academy of Science in 1999. In papers, talks, and interviews following this, Graves began to place her ideas in a feminist framework. A 2001 profile described her as "concerned that a non-feminist view can [adversely] affect how science is done, particularly in her field that deals with what genes determine sex and sex-related characteristics" (White 2001). One might speculate that Graves's position as an outsider, her enhanced freedom, seniority, and legitimacy following her appointment to the Academy of Science and other honors, rising gender awareness in sex determination research, and frustrating experiences explaining and defending her theories under a media spotlight that insisted on seeing them as contributions to the "sex wars," were enablers and preconditions of her ability and desire to speak from a feminist standpoint—in a profession in which claiming a public feminist identity could be a kiss of death—in 2000.

The 2000 paper, "Human Y Chromosome, Sex Determination, and Spermatogenesis: A Feminist View" presents the clearest elaboration of Graves's feminist critique of the *SRY* model of sex determination. Graves argued that researchers' unreflective assignment of masculine qualities to *SRY* led them to ignore contradictory evidence and prefer an unsustainable model of Y chromosomal sex determination over alternative models. Researchers clung to this model even when countervailing evidence should have led them to abandon it. Graves termed this the "Dominant Y" theory (667–668). In the paper, she described three principal ways in which this "macho" conception of *SRY* had misled sex determination research (673). She then proposed an alternative model of the Y chromosome and its role in sex determination.

First, Graves argued that the Dominant Y model led researchers to conceive of *SRY* as a transcendent "maleness" gene, a specialized master gene that reflects the ultimate refinement of male sex determination and is ubiquitous in nature. This caused researchers to expect that *SRY* would be well conserved and that it would act uniquely in the first stages of testis formation. Empirical research, argued Graves, showed just the opposite. *SRY* is poorly conserved, shows a weak, inconsistent transcription pattern, and appears to have different functions in different species. Indeed, transgenic experiments demonstrate that the function of *SRY* can be replaced by other genes with a similar structure in the genome (such as *DAX1*). Instead, Graves argued, *SRY* acts as an important switch in sex determination only by a contingency of molecular evolution and possesses no unique qualities or specialty function. *SRY* may very well be a marginal autosomal gene that became integrated into the sex determination pathway by chance when the Y chromosome evolved. Based on the evidence, *SRY* is better conceived, she suggested, as "a degraded relic of a normal gene that just got in the way of another gene" (674).

Second, Graves charged the Dominant Y model with uncritically attributing aggressive and agentic qualities to *SRY*. For instance, researchers presumed a model of Y chromosome evolution in which *SRY* "specialized" over time into a male-advantageous, and possibly female-antagonistic, gene—a result of a genetic sex war. A desire to see *SRY* in this light, she argued, led researchers to overlook the extent to which genes on the Y chromosome, including *SRY*, have homologues on the X chromosome, of which they are often merely degraded versions. The agentic Dominant Y model also led sex determination geneticists to assume that *SRY* acts as an "activator" at the top of a linear hierarchy. Wrote Graves, "This dominant action has traditionally been interpreted to mean that [*SRY*] codes for some kind of activator that turns on transcription of other genes in the male-determining pathway" (669). Graves argued that the attribution of the masculine quality of "active" to *SRY* prevented researchers from imagining more complex models, or models in which the *SRY* gene serves as an inhibitor, "a spoiler that turns off genes" (674), a model now strongly suggested by current research. Some models of *SRY* action went further, attributing the *SRY* gene with the ability to "overrule" genes in the ovary determination pathway. Once again, as Graves noted, this assumption was later contraindicated by empirical research documenting many examples of genes that can counteract the action of *SRY*, leading to sex reversal of normal XY individuals.

Third, as Fausto-Sterling had some ten years earlier, Graves identified the Dominant Y model as androcentric, devaluing and neglecting female biological processes, leading to explanatory gaps in the theory of sex determination. For example, singular emphasis on the role of the Y chromosome in sex determination caused researchers to overlook or underrate potential contributions from the X chromosome, despite the prominence of X chromosome dosage mechanisms of sex determination in many other species and the discovery of a crucial sex-determining gene on the X chromosome. The genetic pathway of ovarian determination is also neglected. As Graves pointed out, no biological argument is offered for the assumption that ovarian development is a "default pathway"—certainly ovarian development is just as interesting, contingent, and complex as testis development. "[T]here are likely to be just as many genes required for ovarian differentiation and egg development, and so far we know rather little about these genes or how they are switched on in the absence of testis development" (667), she wrote.

A simpler and more explanatorily powerful model, Graves suggested, conceives of *SRY* as a degraded version of a gene on the X chromosome that occupies the role of a genetic switch in sex determination because it happens to be located on a male-exclusive chromosome. Graves emphasized that the genome may contain many genes redundant to *SRY* as well as alternative mechanisms of sex determination, which may involve the X chromosome and may interact with and overlay the *SRY* pathway. For Graves, sex determination is a highly contingent, error-prone, and always-evolving mechanism. Polemically (but underscoring her view that gender ideology has favored a masculine view of *SRY* gene action), Graves called her alternative the "Wimp Y" model of Y-chromosomal sex determination.

In this paper, Graves reiterated and built on arguments incipient in her work since her earliest critique of the *SRY* model of sex determination in 1990. It represents the first instance, however, of Graves's identification of her critique of the dominant *SRY* model of sex determination as a feminist one. The precise nature and source of Graves's feminist identification is not clear. Nonetheless, "feminism" enabled Graves to place her multifaceted critique within a systematic critical perspective. This systematic critical approach makes salient the persistent gendering of biological phenomena and the valu-ing of male over female processes in the *SRY* model of sex determination, revealing gender as a factor in both the construction of the model and its widespread appeal despite its inadequacies. A "feminist view," as Graves de-scribes it, placed a diverse set of critical insights that had motivated Graves's approach to sex chromosome and sex determination research for at least a decade into an easy-to-grasp organizing framework. Graves's "feminist view," then, is effectively presented as a relevant, well-motivated, and insightful critical perspective from which sex determination researchers might evalu-ate scientific models, identify potential sources of bias, and generate alterna-tive hypotheses. Among several channels carrying feminist or gender-critical sensibilities into sex determination genetics in the late 1990s, Graves became among the most forceful, direct, and prominent.

The Normalization of Gender Criticism

Beginning around 2000, a marked shift of tone occurs in the sex determi-nation genetics literature. As the *SRY* master gene model fell out of favor, questions and ideas once at the periphery flooded in from all sides, including gender-critical approaches. The shift was informal and not self-consciously feminist. Rather, a general awareness matured—not evident previously—of the pitfalls of androcentric and gender-dualistic thinking. Researchers took up and absorbed valuable feminist insights, often without realizing that they had done so. This gender-critical consciousness began to be engaged as a mat-ter of course in the intellectual work of the field. I call this the normalization of gender criticism—one model of how feminist critical perspectives might find reception and take root in a scientific field.

The growth and effects of gender criticism are abundantly evident in the set of research questions that have come to occupy the field, changes to the model of sex determination itself, and the framework used by contemporary sex determination geneticists in explaining their research and describing the contribution of their work to biology and to society at large. Whereas "gender-critical" approaches are absent from the sex determination literature in the 1990s, in 2005, Fausto-Sterling's 1989 critique of sex determination models is echoed by prominent researchers in the mainstream literature of the field (though Fausto-Sterling is never cited). Researchers acknowledge neglect of research on the biology of female sex determination as a weakness in scientific theories of sexual development and sexual difference. In addition, researchers seek to avoid language implying that male biological processes are active and dominant while female processes are passive and default. When using the concepts of "sex" and "gender," researchers take pains to resist the implication that biological sex maps plainly to social conceptions of sex and gender. Sex determination literature emphasizes a plurality of sexual phenotypes and multiple pathways to normal sexual development. In a variety of ways, in their scholarship, public commentary, and pedagogy, sex determination researchers signal their awareness of feminist critiques of the *SRY* model of sex determination and their sensitivity to the social consequences of scientific theories of sex and gender difference.

Two sources, transcripts of the 2001 Novartis Foundation symposium, "The Genetics and Biology of Sex Determination" (Novartis Foundation 2002), and a set of interviews of prominent sex determination geneticists commissioned by the Annenberg Foundation for an online biology education project in 2004 (Annenberg Foundation and Oregon Public Broadcasting 2004), provide a remarkable record of the normalization of gender criticism in this field.

Three themes are noteworthy in the 2001 discussions at the Novartis conference: (1) a new, broad consensus on the importance of research on ovarian determination to any sound model of sex determination; (2) the replacement of the "master gene" conception of *SRY* by a multifactorial model of sex determination; and (3) the call for a human-specific model of sex determination, acknowledging the distinctiveness and complexity of sex-gender systems from species to species and the special sensitivities required for research on the biology of human sex and gender (Novartis Foundation 2002).

Whereas the research gap on ovarian determination is mentioned as an aside in scattered literature in the 1990s, in 2001 it is repeatedly and urgently raised in papers and discussions. Lovell-Badge and coauthors write (all quotes from Novartis Foundation 2002):

> Considerable progress has been made over the last 11 years, such that it is now possible at least to formulate models of how sex determination may work in mammals. . . . However, we are no doubt still missing many relevant genes, in particular for the female pathway, both those that can be considered antitestis genes and those that are actively required for the specification of the cell types characteristic of the ovary. (15)

In a closing discussion about future priorities of the field, Koopman names ovarian development as a pressing problem for the field, acknowledging the gap in knowledge produced by the prior totalizing emphasis on the testis:

> In the coming decade, we are likely to see further progress in understanding one of the great black boxes in developmental biology, namely the molecular genetics and cell biology of ovarian development. Efforts to illuminate ovarian development have been overshadowed to some extent by progress in studying testis determination and differentiation. (247)

Male gonad formation was once the primary explanandum and "holy grail" of sex determination research. By 2001 a definitive shift had occurred. The research program was reconceived as identifying the multitude of factors involved in gonad differentiation from a bipotential state. In the transcribed conference discussion, for example, Eric Vilain, now a clinical geneticist at UCLA, prompts researchers to keep in mind that "pro-male" factors are only one research target (47, 49). "Pro-ovary" and "anti-testis" factors (which, importantly, may be distinct) await characterization; without these elements, Vilain argues, the genetics of sex determination remains poorly understood. This perspective, reiterated throughout the conference proceedings by Koopman, Graves, Lovell-Badge, and Francis Poulat (Institute of Human Genetics, France), among others, reveals a widely shared conceptual transformation of the research problem of sex determination.

Consistent with this, the Novartis transcripts also evidence a much-revised estimate of the importance of the *SRY* gene in sex determination. The field's earlier attachment to an all-powerful master "maleness" gene model now appears as a clear blind spot in previous thinking. One (anonymous) discussant points out that the problem with the model now appears obvious in light of empirical counterevidence and basic principles of evolutionary theory, and wonders aloud why Graves's intervention was necessary to make researchers aware of the oversight:

> For model systems where there are genetic tests, we often isolate and identify particular genes, and assign them certain roles. We then tend to think, "Ah, this gene must perform this function in a large number of organisms." . . . We are terribly surprised when we get results such as Jennifer Graves' demonstration that *SRY* is not the be-all and end-all of sex determination, when in fact this is probably a common theme in evolution. (99)

Goodfellow, who in 1992 claimed that the *SRY* gene contained "all of the genetic information that you need to make a male," in 2001 states that it is likely that *SRY* must interact with another gene, and that this interaction itself requires the assistance of cofactors:

> I guess what I am saying is that we have ignored the cofactor molecules . . . for too long. This is why I was emphasizing the possibility that we may be looking at soaking up a cofactor that is needed for the expression of another gene. (40)

In 2001, researchers assign the *SRY* gene a far more modest role in sex determination. Poulat characterizes *SRY* as an interchangeable regulatory element: "We say that *SRY* is only a box. We can exchange this box with other boxes. . . . Basically we have a truncated SOX9 protein, which is also more-or-less a box: nevertheless, in this case we have sex reversal" (36). Similarly, Lovell-Badge et al. describe *SRY* as "acting solely as an architectural factor" (12). Reflecting both the shift to a nonbinary, multifactorial model of sex determination that includes both male and female gonad determination and the trend in biology toward complex regulatory network models of gene action, the language of "master genes" is absent.

Finally, the 2001 conference discussants are newly and keenly aware of the specificities of *human* sex determination genetics. Early enthusiasts championed *SRY* as a tool for Olympic gender verification and the determinant of "what makes a man a man." In 2001, researchers are far more cautious. For example, Vilain reminds colleagues that "a majority of patients with abnormal gonad development remain unexplained genetically" (51). The failure of the *SRY* model to fully explain human sex determination, researchers acknowledge, arises in part from a too-simple binary conception of sex difference and in part from inconsistencies between mouse models and humans. Glossing over discrepancies, at first researchers held to a theory of sex determination as a fundamental and therefore well-conserved mammalian developmental pathway, validating the generalizability of the mouse model system for sex determination research. Researchers in 2001, confronting the breakdown of this model, are more attuned both to distinctions between mouse and human systems of sex and gender determination and to the particular dangers of transferring folk conceptions of sex difference as a simple binary to biological theories of sex determination. In 2001, we see human sex determination genetics developing into a distinct field of expertise and specialists urging colleagues to be mindful of the specificities of the human sex phenotype. Vilain, for example, calls for a model of human sex determination that accommodates an "understanding [of] the tremendous phenotypic variability. . . . We often underestimate all manner of influences, from environment to genetic background" (253). Short adds, "we mustn't be sucked into thinking that [human] sex determination begins and ends with the gonads" (253).

The transcript demonstrates that this new gender criticality is directly linked to increased awareness among researchers of social and political issues raised by the intersex community. Responding to patient advocates, researchers work to challenge their own assumptions about "normal" sex phenotypes and the naturalness and necessity of a male-female sex binary. They appreciate the need for care and precision in research design and language use in sex determination research. For example, in a transcribed discussion (Novartis Foundation 2001) about recent research in human sex determination genetics, Goodfellow says:

> The dialogue that occurs between the medical profession and patient groups is something that the medical profession has to listen to. Not just with respect to this very difficult area, but generally. Treatment can reflect the social prejudices of the treaters. When a particular treatment is chosen because of the prejudices of the people who are performing that treatment, there has to be a social dialogue. The responsibility for the treatment of patients in the UK has changed in my lifetime. . . . Clearly, there is no easy solution to this problem, because unless social attitudes change dramatically we are dealing with individuals who fall outside social norms. . . . [W]e would be wrong not to engage in dialogue with those to be treated. (55)

Goodfellow's alarm about the potential for "prejudices" to influence scientific practice, his sense of responsibility to the intersex community, his awareness of the power and contingency of social norms about gender, and the easy interjection of these issues into a theoretical discussion of sex determination models, demonstrates the cross-talk between the conception of gender as a spectrum advanced by the intersex community and the cognitive work of the field of sex determination research.

Interviews conducted by the Annenberg Foundation in 2004 with leading sex determination geneticists Holly Ingraham, David Page, and Eric Vilain offer a second source documenting the normalization of gender-critical approaches in the field of sex determination research. The interviews echo and elaborate themes of the 2001 Novartis conference, while also presenting a more fine-grained picture of the integration of gender criticism into the models and epistemic practices of the field. These sustained, first-person narratives reveal researchers' own evolving conceptions of sex determination and provide evidence of the broader intellectual framework in which these changes are understood by specialists.

The interviews demonstrate that today's sexuality spectrum, gene dosage model of sex determination is broadly undergirded by a gender-critical conception of human sex and gender. Researchers explicitly link the new model to the development of a changed, more complex understanding of gender in the field, and the old to a set of biased assumptions about the biology of sex. Vilain, for instance, describes the 1980s and 1990s conception of sex determination as "a simplistic mechanism by which you have pro-male genes going all the way to make a male" (Annenberg Foundation and Oregon Public Broadcasting 2004). The model assumed that the male-determining gene contained all that was necessary, Page says, to "impose" masculinization on a bipotential gonad. Page describes this model as "extraordinarily male-biased"; "extremely biased in favor of the male"; "the most obvious hole in our understanding of the development of anatomic differences."

Ingraham, Vilain, and Page all narrate the history of the master gene *SRY* model of sex determination as a lesson in the dangers of building unreflective assumptions about gender into scientific theories. As Page relates, "Biologists have been saying for half a century that female development is a default outcome that somehow all human or mammalian embryos are initially female and then have masculinity imposed on them. I don't think that the available data supports this idea." Vilain explains, "We used to think that females were the result of a default passive sex-determining pathway and we now know that is not true." Ingraham further suggests that the old model reflects biased interests of male researchers, less invested in characterizing "the active processes in females." She discloses, "I wish I could understand it because I am female and I would like to know why I'm female and what are the active components to my gender assignment."

When describing today's model, the researchers emphasize the inclusion of female developmental processes and a dynamic and nonbinary understanding of sex. For example, Vilain says:

> We [are] entering this new era in molecular biology of sex determination where it's a more subtle dosage of genes, some pro-males, some pro-females, some anti-males, some anti-females that all interplay with each other rather than a simply linear pathway of genes going one after the other.

Similarly, Page says:

Both the male and female pathway are very active and require highly orchestrated, highly integrated sets of events, extremely complicated biochemical cascades that we're only beginning to understand.

In these descriptions of the genetic model of sex determination, the researchers' emphasis on the complexity of sex determination, the activeness of both male and female processes, the parity of male and female genetic contributions to sex determination, and the interaction of male and female factors all reflect a deeper shift toward a gender-critical understanding of sex and gender. Vilain says, "there [are] many ways to define sex and each one of them [is] just as equally important as the other." Page says, "[O]ften we fall all over ourselves because of the limitations of the definitions we try to impose" on sex. He adds, "There is no such thing as a simple definition [of gender] and even within a scientific context, sex or gender has been defined at many different levels." Ingraham highlights the diversity of human gender identities, arguing that mouse studies imposed an idealized conception of gender on the research problem and that human sex determination must be contextualized in the phenotypic variability of sexual identity. "[H]ow are you going to find a transsexual mouse? Are you going to ask him [sic]?"

Today gender criticism is part of specialist discourse in the field of sex determination research in a way that it was not in the 1980s and 1990s. As Sinclair, who discovered *SRY* in 1990, said in an interview: "I think humans like things to be ordered, and they get bothered about gray areas and when things become less clear-cut. But these days I don't think so much in black and white about male and female. Now I think of it all as being on a spectrum" (Beale 2001).

It is possible to explicitly link this gender-critical perspective to the cognitive content of sex determination research. Here we have observed gender criticism come to play a part in the larger organizing conception that researchers use to think about sex determination, the descriptive language of sex determination, and the day-to-day work of evaluating hypotheses and interpreting data. In their own words (even if often painfully unaware of the contributions of feminism to their work), we see that researchers have found gender criticism valuable to their thinking, and we can observe gender analysis entering into the standard epistemic strategies for criticism and analysis in this field.

This chapter profiles the social and epistemological advancement of gender criticism in the field of sex determination research during the 1990s. My focus on the gender dimension of sex determination research is, needless to say, not meant to imply that beliefs about gender were the *sole* factor shaping the *SRY* model of sex determination, nor that gender criticism was the sole motive force in the development of a new model. Gender criticism interacted with other factors, including advances in technology, new gene discoveries, and a broader rethinking of "master gene" theories in developmental biology over the past twenty-five years. Nonetheless, the contribution of gender criticism has been significant.

Notes to Chapter 2

Many thanks to Londa Schiebinger, who encouraged me to develop the ideas in this chapter and provided valuable feedback on drafts. Thanks also to Helen Longino, Nora Niedzielski-Eichner, Quayshawn Spencer, and the anonymous reviewer for insightful comments. This research was supported in part by the Marjorie Lozoff Fund, Clayman Institute for Gender Research, Stanford University.

1. The term *mainstreaming* is often used to describe the integration of feminist ideas and methods into the dominant practices of a field, but in this instance the term *normalization* is more appropriate. The field of sex determination genetics experienced a quiet and mostly unacknowledged shift in its epistemic practices. The term *normalization* is intended to highlight this feature of the entry of gender criticism into the field. In contrast, *mainstreaming* generally refers to explicit changes in social and institutional practices in which gender is systematically recognized as a category of analysis, as in changes to hiring and diversity practices, curricula, or the kind of scholarship recognized as prestigious in a field.

2. A further reason for the early and intense interest in the male sex-determining gene may be the dominance of the field by male researchers. This may have influenced both the research agendas and the culture of research and discovery. Bryan Sykes, for example, portrays the search for the male sex determining gene in the late 1980s as a "hunt" and a "race," a "spectator sport where the prize for winning was the glory of being first." Sykes also notes that David Page named his proposed sex-determining gene "DP1007"; writes Sykes, "I am sure I am not alone in noticing the initials and a certain masculine resonance in the last three digits" (2003, 60–66).

3. Graves's Y chromosome degeneration hypothesis, which predicts the disappearance of the mammalian Y chromosome over the next ten million years (Graves 2006), has become a curious flashpoint for cultural anxieties around feminism and male social status. Steve Jones's *Y: The Descent of Men* (2002) and Bryan Sykes's *Adam's Curse* (2003), which symbolically link the degeneration of the Y chromosome to the decline of male social status in the face of feminism, are representative.

3 One Thing Leads to Another

Gendering Research in Archaeology

Margaret W. Conkey

IF WE ARE TO ADDRESS gendered innovations in anthropological archaeology, we would ideally want to consider three interrelated topics. First, certainly one needs at least a brief review of what has been going on in the archaeologies of gender and the feminist practices of archaeology. For some fields, being brief may be all that there is to say. However, archaeology has fortunately witnessed an explosion of sorts, so being brief is not easy. Second, we would also want to explore what "counts" as innovations in archaeology. As with most fields these do shift and change, and what "counts" as an innovation to some may not be so to others. In any event, given that we have so-called gendered innovations, a much longer chapter would want to scrutinize whether these have had an impact, in what ways, and if these have influenced the agreed upon disciplinary standards for innovation. Third, we need at least one case study. Here that will be the focus of the chapter, where we look at a specific scholar and her work as an example of how "one thing leads to another" such that a research program has been irrevocably altered,

Acknowledgments: I am grateful to Londa Schiebinger for her continued consideration of archaeology among the sciences for feminist concern and scrutiny. This chapter was written during my 2004–2005 tenure at the Center for Advanced Study in the Behavioral Sciences, Stanford, California, and I am especially grateful to the Center for unbelievable support. Above all, I am grateful to the now dozens of archaeological colleagues who have made so many important contributions to an identifiable and vibrant community of feministly gendered archaeologies. I regret that rigid space limitations kept me from citing so many important contributions. While Olga Soffer has read one early version of this paper, she is not responsible for what I have done (or not) with her work and that of her colleagues.

and irrevocably engendered. In this chapter, I will discuss one scholar who began her career with one kind of viewpoint; a scholar who never imagined that her teaching would lead to the archaeology of gender and courses cross-listed with Women's Studies or that her research would take the lead toward significant innovations in methods, interpretations, and revelatory new—and highly gendered—understandings of specific archaeological materials.

Anthropological Archaeology, Gender, and Feminist Practices

I never cease to be amazed at how often I get such a quizzical look from people—educated, thoughtful, and even gender-sensitive people—when the concept of "feminist archaeology" is mentioned. What could this be? What kind of thing is that? Is it about claiming that all (or many) great things were done by women? Many find it hard to imagine that we can "see" what women did in the past (equating, of course, feminist archaeology with the roles and activities of women). Somewhat more thoughtful inquirers ask how one can know from "hard" archaeological evidence if women did certain things or had certain roles, even if most never thought to question how most archaeological reconstructions could be so sure as to how the past was the result of men's actions and powers.

But archaeology has had, over the past two decades in particular, a rich, variable, and noteworthy engagement with gender research and feminist theory and practices. I cannot begin to detail this—which it is indeed a delight to report—but can refer you to many texts and edited volumes (for example, Gero and Conkey 1991; Gilchrist 1999; Crown 2000; Joyce 2001; Pyburn 2004), several review papers (for example, Wylie 1992; Conkey and Gero 1997; Wylie 1997, 2001; Conkey 2003; Joyce 2004) and show that the interest is international in scope (for example, Bertelsen et al. 1987, in Norway; Du Cros and Smith 1993, in Australia; Wadley 1997, in Africa).

One can trace these past two decades in terms of various kinds of engagement. There are those studies that are various dimensions of critical engagement with the pervasive androcentrisms that have been documented, ranging from baseline critiques to deepening analyses with specific topics. As well, and simultaneously, have been the ongoing equity critiques (Nelson et al. 1994). Another genre of gender research has been that which constructively has made substantive contributions—and a difference—to so-called conventional topics—such as trade; burials and mortuary analysis; architecture and place; activities and roles, including power; and technological innovations. Even in the most conventional frame for archaeological research—that of the region (for example, the U.S. Southwest) or the period (for example, the Neolithic) or the "significant transition" (for example, to agriculture or to the state), gender and feminist accounts have appeared (for example, Brumfiel 1991 or Pyburn 2004 on "the state"; Crown 2000 on the U.S. Southwest; Watson and Kennedy 1991 or Peterson 2002 on the origins of agriculture).

Furthermore, gender and feminist theory have promoted engagement with topics that are completely new to archaeological inquiry, such as gendered socialization (for example, Joyce 1998, 2000), including children (for example, Baxter 2005), sexuality (for example, Schmidt and Voss 2000) and intimate relations (for example, Meskell 1998), mothering and midwifery (Wilkie 2003), among others. To varying extents, gender work has "gotten traction" (after Wylie) in almost all domains of Anglo-American archaeology. We have also witnessed the emergence of new conceptual and theoretical frameworks for understanding core aspects of past human life that have been directly mobilized by a gender-sensitive and feminist engagement, such as kinship and house societies (Joyce and Gillespie 2000) and technology (Dobres 2000). As well, there are considerations of intersectionalities of feminist archaeologies with relevant theoretical perspectives, such as with Black feminism (Franklin 2001) and with Indigenous archaeologies (Conkey 2005). There are also engagements with practices, pedagogies, presentation of research, community archaeology, and accountability, especially to descendant communities (for example, Conkey and Tringham 1996; Watkins et al. 2000).

So, you might say, what's the problem? While all of this work and all of these new insights are nothing to be belittled, some of us have our eyes on something of a prize, one that would have nothing less than transformative impacts on the practices of archaeology. "Doing" gender in archaeology is still somewhat marginalized, even ghettoized, and "done" almost entirely by women archaeologists. Articles in journals highlighting gender or with a feminist approach are still quite rare; most work is in edited volumes. Not every major PhD-granting institution has a female archaeologist, despite plenty to go around, numerically, and there are plenty of "gender troubles" in employment and promotion. Superlative theorists who incorporate feminist approaches find it hard to get positions, there has been only one job advertisement that explicitly lists feminist archaeology, and the gender of those doing theory is still predominantly male. The adoption of many feminist virtues of research practice (after Longino 1994 and Wylie 1995) is still elusive and often countered by authoritarian and absolutist discourses that proclaim rather simplistic views of the past, often without regard for, much less accountability to, the subjects either of the past or their descendants in living communities of today (although the politics and voices of Indigenous archaeologies are making this latter practice less viable). While we may indeed be reaching for the sky, many of us seek an archaeology that is fully reflexive and much more open to revision.

Many problematic domains persist, especially when it comes to interpretations of the "deep human past," which are still quite unaffected by the feminist critique and yet most problematic because they are appealed to as integral to "what it means to be human" and are drawn upon to naturalize and legitimate many deeply problematic, often patriarchal (sexist, racist, and classist) dimensions of contemporary cultures. Further, the archaeology of human evolution and of deep prehistory are more often at the interface with the public—in "lay public" journals, in ads, and in newspapers and television "documentaries." But before turning to a case study as to how one might make something of a difference, even for the "deep past," a few words regarding "innovations" in archaeology are in order, if only to anticipate what a feminist intervention might look like.

What Counts as an Innovation in Archaeology?

I am discussing here the archaeology done primarily by anthropologically trained archaeologists, less so by classicists or others who are perhaps more rooted in a historical and humanistic tradition. Many other approaches to gender in the past or to other disciplinary practices and preferences are necessarily not included. But anthropological archaeology of the Anglo-American genre has a long history of alignment and self-definition with archaeology as a scientific practice, not just as an inquiry that "uses" scientific methods and techniques, such as Carbon-14 dating or soil chemistry analyses. Most recognized disciplinary innovations are in the domain of techniques, methods, or methodologies, and much of the conceptual and theoretical work (if one can really separate methods from theories) has been drawn from sources external to archaeology or is dependent upon the successful or viable applications of said theory (for example, evolutionary theory, practice theory) to archaeological data or questions.

We can note that "discovery" still holds the trump card as innovation. This is not surprising given the integral practices of archaeology as being about searching (for new evidence or new patterns) and the powerful (and problematic, for feminist analysis) central role played by excavation in the disciplinary identity and regimes of value. Any discovery is further enhanced if the find in question can also be shown to be the "earliest" or "the first" manifestation of something—the earliest stone tools, the earliest evidence for rice agriculture, the earliest house structures, and so forth. Many go to great pains to characterize their discoveries within the rhetoric of an origin. Most of these origins or discovery claims have been highly gendered male, directly (Watson and Kennedy 1991; Conkey and Williams 1991), or, in the absence of an explicit consideration of the social implications or social contexts of a discovery, the gender (age, faction, class, etc.) implications are muted or ignored (Brumfiel 1992). Yet, in the context of a long history of representing innovations and action in the past as being predominantly a male affair (if only because the important markers of such innovation and action are gendered male—the rise of and control by chiefs, political expansionism, new durable technologies of weaponry, metallurgy, etc.), even if such accounts of origins are not explicitly gendered, they are usually assumed to have been the result of male action.

Additionally, new methods and techniques frequently count as innovations. Even the most theoretically oriented archaeologist recognizes that we have—and should have—forensic strengths, and new ways to wrest more cultural insights or "blood from stone" are highly valued. Many such innovative techniques are often derived from ancillary fields. For example, the exciting breakthroughs in understanding how some Ice Age cave art images in southwest Europe were made came from technical researchers at the Louvre who had the capabilities (and machinery and methods) to identify the composition of pigments used and the variations in the recipes of components that made up any given pigment. The identification of different "recipes" in turn allows for inferring connections between different sites on the landscape where recipes appear to have been the same. Additionally, the documentation of the variations and complexities in how pigments were actually made provides an empirical baseline for making claims about the ecological and material knowledge systems of prehistoric people (attesting to the specific ways in which they transformed raw materials—manganese, ochres, biotite, etc.—into viable pigments that would bind and "stick" to the walls) that in turn could contribute to wider inferences about the social relations of production. And, of course, as has been addressed elsewhere (for example, Russell 1991; Conkey 1997) the practices of "making art" have been overwhelmingly gendered male.

Often, an innovation in archaeology will be in the form of a rewriting—based on empirical evidence, often newly identified—of some part of the culture historical narrative. Examples here would include Kealhofer's (2002) revised trajectory for the development of agricultural systems in southeast Asia (from a single unilineal path once rice is domesticated, to a two-stage path) or Kirch's suggestion (Kirch and Sharp 2005) that the rise to power of the chiefs in Hawai'i took place in a much more rapid (than gradual) manner (based on new dating techniques used on coral offerings). Not surprisingly, such "new" versions of historical (or evolutionary) narratives are presented in terms of, based on, or motivated by a new discovery, something revelatory, a "find," or a new synthesis of materials and evidence. In some contrast to the "new finds" approach, one can take up a gender-sensitive viewpoint using extant archaeological materials that can not only be looked at in a new way, but can yield a new account, an-other story. Examples here are many, such as Brumfiel's (1991) analysis of Aztec weaving and cooking practices, which shows how much of the support for the Aztec empire was based on women's labor; or Peterson's (2002) rewriting of the major transformation we call the "origins of agriculture" from a gendered perspective that looks, for example, at how bodily practices and physical labors leave their "mark" and allow for new insights into the roles—and labors—of women.

Lastly, there are theoretical innovations in archaeology. One of the most explicit and striking in Anglo-American archaeology, for example, took place in the early 1960s, now called the "New" or Processual archaeology. This innovation involved an explicit shift in the core concept of "culture" (from culture-as-normative to culture-as-adaptive system) with subsequent redefinitions of research objectives and research design. Almost always, such theoretical innovations must be accompanied by specific application to an archaeological situation, data set, or way of working. The ways in which this particular theoretical formulation inhibited the engagement with gender and feminist issues have been discussed (for example, Wylie 2001). In what is widely recognized as a visibly placed early call (Conkey and Spector 1984) for getting a robust and organized archaeological consideration of gender off the ground, we authors were required by reviewers to have an application, a method, a way to "do" a gender-theory informed archaeology. Of course, there have been some theoretical developments since those of the 1960s and 1970s. One of the most powerful, gender-inspired critiques was that of Brumfiel (1992), arguing for "breaking and entering the ecosystem: gender, class and faction steal the show"! Others include views (lumped under the label of post-processual archaeology in the Anglo-American world, Johnson 1999) that have been more receptive to and compatible with feminist archaeologies (Engelstad 1992). This association has, however, been a two-edged sword, since, even today, the association of gender or feminist work with this post-processual set of theoretical perspectives has, for many, relegated feminist archaeology to a (misinformed) view as relativistic and "unscientific" (see Wylie 1992).

Of course, much more can be said about what "counts" as an innovation in archaeology, and what the implications are and have been for any gendered innovations. On the one hand, there has been relatively little discussion about feminist theories and archaeological innovations (but see, for example, Franklin 2001, or as discussed in Conkey and Gero 1997). On the other hand, there has been considerable debate and discussion about the techniques, methods, and methodologies that might render gender (and especially women and children) more "visible" archaeologically. Not surprisingly, some of us have voiced that feminist archaeology is not reducible to the discovery of "methodological breakthroughs" that would suddenly render women and gender visible. Often this call for methods or techniques has gone on as a discussion regarding the centrality or necessity of "gender attribution," that is, being able to attribute specific artifacts, structures, features, activities, and roles to specific genders, though usually this means women (Dobres 1995; Costin 1996).

There has long been a demand for the so-called smoking guns needed for an archaeology of gender—for example, burials (in which there can be highly probabilistic identification of the sex of the interred) and imagery (of males, females, etc.) on monuments or murals, and as figurines and the like. We have had, it seems, little problem in attributing a great deal of the archaeological record to men (the more salient stone tools, the hunting of big game, the making of "art," the development of power politics, the building of pyramids and mounds, the invention of writing by priests or temple accountants, domesticating gourds in order to have them available for shamans' rattles, etc.). It is perhaps not that archaeology needs to be gendered—it has been "saturated" with gender; it is more the case that it needs re-gendering, starting, of course, by questioning notions of gender that are limited to a bipolar male/female or an uncomplicated men and women. Of course, some thoughtful archaeologists have often recognized that many archaeological sites, as residential loci (villages, houses, gathering places) and abundant archaeological materials (ceramics, for example) have a very high probability of being, respectively, contexts within which men, women, and children were "at work" (and at play!), and the products of gendered labor.

One place to scrutinize the possibility or actuality of gendered innovations is to look at what archaeologists actually "do," interpretively, with new finds, discoveries, new techniques, or new ways to look at things. For this, I present below a "case study" of a colleague and her work over the past twenty years; someone who works in that "deep time" of some 25,000 years ago in what we call the Ice Age—a period that lacks historical and ethnohistorical documents, which are so often the crucial handholds for interpretation. Yet this is a period burdened by long-standing, deeply entrenched, difficult-to-dislodge androcentric paleovisions of humanity (for example, Gifford-Gonzalez 1992; Moser 1998; Dobres 2004).

In considering both the foregoing listing of innovations in archaeology, and in reading the following discussion about a single archaeologist, it is crucial to point out that the practice of archaeology is never that of a single individual, although it seems as if individuals are the ones who "make" the discoveries, who are credited with the "finds" and the new techniques, and often characterize the theories (for example, Binfordian archaeology). What is really important in assessing innovations in archaeology is the structural underpinnings, the institutional and funding contexts of discovery, and the distributed nature of how archaeological knowledge is produced. Archaeology is so collaborative, so teamwork dependent, so multidisciplinary that innovations cannot possibly happen from the labor of a single individual. While I focus below on one archaeologist and her work, I will include consideration of how her work is necessarily enmeshed in a network of collaborations and previous research, and why it is that it is her work and her authorship that "shows up" perhaps more so than the assembled collaborators and specialists with whose work her own is interdependent.

Olga Soffer: Rethinking the Ice Age, Re-Visioning Gender, Revisiting Venuses

Olga Soffer is a professor of anthropology at the University of Illinois, where she is one of two female archaeologists. She became an archaeologist after a first career as a fashion coordinator and special events manager for a New

York department store, bringing to her graduate program in the mid-1970s at the City University of New York an enviable ability to speak several languages, such as Russian and Serbian. Soffer's dissertation (in 1984) was a comprehensive compilation of empirical evidence and prudent interpretation regarding the lifeways of people who lived on the Russian Plain during some 30,000 years before the climatic shifts of the Holocene, at some 10,000 years ago— what we call the Upper Paleolithic (or last phase of the Old Stone Age). This was an award-winning dissertation in published form (Soffer 1985a), and its approach was quite mainstream for the early 1980s among Anglo-American archaeologists working on the Paleolithic. Using her language skills and an archaeological record—on the Russian Plain—that was marginal to the so-called heartland of the Upper Paleolithic (southwestern Europe), she was focused on documenting and understanding the increasing complexity of social organization of mobile hunting-gathering populations, arguing that our extant models have been too simple, with too much stress on the romanticized notion of hunter-gatherers as egalitarian.

One might suggest in hindsight that Soffer is already at the edge of what would become some key principles of a feminist approach to archaeology: a critique of simple and taken-for-granted models, looking for the complexity in both evidence and interpretations, thinking about social differentiations, and bringing into the literature evidence and (alternative) scenarios from "the margins" of the preferred research areas that had defined the paradigm for what life was like in the Ice Age.

Yet, this was research within the Anglo-American framework of the 1970s and 1980s: her analysis begins with the environmental setting (and climatic fluctuations) as a justifiable context within which social stress would have been at work, which itself required or fostered an increase in information flow between groups leading to an intensification of social interaction that, in turn, is associated with appearance of art and a quantitative increase in ritual behavior. That is, this is a systems model at a macro-scale, with environmental but not much historical specificity or contingency (what Tringham [1991] would have called research about "faceless blobs"). Any attention to individual agency or social practice was phrased in terms of how much labor was involved to construct some of the rather phenomenal (and heretofore unknown or underappreciated) mammoth bone dwellings they constructed.

Since it is her subsequent (and recent) work with material culture and the so-called Venus figurines that will attest her gendered shifts, it is of note that her approach to style and material culture at this mid-1980s time (Soffer 1985b), including the female or "Venus" figurines, discussed them in terms of their being status items; ways to control and manage scalar stress, differential access to resources, labor investment, and the standardization of production of some items; and in terms of their being linked to different manifestations of social hierarchy across a wide region from present-day Vienna to the central Russian Plain. Again this is pretty standard for archaeological accounts that consider culture as adaptive, material culture as "solutions" to social and environmental factors (and stresses), albeit, perhaps in Soffer's case, with a little extra emphasis on "the social." While such approaches do not necessarily exclude gender or feminist concerns, they consistently tend to "disappear" gender (after Longino 1994) and other more micro-scale, dynamic, on-the-ground aspects of human social life.

I have yet to track exactly how Soffer came to engage with her next projects, which have come to focus on a set of archaeological sites in the present-day Czech Republic or Moravia, dated to between 24,000 and 29,000 years ago (maximum range, so think 26,000 years ago), although as understood from a grounding in—and often in important comparative reference to—quite similar archaeological materials from major sites (for example, Avdeevo, Kostenki) on the Russian Plain dated to as much as 4,000 years later. Her own cultural and linguistic background, and a "realpolitik" decision on her part (as an older student, single mother) to "do" her Paleolithic archaeology in a less populated (by archaeologists) region than the ever-popular Dordogne (southwestern France) certainly promoted her continued focus on this region and its sites, whether before or after the Warsaw Pact world. However, in terms of the archaeology, material culture, and social worlds of the prehistoric Paleolithic peoples that played out, as they were, on a regional scale, this shift from the Russian Plain to the then-Czechoslovakia was not a significant shift.

Basically, Soffer came to focus on archaeological materials—fired earth (or "ceramic") artifacts—that are themselves considered to be technological innovations, but that had not been appropriately heralded as such. No application of certain analytic techniques to these materials had been carried out (to determine the manufacturing methods and firing temperatures, for example), nor had they been used for a more ambitious (but not unwarranted) suite of interpretive implications. Since the early twentieth-century

(1920s) excavations at the sites of the Dolní Věstonice locality in the Pavlov hills south of Brno (Czech Republic) (as well as at several other sites), ceramic artifacts had been known, although these are not pottery (jars, bowls, containers), which is almost always associated with the later periods of the Neolithic and the development of agricultural villages. And even though excavations at the Dolní Věstonice I site had revealed two walled structures used as kilns, even as merely a technological mastery or innovation, these finds had not been promoted or given their due in the history of technology—this is thousands of years "too early" for ceramic technologies and kilns! Such finds were both anomalous and, as far as one could tell, relatively unique, especially in their abundance (only six other examples from across the breadth of Eurasia had been reported for time periods stretching over thousands of years).

There are two relevant aspects to Soffer's work with these some 10,000 ceramic artifacts. First, in conjunction with a ceramics materials analyst from the Smithsonian (Pamela Vandiver), Soffer and her Czech colleagues (Vandiver et al. 1989, 1990) were able to demonstrate precisely how these "cooked earth" artifacts—including figurines of animals and a very famous so-called Venus figurine (Figure 3.1)—were made: the firing temperatures of the kilns and the nature of the subsequent thermal shock firing many of them—primarily clustered inside the kilns—were subjected to. This, in turn, provided the empirical baseline for challenging the prevailing modernist assumptions that the makers were trying to produce durable images in clay, and that the object of their labors was to produce a finished object that itself was the desired product or cultural goal—to be viewed, displayed, held, "objectified." This notion of "the object" could be challenged because, as they have shown, most of them were intentionally fired so as to shatter (with a sizzle and a pop!), often fragmenting into flying pieces of ceramics. The high fracture rate observed (and the structural nature of the fractures, see Vandiver et al. 1989) led them to infer that what was important was not the final durable product—the objet d'art—but rather the process of making and firing the objects. We again see how Soffer's work with long-known, but marginal, materials and sites, and a willingness to challenge fundamental (but problematic) assumptions about the intentions of past peoples in making figurines, including one of a human female, characterize her approaches.

Second, although their original study focused on the over 3,700 broken fragments of figurines (almost all of animals), from the site of Dolní

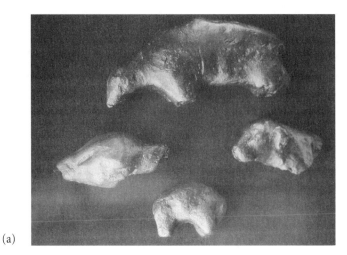

(a)

(b)

FIGURE 3.1 Early finds from Moravian sites, made from baked earth clay.
(a) Animal figures baked in earth clay, Dolní Věstonice, Moravia. (b) Female
clay statuette, Dolní Věstonice, Moravia. Reproduced from O. Soffer, J. M.
Adovasio, and D. C. Hyland, 2000, "The Venus Figurines: Textiles, Basketry,
Gender and Status in the Upper Paleolithic," *Current Anthropology* 41: 511–537,
Figure 3, page 516, which are drawn "after Klíma 1991, fig 15." Published
by University of Chicago Press © 2000 The Wenner-Gren Foundation for
Anthropological Research.

Věstonice I, they catalogued some 2,000 small (4–10 mm) gray pellets of ir-
regular shape to which Soffer would subsequently turn her attention (Figure 3.2). Of course, where would a good story go without a bit of serendipity,
which plays the next part in this account. As Soffer herself remarks about
what happened when an archaeological colleague from out of town visited
her: "we ran out of videos to watch and so I offered to show Jim [Adovasio]
some slides of these little ceramic fragments from the Moravian sites." As it
happened, Adovasio has long worked with basketry, twining, weaving, and
other "perishables" of human cultures. And, on these tiny pellets he thought
he could see clearly the traces of impressed fiber technologies—that is, things
made from plant fibers into what might have been mats, baskets, or other
"woven" goods.

Let me jump from this evening slide show to what Soffer and colleagues
have done with this, showing, I believe, how not only "one thing leads to another" but how this does not merely end up with a demonstration that prehistoric peoples made things with fibers (as we always assumed), but also how,
when taken up in a gender-sensitive context of inquiry, we have before us a
challenge, with empirical and analogical support, to the long-prevalent interpretations of "Venus" figurines, and some exciting ways to open up the inquiry into gender during the Upper Paleolithic. In pursuing their inference of
fiber technologies as impressed onto clay fragments that are the likely remains
of clay/earth floors of dwelling or working places, Soffer and Adovasio, along
with David Hyland, sought confirmatory lines of evidence in other archaeological domains, including a possible attestation to the wearing of "textiles"
on the few human depictions in the Upper Paleolithic, namely the "Venus"
(and other human) figurines.

In an article, "The 'Venus Figurines': Textiles, Basketry, Gender and Status
in the Upper Paleolithic," Soffer, Adovasio, and Hyland (2000) begin with a
critique of the androcentric bias in both popular and scholarly representations
of Upper Paleolithic life, gender roles, and activities. Unfortunately, this is still
often necessary in archaeological, especially Paleolithic, research. They also
broach right away one of the key issues in a gendered archaeology, namely, the
entire issue of "visibility." There is another full paper to be written on such a
topic, but, as alluded to above, one long-standing challenge to the inference
of women and gender in much archaeology, especially that of the "deep past,"
has been that women's work and roles (!) are not visible. Of course, this is often derived from the problematic assumption that all activities that result in

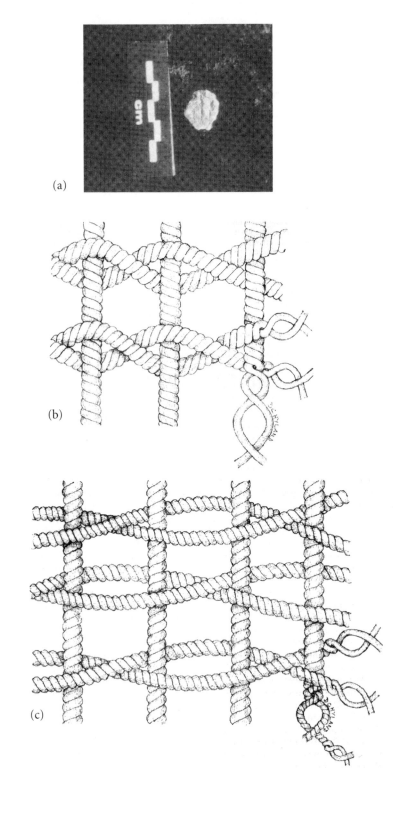

(a)

(b)

(c)

the accumulation of (the often best preserved materials of) bone and stone, for example, were men's work yet we do know that women are often those who process or butcher meat (Gifford-Gonzalez 1992) and that they certainly made stone tools (Gero 1991; Brandt et al. 1996). (For a detailed documentation of gendered labor in the Paleolithic of southern Germany, see Owen 2005.) With plant remains, extending to fiber-based technologies such as weaving or plaiting, there are not just preservational biases and "missing" evidence but, as they note, "deficient recovery techniques" (Soffer et al. 2000). These may come from the double jeopardy of "not thinking to look" (for such evidence), perhaps because of the association of the activities and technologies with other-than-masculinized heroic ancestors. (Whoever saw a headline proclaiming the earliest evidence for sewing?) These are also perhaps the kinds of inventions that are the less visible or invisible (and taken for granted) innovations that are viewed as the more mundane (Suchman 2005).

Archaeology has long suffered from "the fallacy of misplaced concreteness." Among the many goals of a feminist archaeology, one would be to extricate archaeology from the trap of a focus on and fetishization of the archaeological trace as a thing in itself (after Byrne 2003), and to address the problems of visibility in two senses: (1) this apparent invisibility of women and gender (and other contained, silenced, erased people and contexts), and (2) the optical illusion of visibility. That is, okay, so there are now women, men, children, but, look again: they are depicted in roles, attitudes, relations

FIGURE 3.2 Clay pellet and examples of the twining techniques (Pavlov site, Moravia). (a) Type I specimen of baked clay pellet with textile impressions. Photo by Olga Soffer, reproduced from J. M. Adovasio, B. Klíma, and O. Soffer, 1996, "Paleolithic Fiber Technology: Data from Pavlov 1, ca. 26,000 BP," *Antiquity* 70: 526–534, Figure 3b, page 529. Reprinted with permission of Antiquity Publications Ltd. (b) Diagram of the textile impression from Pavlov site, Type I specimen. Drawing by D. Hyland, reproduced from J. M. Adovasio, B. Klíma, and O. Soffer, 1996, "Paleolithic Fiber Technology: Data from Pavlov 1, ca. 26,000 BP," *Antiquity* 70: 526–534, Figure 3a, page 529. Reprinted with permission of Antiquity Publications Ltd. (c) Open diagonal twining, S-twist, Pavlov site. Drawing by D. Hyland, reproduced from J. M. Adovasio, B. Klíma, and O. Soffer, 1996, "Paleolithic Fiber Technology: Data from Pavlov 1, ca. 26,000 BP," *Antiquity* 70: 526–534, Figure 4a, page 531. Reprinted with permission of Antiquity Publications Ltd.

that are all-too-often merely extensions of stereotypical/problematic ones of the present.

To skip to the "results," of Soffer's work with Adovasio and Hyland (see also Adovasio et al. 1996; Soffer et al. 2002), the 2000 paper presents the following:

1. A summary of the evidence that they have accumulated for the existence of not just perishable technologies but for the complex and multiple ways of weaving and twining, for the weaving of textiles, the plaiting and coiling of baskets, the production of cordage and nets, as revealed by the impressions on some 78 fragments of impressed clay fragments from Dolní Věstonice (I) and Pavlov I. The range and variation is extensive indeed: single-ply, multiple-ply, braided cordage, knotted netting, plaited wicker-style basketry; non-heddle loom woven textiles, including simple and diagonal twined pieces; and plain woven and twilled objects (Figure 3.2). That is, woven textiles, baskets, and nets are represented, and seams suggest textiles were sewn together to produce more complex structures, such as clothing and bags. These are not "primary essays in the craft" (Soffer et al. 2000) but are very well-made items. Paleobotanical analysis for the site has documented that the specific climatic contexts within which many usable species for such fiber technologies existed and that some such species could be attested to by actual plant remains (Mason et al. 1994).

2. In a systematic and detailed examination of the so-called Venus figurines (and other humanoid statuettes) they show iconographic evidence on many (but not all!) for woven clothing, including several types of headwear, various body bandeaux, and at least one type of skirt. They argue that these plant fiber garments were exquisitely detailed, and selected for such detailed representation, such that one might thus infer the important role played by textiles in some Upper Paleolithic cultures. Furthermore, these "clothing" representations are quite varied across Europe—destabilizing the assumed model of a homogeneous class of material culture—"Venus" figurines—referable to fertility or erotic beliefs (see also Nelson 1990; Dobres 1992 on "Venus" diversity).

3. By asking how these fiber technologies were produced, what their functions were, and who made them and used them, they discuss the basis for associating these technologies with women, and with power, prestige, and value.

In addition, Soffer and colleagues go back to assemblages of other kinds of artifacts, often previously explained away as "decorative art" or "hunting weaponry" and show how they could be equally well (if not better) explained as net spacers, loom weights, spindle whorls, or as grass combs. And they use this research as a baseline for studying ethnographically documented bone and antler items used in weaving, basketry, and netting technologies, as a comparative baseline for reassessing the functions and uses of objects in the relevant Moravian archaeological assemblages (Soffer 2004). They are able to show that use wear patterns on some Moravian artifacts from several sites are very comparable to those on similar items (for example, battens) known to have been used for weaving in ethnographic contexts (for example, by Navajo weavers).

Some Concluding Thoughts

There are three levels of important points here. First, it is important to keep in mind the very powerful role that the "Venus" figurines have had in generating, sustaining, and continuously mobilizing specific gendered (and raced, see for example, Conkey 1997; see also Dobres 1992; Mack 1992) understandings of our human ancestors in Eurasia. We should not discount the disproportionate attention they have been given, among thousands of other artifacts and even figurines, in all sorts of pervasive grand narratives drawn upon and created by all sorts of interested parties who use the past for a variety of sociopolitical and cultural purposes.

Therefore, insofar as the interpretation of the "Venus" figurines are concerned, the work by Soffer and her colleagues is a crucial intervention into the long-standing, pervasive, and almost always biologically based interpretations of these depictions of females. Past interpretations have tended to minimize the variations (and almost never really considered that the variation might be patterned in culturally meaningful ways) or have emphasized the variations in body parts alone. They have sought essentialized interpretations, such as fertility figures, or mother goddesses, as paleo-erotica (made by men and for men, Guthrie 1984), gynecological primers (Duhard 1989), self-portraits (McDermott 1996), or signifiers of alliances between groups (Gamble 1982). A great deal of angst has been spent on how to account for the adiposity (only of some of them, however), especially among hunter-gatherers in the (presumably difficult) Ice Age (for example, Trinkaus 2005).

But what Soffer and colleagues have argued is that, it is not their anatomical features (breasts, lack of full legs, no face, vulvas or not) that differentiates them and in patterned ways, it is the detailing of the clothing that is both a representational focus and, most likely, one key to their cultural significance. Soffer and colleagues draw from contemporary theory on material culture, on the ways in which figurines may well be a "medium for the active construction of social identity" (after Lesure 1997, 229; see also Joyce 1993, 256), and how that which is selected for representation may be important clues as to what is being "talked about" in social life. Once one accepts that "the body" is an important domain for archaeological inquiry—as a feminist perspective might suggest (for example, Joyce 2005)—especially that the cultural body has a social skin, all sorts of new ways of looking at such figurines become possible. Furthermore, they have shown that, in such cases as the very well-known head of the "Venus" of Willendorf (Figure 3.3), what is represented there in such fine detail that they can see (with the use of the microscope and an understanding of the technologies of weaving) is not some sort of hairdo, but a cap, a spirally or radially worked item (see also the head from Kostenki I in Soffer et al. 2000). This depiction of a cap, in all its technological details, could only have been done by someone who has actually done such weaving. That is, "whoever carved the clad 'Venuses' was intimately familiar with fiber technology" (Soffer et al. 2000, 525). Drawing from ethnography about weaving and gender, the fact that none of the very few male (or abundant unsexed) figurines have any clothing depicted on them at all, and from a number of other lines of evidence, Soffer will push—not without basis—this interpretation into a discussion of gendered labor, agency, and the value of that labor.

Another move—where one thing leads to another—has been the extrapolation from the evidence for knotted cordage that might well sustain the probability and likelihood of the use of nets, and even for hunting. As has been amply documented ethnographically (for example, Satterthwait 1987), even large game can be successfully taken with communal nets. The way that the existence of such a technology itself intervenes into the overworked stereotype of "man-the-hunter" (with thrusting spear in hand) should not be underestimated.

Second, we do need to stress the distributed nature of archaeological inquiry in this specific case. The innovations suggested by Soffer and colleagues rest minimally on excavations that, in turn, provided materials for many subsequent specialist analyses (especially those of Vandiver, Adovasio,

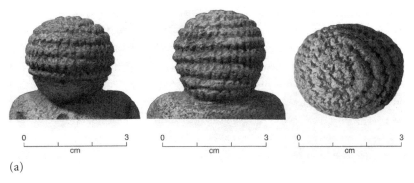

(a)

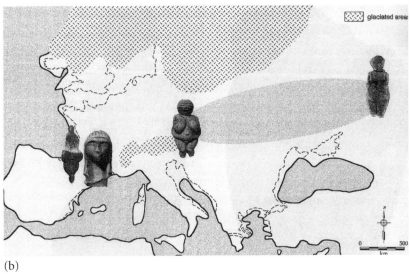

(b)

FIGURE 3.3 Venus wear: Willendorf (Austria) and elsewhere. (a) The spiral woven cap on the "Venus of Willendorf." Reproduced from O. Soffer, J. M. Adovasio, and D. C. Hyland, 2000, "The Venus Figurines: Textiles, Basketry, Gender and Status in the Upper Paleolithic" *Current Anthropology* 41: 511–537, Figure 4, page 517. Published by University of Chicago Press © 2000 The Wenner-Gren Foundation for Anthropological Research. (b) Venus wear map: in the west, knotted snoods and skirts; in the east and central Europe, twined caps and bandeaux. Reproduced from Soffer et al., 2000, Figure 11, page 522: "Distribution of the different types of clad Venus figurines," *Current Anthropology*. Published by University of Chicago Press © 2000 The Wenner-Gren Foundation for Anthropological Research.

Hyland, and archaeobotanists [Mason et al. 1994]), and all that it takes to sustain those institutionalized settings and technical analyses. Additionally, previous ethnographic work with artifacts that were, of course, originally the labor of Navajo weavers, and the curation of such for Soffer's analyses (Soffer 2004) provide the basis for which she could then develop an empirical component that is crucial to a robust interpretation. And while the particular accounts may have Olga Soffer as lead author and have been assembled by her as the lead or only author, these are surely put forth in the context of discussions, debates, and others' ideas as well as labors. So, why have I elevated Soffer here? What are the activities and rationales through which she, as only one actor in a complex web of distributed scholarly labor, is being put into the widest public view here?

When one looks at her career or scholarly trajectory, what may well be the contribution and the innovation of the moment may not be "the" interpretations per se—about Stone Age statuettes, about previously unevidenced prehistoric technologies (for example, weaving), about plausible expansions of gendered labors in the "deep past" and so forth—but, rather, the ways in which multiple contributions and scholarly practices have been configured and reconfigured, what Suchman (2005) calls "collective sociomaterial infrastructure building." To detail this for the Soffer and colleagues example requires more resources than I have at hand, but it is surely absolutely crucial to understanding a gendered innovation such as the "new" interpretation of the prehistoric past as articulated by Soffer and multiple colleagues. I honestly cannot specify the sociomaterial relations within which this particular distributed agency evolved, but it would be an interesting and informative project—for this and for most archaeological knowledge.

Third, at the level of assessing gendered innovations, I have selected the Soffer example for several reasons. First, this is not a scholar who came easily into the gender boom of the 1990s, but she is one who has long been engaged, probably unwittingly, with some aspects of what it might mean to "do social science/archaeology as a feminist" (Wylie 2001). I doubt she ever envisaged that by 2000 she would be teaching a class on Women in Prehistory cross-listed with Women's Studies (or taking herself the feminist theory class at Illinois, on a special faculty development program). But to me, this is another example of what Joan Gero and I found worked out so well in the 1988 conference that led to the 1991 edited volume, *Engendering Archaeology* (Gero and Conkey 1991). Here we invited numerous colleagues (some of them, by their own subsequent accounts, "kicking and screaming" [Tringham 1991]) to take their own empirical work, with which they were intimately familiar, and ask questions about it—from the perspective of gender, what gender has to do with it, or from a feminist perspective—even if they had never imagined or thought about "their specialties" that way before.

Soffer's work over the past decade has used an empirical richness—and much of it not of her own individual discovery, but surely mobilized by her energy and abilities to "think outside the box"—to question and destabilize long-standing assumptions. Not all or even most scholars would make the move from textile impressions on clay fragments to a consideration of what Soffer (Soffer et al. 2002) sometimes calls "Venus wear" (perhaps this is her fashion industry background coming through!). Of course, it is not insignificant that the recognition of clay-like technologies with the impressions of finger or palm prints had been made long ago at these sites and elsewhere but never taken up in a climate of Paleolithic studies that privileges the "hard" matters of stone (technologies) and bone (both technologies and subsistence). In fact, although even the "lines" of the textile impressions had been noted (at least in some early drawings), the actual recognition of these elements as being textile impressions took Adovasio's expertise and Soffer's collaboration. All the scholars involved have basically ridden away, so to speak, on the proverbial interpretive "wheel" that was "invented" with this recognition. To cite the work of Soffer and colleagues as a gendered innovation is to remark upon how it has opened up questions and possibilities—even within Soffer's own research trajectory: "What is inventive is not the novelty of the artifacts in themselves, but the novelty of the arrangements with other activities and entities within which artifacts are situated" (Barry 1999, 4)).

Although Soffer would firmly note that this extensive clay or ceramic technology at the Moravian sites is surely the oldest documented ceramic technology in the world—classic archaeological discourse for gaining requisite innovation attention—her own innovations and contributions lie not in the claim as an end in itself, but in showing how those prehistoric peoples themselves were engaged in the "ongoing collective practices of socio-material configuration and reconfiguration in use" (Suchman 2005). For feminist archaeologies, Soffer's expansive approach was crucial in making sure that a consideration of gender was not only possible but integral to what are reformulations of our questions, to a reconsideration of our methods and of our extant archaeological assemblages, to going beyond just a new and differently gendered account to one with the potential to reconfigure the practices of Paleolithic archaeology.

Archaeologists actually have something of a responsibility, and it is basically a feminist responsibility, nicely summarized by feminist anthropologist Henrietta Moore:

> [I]t is the archeologists rather than the post-modernists to whom we look to sustain our awareness of the plurality of social times. (Moore 1995, 53)

4 Sex Matters

Letting Skeletons Tell the Story

Lori D. Hager

R ECONSTRUCTIONS OF LIFE in the past often begin with identifying the sex of skeletal remains. Sexing an ancient skeleton as
male or female holds immediate consequences for interpretations of that specific individual, and for humans more generally. That "Lucy" was female and
"Kennewick Man" male immediately establishes the identity of these bones as
individuals, as representatives of their sex, and as representatives of their species. When sex is assigned, a skeleton ceases to be simply a biological remnant
preserved by the idiosyncrasies of time and suddenly becomes embodied as a
man or a woman with a distinct cultural identity—often one assigned by us
and having to do more with our culture than its own. Skeletal analyses are
both informed and driven by the sex they are assigned.

When the sex of a fossil is identified, modern humans conjure up visions of the past—as attested by the many dioramas recreating ancient life
in museums throughout the world. Visual images are powerful tools that present life in former times. These, however, are often taken as "the way it was"
rather than as one interpretation among many (Conkey 1997). In the well-
known image of "Lucy" and her mate at the American Museum of Natural

I would like to thank Londa Schiebinger for inviting me to participate in this volume and for her
incredible patience. For the many years of discussion on these issues, I have been lucky to have
Meg Conkey as a friend and colleague living nearby. As I was working on this chapter, the great
feminist Betty Friedan died on her 85th birthday. I thank her for recognizing the possibilities of
women's lives and the lives of the many daughters yet to come. As always, thanks to John Holson
for his continual support.

History (see Figure 1.4, this volume), the sex of "Lucy" as female is central to that reconstruction of life even though what is seen is not based on evidence (Zihlman 1997). The sex roles in the past are clear from this portrait. Pair-bonds are common. Females are small and need protecting; males are large and do the protecting. What might that diorama look like if "Lucy" had been sexed male?

In practice, archaeologists and paleoanthropologists are faced on a continuing basis with skeletons or fossilized remains that are in need of sex determination. Given the importance of sexual identity to our interpretations of the past, sex determination of skeletal material should be solid. However, misidentification of skeletons as males or females does occur in large part because of poor preservation of the specimens (Walker et al. 1988), but also because of various forms of cultural bias. Kenneth Weiss (1972) first noted bias in the sexing of skeletons from archaeological and fossil collections. He showed that more male assignments are made than female ones, particularly when the skeleton shows signs of strength by being large and robust. Weiss suspected that the "larger-smaller" nature of many non-pelvic traits produces a higher percentage of male assignments than would be expected in the population. This results in many well-developed females being mistakenly diagnosed as males. Skeletons of intermediate size and robusticity are particularly vulnerable to misidentification because these skeletons often represent females who fall outside the "normal" range of variation. Weiss also noted age-related bias favoring male assignments. This important study quantified an underlying bias in sexing skeletons derived from long-standing cultural beliefs about the physical nature of men and women.

The view of women as physically smaller and less active relative to men has been a prevailing theme in Western societies for hundreds of years. Londa Schiebinger (1987) documents how eighteenth-century European anatomists were complicit in defining the nature of women as belonging to motherhood and the home by illustrating female skeletons as they thought they should be rather than how they actually were. Traits considered to be female/feminine such as a small skull, short stature, small body build, but large pelvis, were emphasized and even exaggerated. In the late nineteenth century Charles Darwin (1871) articulated a rigidly Victorian view of males and females within his sexual selection theory that has been highly influential in biology, and specifically in defining the nature of humans (Hubbard 1979; Fedigan 1986). He believed human females to be nurturing, maternal, reclusive, and altruistic while he saw human males as forceful, assertive, courageous, inventive, and energetic. Males were larger than females because of male-male competition for females and because males must also provide for the females. The female role was reproductive—focused on bearing and nurturing children—while the male role was active and complex. Darwin viewed human evolution as driven by males with females evolving by the "equal transmission of characters" or on the "coattails" of males.

In human evolutionary studies, the influential "Man-the-Hunter" model of the 1960s closely followed this theme by relegating females to the background and males to the foreground. Hunting and other typically male activities were thought to account for the entire evolutionary trajectory of humans from bipedalism to large brains to technological innovations. Anthropologists and archaeologists of this time barely discussed females' roles beyond reproduction (Washburn and Lancaster 1968) even though the important role of women to subsistence in traditional modern societies was just becoming a topic of interest (Lee 1968).

With the majority of anthropologists wedded to the "Man-the-Hunter" model of human evolutionary events where men were driving evolution and women were nearly absent, Sally Slocum (1975) and Nancy Tanner and Adrienne Zihlman (1978) rightly asked: Where are the women and what were they doing? With these simple yet vital questions, women scientists along with a few male ones considered the evidence from a viewpoint where women were central, not peripheral, to life in the past. The "Woman-the-Gatherer" model promoted the view of women as active agents of evolutionary change. Caregiving was only one part of the daily life of early hominid females, which required that they use the landscape as the males did in search of food, water, and shelter, in avoidance of predators, and in the making and using of tools. The "Woman-the-Gatherer" model challenged the passive nature of women and, by doing so, one half of the species became recognized as active contributors to the evolutionary history of humans.

Glynn Isaac (1978) also recognized the critical economic role of women in modern hunter-gatherer societies ignored by the "Man-the-Hunter" model. In Isaac's "Home-Base" hypothesis, there was a clear sexual division of labor of early humans with males hunting and females gathering. But Isaac envisioned the interdependency of males and females as each returned to the communal camp to share the collected resources. Both men and women were central to daily life in this relatively egalitarian model. The lack of archaeological evidence for the "home-bases," however, limited the acceptance of the model in its strictest sense.

The essential contribution of women in the human evolutionary story was not widely accepted, and the "Woman-the-Gatherer" and "Home-Base" models were soon followed by the "Man-the-Provisioner" model (Lovejoy 1981). Similar in some ways to the earlier "Man-the-Hunter" view of the past while at the same time co-opting features from the "Woman-the-Gatherer" view, Lovejoy's model reestablished the centrality of males in human evolutionary events and relegated females to reproduction and little more. Males provide food for the females in exchange for sex and assured paternity of offspring; females pair-bond with the males so they and their offspring will be provided for. Although Lovejoy's model has been criticized in many of its details and its lack of evidence (Hrdy 1981; Fedigan 1986; Falk 1997; Zihlman 1997), his hypothesis continues to be given serious consideration in popular introductory textbooks when discussing the origins of bipedalism and sex roles in early human prehistory (Jurmain et al. 2005).

Even though the "Woman-the-Gatherer" model was by no means adopted by the majority of the discipline, its influence has been significant. In an atmosphere where female roles were being questioned in related fields such as primatology (Lancaster 1975) and social-cultural anthropology (Reiter 1975; Rosaldo and Lamphere 1974) the "Woman-the-Gatherer" model opened the debate on the role of women in human evolution, and once started, it has not stopped. The "Man-the-Hunter" model crumbled once the bias and the lack of evidence were exposed. The important questions raised by the "Woman-the-Gatherer" model in concert with a changing view of females in related fields has influenced a new generation of researchers who do not systematically ignore or diminish the role of women in prehistory.

An examination of men and women in more recent prehistory by archaeologists has been profoundly affected by the landmark paper from Meg Conkey and Janet Spector (1984). In this paper, Conkey and Spector argue that gender has an effect on the reading of the archaeological record and, at the same time, gender is a crucial element of the record. A new view of women in prehistory that includes a variety of significant and important activities by women emerged from this important paper (see Gero and Conkey 1991; Du Cros and Smith 1993; Conkey, this volume). For many, the passive or absent female has been replaced by a complex and dynamic participant in life. Moreover, assumptions about males and females in the past have been challenged on many levels so that sex roles in the past are not dependent on present views of men and women.

A view of women as active, engaged members in past human societies has emerged from these pivotal studies in human evolution and archaeology. But have these studies changed the "cultural stereotype" that sees males as large and robust and females as small and gracile? If the current view of prehistoric females is active and engaged, is this reflected in the sexing of skeletons? Is the bias noted by Weiss (1972) still present?

Sexing Skeletons

Sex is determined through a serious studying of the skeleton based on the standards established by forensic anthropologists, physical anthropologists, and others (see Krogman and İşcan 1986; İşcan and Kennedy 1989; Mays and Cox 2000; Walrath et al. 2004). At its roots, sex determination in skeletons is about biological sex where the goal is to link the expression of phenotypic traits with the X and Y chromosomes carried by the individual. The best sexing criteria on the skeleton should exhibit bimodal distributions where the overlap of trait expression between the sexes is low. Based on differences due to reproduction, many pelvic traits in humans are indeed bimodal and do sort skeletons into males and females with high accuracy. Pelvic traits are the most reliable sex indicators present on the human skeleton although enough population differences exist to warrant caution in comparisons between samples (İşcan and Kennedy 1989; Mays and Cox 2000). Other traits are used to sex skeletons, particularly in the absence of the pelvis, including traits on the skull and lower jaw. Some of these traits are more accurate than others in sex determination, but all are less reliable than those of the pelvis.

Body size and bone robusticity are two non-pelvic traits routinely used to determine sex. These traits contribute to the male-bias sex ratios noted by Weiss (1972). Size and robusticity may be useful when population-level variation is considered, but their predictive value for sex determination is otherwise low because both biological and environmental factors are responsible for bone growth and bone degradation. With a basic morphology situated in biology, bones respond to the ebb and flow of exercise, diet (good, poor, or intermittent), physiological stress, disease, and trauma. Bone biology is clearly affected by activity and nutrition in terms of muscle strength, bone mineral density, and body size (Bassey and Ramsdale 1994; Soderman et al. 2000). Anne

Fausto-Sterling (2005) correctly argues that bone biology is a good example of the interplay between genetics, hormonal influence, and the environment because both biology and life experience are responsible for the ultimate course taken in human bone development.

In sexing human skeletons, physical anthropologists have treated differences in body size and robusticity as if they are discrete traits, but in reality, these traits show a continuous distribution with considerable overlap between the sexes (Krogman and İşcan 1986; İşcan and Kennedy 1989). Scholars have not always considered or appreciated that females might practice hard physical labor in life where strong, robust bones would be present. While moderate levels of dimorphism exist in modern humans, no evidence suggests that all females will be small and gracile and all males will be large and robust. To the contrary, the mechanics of bone biology suggest that both males and females will vary in size and robusticity. Physical anthropologists have documented and acknowledged the complex nature of bone development, but in practice they often consider size and robusticity in determining the sex of skeletal material.

This is particularly true in paleoanthropology where the sex of fossil hominids is often based on the overall size and robusticity of the specimens and, where available, pelvis size and shape. Unlike archaeologists who deal only with *Homo sapiens* when making decisions regarding sex, paleoanthropologists must consider multiple hominid species where size and robusticity are also important factors in distinguishing the genus and species. Do differences in size between specimens represent differences in males and females of the same species, or do they reflect differences between more than one species? When the fossils are considered members of the same species, sex is assigned based on the "larger-smaller" scale for males and females.

In the past, paleoanthropologists have postulated a close but mistaken association between size and sex in fossils. While the "Man-the-Hunter" model prevailed in the late 1960s and early 1970s, for example, *Australopithecus africanus* and *Australopithecus robustus* were thought to be the female and male counterparts of the same species (Wolpoff 1971). Size differences were significant with the males being quite large and robust compared to the gracile females. This view was short-lived in the light of the mounting fossil evidence, but the idea that there might be large size differences in hominids due to sex has been a recurring theme in human evolutionary studies. Today, not only are these fossils considered different species but many call further for a genus-level distinction, replacing the genus *Australopithecus* with *Paranthropus* for the robust specimens.

In a similar fashion, Louis and Mary Leakey simultaneously used size to determine sex and to determine the genus and species for the hominids from Olduvai Gorge, Tanzania. At the time, this was the common manner in which paleoanthropologists determined sex in fossils where size differences between males and females were expected. In the 1960s and 1970s, many new fossils were found and placed into a new genus and species, *Homo habilis*, or "Handy Man" because of the association of these fossils with stone tools (Tobias 1965). Paleoanthropologists attributed the clear size variation between the specimens to sex differences (Walker and Leakey 1978). Later, they revised their viewpoint when it was recognized that the variation was due to more than size alone, resulting in the large and small specimens being placed into separate species (*Homo rudolfensis* and *Homo habilis*) (Wood 1985). Scientists based their revision on a reevaluation of the complexity of variation in the fossil record as they discovered additional fossil specimens and to a growing recognition that sexing skeletons based on size alone could lead to erroneous conclusions. At this time, body size dimorphism was a leading issue in paleo-anthropology, mainly because of "Lucy."

Paleoanthropologists used body size and pelvic morphology in sexing the now famous hominid fossil named "Lucy." A prize find in the 1970s, this fossil has garnered worldwide attention ever since. Because of the immediate sexing and naming of the fossil, few have questioned whether "Lucy" was a female. The story of why "Lucy" and not "Sgt. Pepper" is well known (Hager 1991, 1997; Zihlman 1997; Schiebinger 1999): within twenty-four hours of finding the skeleton, which included parts of the pelvis, and well before systematic analysis of the remains had been made, Donald Johanson and his colleagues had declared the skeleton a female, "Lucy" after the Beatles song, thus sexing (and gendering) this individual forever.

Later, Johanson and others undertook a full analysis of the skeleton, confirming their original interpretation of the skeleton as female. The placing of the specimen into a new species prompted a renewed look at the nature and extent of sexual dimorphism in early human ancestry (Day et al. 1980; Kimbel and White 1988). When other physical anthropologists studied further the hipbone, sacrum, and reconstructed pelvis of "Lucy," several aspects of the specimen actually looked more male-like than female-like (Tague and Lovejoy 1986; Hager 1991). These results were at first surprising. Did this mean

"Lucy" was actually a male and that the small size of the skeleton influenced the sex determination? Or did it mean that the modern traits being used to determine sex were not relevant to this species?

In fact, both are true. Johanson and his colleagues used the diminutive size of the individual to identify the sex of the skeleton as female in a manner consistent with the "larger-smaller" concept of males and females (Kimbel and White 1988). They emphasized the small size of "Lucy" once larger specimens were discovered at a site nearby. At the same time, Johanson used modern pelvic criteria to sex "Lucy" (Johanson and Edey 1981; Johanson et al. 1982) but physical anthropologists now question the relevancy of these criteria to nonmodern hominid species.

When the pelvis is available, physical anthropologists have tended to apply modern sexing criteria to the fossil specimens. My examination of fossil hip-bones ranging in age from several million years ago until several thousands of years ago reveals, however, that modern sex differences in the pelvis were a late evolutionary development (Hager 1991, 1996). Sex differences in the early hominids, like the australopithecines, were not like sex differences in modern humans. Sex differences in modern humans result from selection on the female for a large pelvis where reproductive success depends on the successful birth of a large-headed neonate (Rosenberg 1992). The australopithecines were small-headed and therefore pelvic dimorphisms based on parturition were minimal. The pelvis of early hominids should not be expected to have the same kinds of sex differences as modern humans and therefore should not be sexed as male or female based on these modern criteria. Beginning some two million years ago, the hominid brain shows a significant expansion in size, and this is when modern sex differences in the pelvis appear in some fossil hominids. The pelvis of "Lucy" is unique to the species and it is best evaluated with this in mind.

Establishing sex early in an analysis of any given fossil begins the reconstruction of that individual and, at the same time, drives it. It is important to understand the extensive consequences that the sexing of "Lucy" as female held for all other interpretations of the species *Australopithecus afarensis* and of sexual dimorphism in early human evolution. For example, Johanson and his team found additional fossils in other locales in Hadar, Ethiopia, where "Lucy" was discovered. Many of these new specimens were quite a bit larger than "Lucy." Because "Lucy" was small and designated female, the large ones became "males." Johanson attributed the considerable size variation between specimens to sex differences, and even today, *Australopithecus afarensis* is considered to be a highly sexually dimorphic species where males and females may vary as much as modern orangutans with males being twice as large as females (McHenry 1991). That our earliest hominid ancestors are considered highly dimorphic with regard to sex is the direct result of the small hominid named "Lucy" being sexed female.

When sex differences are high in our ancestry, with males being perhaps twice as large as females, the inequality of males and females is emphasized in both a physical sense and a social sense. High sexual dimorphism reinforces the perception of females as small and subordinate and males as large and dominant. Figure 1.4 (see Schiebinger, this volume) is a good example of how life in the past is reconstructed when males and females show significant differences in body size. The image promotes Lovejoy's model with "Lucy" pair-bonded and with the male in the dominant, controlling role. For these reasons, the sex determination of early hominids has an underlying significance beyond the fossils themselves.

Several paleoanthropologists, however, dispute the single-species hypothesis relative to the *afarensis* material. They disagree with the claim that the observed variation can be accommodated into one sexually dimorphic species, and they argue instead that the small fossil specimens once thought to be females, including "Lucy," are actually a different species from the larger specimens (Day et al. 1980; Zihlman 1985). This interpretation of the *afarensis* material does not immediately suggest that "Lucy" was a female or that sexual dimorphism in our ancestry was high. In this interpretation, "Lucy" may or may not have been a female, but the determination of this does not depend on the small size of the specimen.

The importance placed on the size of the specimen for sex determination has been extended to juveniles. A relatively new skeleton of *Australopithecus afarensis* from Ethiopia has been sexed female even though the individual is considered to be approximately 3-years old at the time of death (Alemseged et al. 2006). In modern humans, it is extremely difficult to accurately sex prepubescent juveniles due to the lack of sexually differentiating traits in their skeletons, thereby making the sex determination of a 3-year-old hominid highly questionable where the pattern of ontogenetic development is even less secure.

Sexual dimorphism and its relevancy to all levels of interpretation of the hominid fossil record are demonstrated by new fossil finds of early *Homo* specimens from Kenya (Spoor et al. 2007). Reinforcing the concept of high sexual dimorphism in our ancestry, a small *Homo erectus* skull has been sexed as female based on the "larger-smaller" scale for fossil skulls. This interpretation ensures the specimen is taxonomically placed into *Homo erectus* and that the species is recognized as a single, sexually dimorphic one.

Sex determination of early hominids is admittedly difficult. On the one hand, the most reliable modern sexing criteria of the pelvis are not relevant for sexing the early hominids. On the other hand, using size and robusticity to determine sex may result in biased sexing because the traits are based on the "larger-smaller" concept of males and females of an unknown scale. Refining sexing criteria for increased accuracy depends on recognizing traits that are biased. This can only occur when paleoanthropologists question sex determinations based on long-standing viewpoints of males and females in the past. The reevaluation of sex determination in fossil hominids stems from the recognition that bias exists, even if it is difficult to recognize, and that reconstructions of life in the past are profoundly affected by these sex determinations.

Modern humans display moderate levels of sexual dimorphism and modern sexing criteria are more accurate. Skeletons of modern humans from archaeological sites tend to be more complete and better preserved compared to the fossil hominids. In addition, the sample sizes are often large so that consideration of population variation is possible within a particular environmental and cultural context. Skeletal sex determination in burials is the foundation for the study of gender at archaeological sites. Interpretations of male-female patterns in grave goods, levels of activity, diseases, trauma, and survivorship all depend on accurately sexed skeletons.

Denise Donlon (1993), a participant in the Women in Archaeology conference in Australia in 1992, followed up on Weiss's findings (1972) of male-sex bias in sexing human skeletons. Examining the sex ratios from several archaeological samples of Australian Aborigines recovered from the 1950s to the 1990s, she found that the percentage of skeletons sexed males was well over the 50 percent expected sex ratio and even approached 90 percent at one site. Donlon noted that the bias in sex ratio toward males may be due to differential burial practices, but she does not rule out a bias against females when sexing robust skeletons. Moreover, Australian Aborigine samples were more likely to be sexed male than non-Aboriginal ones, indicating that the robust skeletons of male and female Aborigines contribute to sex determination.

Karen Bone (1993) also addressed the bias first identified by Weiss (1972) by analyzing large numbers of burials from archaeological sites in North and

South America. Bone noted that since the 1970s physical anthropologists have privileged pelvic traits over non-pelvic ones in efforts to increase the accuracy in determining sex. She believes this has led to a reduction in bias in the sexing of skeletons. Male-biased sex ratios increase, however, whenever physical anthropologists used subjectively scored non-pelvic traits. Bone also found that other sex-bias ratios were due to different ways men and women were buried.

Phillip Walker (1995) has explored issues of poor preservation and sex bias by examining archaeological specimens in conjunction with historical documents. Focusing specifically on cranial morphology, he found bias in how skeletons were sexed, a "sexism in sexing," as he put it. Walker noted that older females were not accurately represented in archaeological samples because of the changes that occur in postmenopausal female skulls. These females are often misclassified as males because cranial robusticity increases as the female ages. Moreover, Walker's comparative samples suggested that some young males may also have been misidentified as females due to the gracile nature of their cranial features that become more robust with age.

Walker (2005) noted similar age-related changes for the pelvis. Specifically, he found that the greater sciatic notch, an important sexing criterion, changes from a more feminine form to a more masculine one as the individual gets older. As with the cranium, older women tend to be assigned to the male category and younger males to the female one.

Walker believes this pattern of "sexism in sexing" is not overt but rather it is based on the unconscious "cultural stereotype of 'typical' female morphology" that sees males as large and robust and females as small and gracile (1995, 36). More than twenty years after Weiss's landmark study (1972), Walker demonstrated that bias in sexing skeletons is still present because archaeologists are unable to recognize or accept robust females in the samples. Moreover, Walker's study shows that the "larger-smaller" perception of males and females continued even after the recognition that older women have robust skulls and that many prehistoric women led active, dynamic lives and had potentially robust skeletons.

Although bias against robust females does continue, the recognition of potential male bias in sex ratios from non-pelvic traits from studies like Walker (1995) has prompted several researchers to reevaluate how sex is determined (Murail et al. 1999; Kjellström 2004). Increasingly, scholars have rejected the automatic assumption that females are passive and inactive that drove much of earlier archaeology and paleoanthropology. Instead they leave open the option that prehistoric females may be large, robust, active, and strong in both muscle and bone. Moreover, they are careful not to misidentify skeletal material by overlooking the age-related changes in older females and in younger, gracile males. Studies today reject most subjective indicators related to bone size and robusticity that have been the main sources of male bias in sex ratios. Scholars working in these areas today strive to eliminate nonquantifiable traits for sexing skeletons where males and females overlap in their expression, and in so doing they hope to reduce or eliminate the male bias.

Numerous studies in bone biology on modern men and women in a variety of disciplines have prompted physical anthropologists to revise cultural stereotypes surrounding notions of robust males and gracile females. Understanding the complex nature of bone biology in modern men and women where many factors contribute to bone development and degeneration has increased significantly in the last twenty years (Fausto-Sterling 2005). Walker (1995), for example, addressed bias related to changes in the postmenopausal skull of females as a direct result of our increased knowledge of older modern women and their bones. The more we know about bone biology in modern men and women, the better we can address preconceptions of males and females in the past and the bias in sex assignments that resulted from these views.

Letting Skeletons Tell the Story

The human skeleton has a story to tell even after the individual dies. The goal in identifying sex is to pay attention to the facts embedded in the skeleton first and foremost. Gender analysis, particularly in archaeology, reminds us that the skeletons from the deep past are not part of our culture and that, through our interpretations, they should not come to embody preconceptions that govern our culture today.

Paleoanthropologists' long-standing practices of naming ancient human skeletons have added to the difficulties in retaining an objective stance in interpreting the meaning of fossils. Names situate specimens within a cultural context. By assigning the highly gendered "Lucy" to the specimen soon after it was found, "her" sex and gender became etched in stone. Even as early as the 1890s, fossils were named in ways that identified their sex and held immediate gender implications. Consider the images conjured by the names "Java Man," "Piltdown Man," "Peking Man," "Cro Magnon Man," and "Mrs. Ples."

Or those associated with the names Louis and Mary Leakey bestowed on their hominid finds coming out of the well-known Olduvai Gorge site in Tanzania beginning in 1959: "Nutcracker Man," "Jonny's Boy," "George," "Cinderella," and "Twiggy" to name a few of the more famous ones (Leakey 1984). "Millennium Man," an early bipedal hominid found in Kenya in 2000, is a recent example (Pickford and Senut 2001).

Names resonate with the people and help the general public connect with the bones that scientists promote as human ancestors. People like to refer to these skeletons in terms they can understand and identifying the sex of a fossil becomes an important part of this process. But the names immediately seal the sex/gender of the skeletons, whether or not scientists have fully analyzed those characteristics. In many instances, these gendered names unduly gender our vision of our own past. While scientists continue to name the skeletons they unearth, some progress has been made relative to the naming of female skeletons. Today, when a skeleton is sexed female, paleoanthropologists tend give it a "feminine" name or other designation such as "Woman." This reflects a shift away from the use of the generic "Man" in the public and scientific arenas—a shift that resulted in large part from feminist critiques of such practices.

When scientists discover skeletons from past humans and determine their sex, the history of the sexes is changed, even if ever so slightly. Each new discovery reveals a little bit more about men and women in the past, and since we are their legacy, we come to know a bit more about ourselves. The story is inevitably complex because genetics, hormones, and life experience of an individual together shape a skeleton and the markings of its sex. Identifying sex in skeletons may be difficult because of these factors, but the story that unravels from these "readings" can often be extremely rich. Letting skeletons tell their own stories freed as much as possible from modern-day preconceptions of gender is the only way we will come to understand fully males and females in the past.

In the future, it is likely that analysis of genotype will replace phenotype in determining sex in skeletons. Ancient DNA studies have grown significantly over the years and, with new methods and techniques, this may prove an extremely promising way to determine sex in skeletons. The study of ancient DNA from archaeologically derived materials has already yielded results for genetic sex, including the sex of juvenile skeletons (Kaestle and Horsburgh 2002), although significant difficulties remain in the application of these methods to the everyday analysis of bones by the paleoanthropologist and bioarchaeologist (Brown 2000). Innovative new techniques combined with new critical views of females should result in increased accuracy in sexing skeletons.

There is no doubt that gender analysis has brought important changes to paleoanthropology and archaeology over the past thirty years. Gender analysis has enriched our understanding of our earliest hominid ancestors, and, in particular, what it has meant to be male and female in the course of human evolution. These changes have been brought about by asking relatively simple but essential questions: Where are the women and what were they doing? Is there a bias in the sexing of skeletons? What is the nature of this bias? That the bias against females has been recognized and that women are now viewed as active participants in the life of our ancient ancestors suggests that these changes are here to stay. As gender analysis moves forward, what further insights will it bring?

5 Change around the Edges

Gender Analysis, Feminist Methods, and
Sciences of Terrestrial Environments

Louise Fortmann, Heidi Ballard, and Louise Sperling

WE ARGUE HERE that (1) recognition of anthropogenic effects on contemporary landscapes and ecosystems in the context of a series of scholarly and political events created a space in which women's work and knowledge became visible to some scientists and (2) this enabled gender analysis and feminist research methods to affect the process and content of terrestrial environmental sciences. Our case studies come from forest ecology and plant breeding, but our argument applies more generally. We show that just as women plant crops around the edges of men's crops, gender analysis and feminist methods have made changes around the edges of practice in these sciences.

In contrast to a field like physics, it is impossible to discuss the terrestrial environment for very long without reference to humans. Since the atmosphere transports human influences over space and time (Matson 1996), it isn't even necessary for humans to be present in a particular place at a particular time

Thanks to Londa Schiebinger for the invitation to think about this exciting topic. This chapter has benefited from input from a multidisciplinary group of scholars. Scientists from the International Center for Tropical Agriculture (CIAT), pathologist Robin Buruchara, and plant breeders Steve Beebe and Roger Kirkby provided invaluable information and feedback on the Rwanda PPB section. Conversations with political scientist and activist Irene Tinker and anthropologist Donald Moore informed the section on early feminist work and activism on women and agriculture. Conversations with policy analyst Emery Roe and philosopher Alison Wylie were helpful. Special thanks are due to Don Collins, Floral Greens Harvesters, and Rwandan Bean Experts, partners in the two research projects described here.

for their influence to be evident and enduring in that ecosystem.[1] The recognition of the predominance of human dominated ecosystems (Vitousek et al. 1997) has led terrestrial environmental scientists to recognize the importance of social structures and processes in their work. This is particularly true in the case of working rural landscapes where the actions of farmers, foresters, hunters, and others affect terrestrial ecosystems. Thus knowledge about agrarian production systems is relevant to terrestrial environmental sciences.

Gender Analysis and the Terrestrial Environmental Sciences

As Bocking (2004) noted, research agendas create areas of ignorance (see also Chambers 1983, Frickel and Vincent 2007). Research on agrarian production systems proceeded for decades on the assumption that men were farmers and foresters while women were housewives. This created a huge area of ignorance regarding what women knew and did in and to local ecosystems.

The 1970 publication of Danish economist Esther Boserup's classic book, *Woman's Role in Economic Development*, serves as a useful benchmark for the scholarly work that was starting to chip away at this area of ignorance.[2] Boserup was not the first scholar to recognize that women worked. Indeed, in the bibliography of *Women's Role* she cites not only classical ethnographies but also a large number of empirical studies of that time, often sponsored by national governments or the UN and many written by women, on the status and work of women. But she differed from earlier authors in that she was an internationally known economist in a time when economics had started to come into its own. In addition, Boserup was writing about the importance of women's work to development and the adverse effects some development efforts were having on women at a time when multi- and bilateral development aid had become well established on the international stage and had just shifted from an emphasis on infrastructure to basic human needs. Thus, hers was a voice with at least some weight. An important development followed on the U.S. scene in 1973 when U.S. Senator Charles Percy introduced what came to be known as the Percy Amendment to the Foreign Assistance Act.[3] The Percy Amendment required the U.S. Agency for International Development (USAID) to integrate women into projects in four categories including agriculture. To the extent that the Percy Amendment was actually implemented, it created a need for information on women's role in agrarian production systems.

The two decades following Boserup's book witnessed a steady stream of scholarly work, almost exclusively done by women, chipping away at the large area of ignorance by documenting women's work in agrarian production systems. Any list of these scholars would necessarily be partial but would include the following: in farming, Meena Acharya and Lynn Bennett (1981), Elizabeth Croll (1985), Jean Davison (1988), Carmen Diana Deere (1982), Ruth Dixon (1978), Louise Fortmann (1981, 1984), Carol MacCormack (1982), and Shimwayi Muntemba (1982); in agroforestry, Louise Fortmann and Dianne Rocheleau (1985) and Dianne Rocheleau (1988); and in forestry, Bina Agarwal (1986) and Carol Colfer (1981).

Consistent with Donna Haraway's (1999, 175) injunction to "feminists . . . to insist on a better account of the world," this research made the work of women farmers, agroforesters, and foresters visible to state agencies and donors as well as to other scholars. They asked: What work do women do? What resources, in what quantities, do they have to work with? What are they responsible for? What are their practices? What costs do they bear? What benefits do they achieve? The account of the world that emerged was one of women whose work and knowledge were essential parts of rural livelihood systems.

In the late 1970s more systematic attention began to be paid to the knowledge of agrarian producers under the rubric of traditional knowledge or indigenous technical knowledge (ITK) (compare Brokensha et al. 1980).[4] As ITK became a growth field (particularly related to conservation), scholars (mostly gender specialists) identified and made visible the contemporary specialized knowledge of women[5] including but not limited to medicinal plants (Lewis and Lewis 1990, Caniago and Siebert 1998); ecological, political, and social knowledge as survival drought skills (Rocheleau 1991); forest ecology (Leach 1994); ethnoveterinary medicine (Davis 1995); food (Kuhnlein and Receveur 1996); and bush skills (Ohmagari and Berkes 1997). Gradually the importance of women's work and knowledge began to appear, albeit often just in passing, in work that was not written by gender specialists. In the fields of forestry and conservation this included, among others, Westoby (1989), Campbell (1996), and Hulme and Murphree (2001).

The question then arises, having been facilitated by these political and intellectual events of the 1970s onward, could this steadily accumulating mass of gender analysis affect the terrestrial environmental sciences? One pathway might have been through the incorporation of, for example, women's knowledge about the properties and stewardship of plant and animal species into conventional scientific research.[6] We leave the analysis of this pathway for others. A second pathway proved to be incorporation through feminist research methods. We address this in the next section, focusing on participatory research methods.[7]

Feminist Research Methods and the Environmental Sciences: The Case of Participatory Methods

We start from the assumption that, at their best, participatory research methods in the biophysical sciences are feminist methodologies. Is this a valid assumption? A detailed answer is far beyond the scope of this chapter. However, the assertion that such methods are unquestionably feminist is solidly grounded in feminist analyses of science. The inclusion of people with different kinds of knowledges and different ways of knowing in participatory biophysical research embodies the greater inclusiveness called for in Longino's (1990, 2002) model of objectivity. As shown in the two case studies below, participatory researchers understand that they cannot do rigorous, meaningful research without the collaboration of people with different kinds of knowledge. Thus, participatory biophysical research embraces Haraway's (1999) concept of *situated knowledges* and *multiple ways of producing knowledge.* Participatory researchers also assume with Haraway (1999, 1176) that objectivity is not the god-trick of seeing everything from nowhere but rather that objectivity is necessarily embodied and, therefore, all knowledges are situated and partial. Participatory biophysical research is constituted through specific places and embodied knowledge. Finally these methods embody characteristics that feminist scholars such as Bug (2003), Conkey (2003), Cosgrove (2000), Deutsch (2004), Katz (1994), McDowell (1992), and Wolf (1996) consider to be attributes of feminist science and feminist research methods. Specifically, participatory biophysical research is inherently *collaborative.* It is intentionally *not exploitative* of research partners. It is, of necessity, *knowingly embedded in a social and political context, which is taken into explicit account in the research process and reflective practice.* Interactions with research collaborators lead participatory researchers to *assess their categories and assumptions critically and mutually.* Similarly, because the lived experience of research collaborators is complex and heterogeneous, conventional researchers must grapple with heterogeneity and particularity in their research. In some contexts, participatory biophysical agricultural research, including participatory plant breeding in Africa where women do the vast majority of agricultural work, makes visible the situation, work, and knowledge of women and girls.[8]

Anti-feminist scholars before (and unfortunately after) Boserup developed accounts of the world that consisted of and privileged male agency, knowledge, and efficacy. Feminist biophysical researchers have produced a better account of the world by repicturing it through women's agency, knowledge, and efficacy, *and* often in ways that implicitly or explicitly contested earlier versions. Examples of this approach in forest ecology and plant breeding follow.

Participatory Forest Ecology[9]

In 2001, a small group of non-timber forest products (NTFP) harvesters founded the Northwest Research and Harvesters Association (hereafter, the Association) in the Pacific Northwest's Olympic Peninsula, Washington State. They were trying to access the NTFP resources growing on both public and private industrial forestlands and to collaboratively manage and monitor these resources on which they depend for their livelihood. Later that year forest ecologist Heidi Ballard formed a partnership with the Association called the Olympic Peninsula Salal Sustainability and Management Research Project (hereafter, the Salal Project) in order to undertake dissertation research. Salal, *Gautheria shallon* (called "lemon leaf" in the floral trade), is sold commercially in the multimillion dollar floral greens industry. The president of the Association, Don Collins, and Ballard decided to conduct research on salal harvest sustainability on which there had been no published scientific research as floral greens species have traditionally been considered weeds by foresters.

Because studying the ecology and management of non-timber forest products (of which floral greens including salal are one) is a relatively new pursuit for ecologists in the United States, Collins and Ballard decided that participatory research combining harvester ecological knowledge with conventional science was essential to the research design process. The salal harvesters and Ballard each held knowledge and experience that the other did not, such that neither could conduct this research effectively without the other. Harvesters[10] played an active role at every step in the research.

Framing the Research Question
Initially Ballard intended to focus the research on the incentives for, and effects of, harvesting different commercial grades of salal. The research was reframed to include harvesting intensity when interviews with harvesters revealed the effect of resource tenure on harvesting practices.

Harvester Hypotheses   The project began with collaborative hypothesizing about how salal responds to different intensities of harvesting. Harvesters suggested that when people picked 100 percent of the commercial-quality product in a given area ("Heavy Intensity harvest"), it involved removing mature stems along with new leaf buds. Thus, if they were picked every year for several years in a row, growth would decrease. They explained that because the plant would not be able to maintain growth levels over time, this harvest method would not be sustainable. Harvesters hypothesized that removing only 33 percent of available commercial shoots ("Light Intensity harvest") every year would not decrease growth because not all the new leaf buds were removed. When Ballard suggested testing these two methods in a controlled experiment across different kinds of sites, several harvesters volunteered to help with the experiment.

Experimental Design   Harvesters contributed substantially to the experimental design of the Salal Project due to their considerable ecological knowledge about the effects of stand conditions on understory[11] species, particularly commercial-quality salal. Nearly all harvesters described the stand conditions, such as dominant tree species and amount of canopy closure, required for producing commercial-quality salal. Many harvesters described relationships among understory species, noting that salal is found in association with some shrub species but not others. Several harvesters described elevation, soil moisture, and other soil conditions as important factors for salal growth and quality. These factors were known by conventional forest ecologists as some of the factors that determine understory species distribution and dominance in the region, but how these factors affect the distribution of commercial-quality characteristics was less familiar to conventional scientists. With the addition of harvesters' knowledge of overstory, understory, and environmental characteristics that affect salal growth and commercial quality, the experimental design that had relied solely on a review of the literature and discussions with ecologists was significantly altered. Research sites chosen by harvesters varied by elevation and forest stand type. Most important, harvesters and Ballard collaborated to identify and operationalize variables not commonly found in the conventional scientific literature that would specifically measure impacts of harvest on the plant. In the summers of 2001–2003 harvesters worked as field assistants, collecting and recording data. The harvesters' ecological knowledge was complemented by the statistically robust experimental design and plant ecology field methods that Ballard's conventional science background provided.

At the start of the Salal Project, several ecologists suggested that Ballard's harvest experiments should be done in a greenhouse under controlled conditions. While an effective way of reducing variation, controlling environmental and anthropogenic variables, and measuring accurately the effects of biomass removal on salal regrowth, this approach ignores the actual harvest practices of harvesters across the Olympic Peninsula. Without harvester collaboration, Ballard's research would have been of limited practical, management, or policy value.

Defining Harvest Treatments   The collaborative definition of harvest treatments based on the relationship between harvest practices and tenure resulted in an experiment that both reflected real-world practices and also relied on standardized ecological guidelines for biomass removal experiments. In the fall of 2001 and 2002, harvesters applied the harvest treatments, including weighing and taking samples of the harvested product. The precise definition of "available commercial shoots" had to represent harvest practices accurately, while quantifying the amount of biomass removed had to satisfy the standards of consistency in ecological research. To achieve both, a core group of harvesters and the university researcher collaboratively determined the harvest treatments and applied them over the three harvest seasons of the study. Methods from the literature had to be modified to encompass the parts of the plant actually harvested. Harvesters (who kept and sold the experimental harvest after it had been measured) had to accommodate efficiency of harvesting with the demands of thoroughness and uniformity of biomass removal. Rather than representing a loss of validity, this accommodation represents a successful navigation of two sets of standards, resulting in a more valid experimental design. Further, because the treatments were defined as an outcome of specific access conditions for harvesters, the experiment had a direct link to management and policy.

Interpreting the Data   In September 2003, twenty harvesters in the Association gathered to interpret the harvest yield results for each year for each experimental site, using large bar graph representations of the results. With instructions and discussions on how to read bar graphs and several harvesters serving as Spanish translators and facilitators of small group discussions, harvesters discussed why some results differed from their hypotheses, why sites responded differently to the same harvest treatments, and how the results could be used for management recommendations. The participation of harvesters in analyzing the yield data produced unexpected results. Most respondents described insect damage and several different fungal diseases that afflict the plant, including hypotheses on what conditions cause the spread of different diseases. Since the commercial value of salal depends on leaf quality, any disease or other blemishes on the leaves are of great concern to most harvesters. Their observations played an important role in designing the variables to be measured during the experiment, as well as interpreting the results that seemed inconsistent if insect and disease spread were not considered.

Contributions to Management and Policy   Harvesters' knowledge and experience were instrumental in developing management recommendations made to local forest managers. Their insights are, at the time of writing, being applied to the management recommendations the project is producing. By involving harvesters in the analysis of the results, Ballard hoped to "broaden the bandwidth" of questions of validity and rigor in research (Bradbury and Reason 2003) by challenging managers and scientists to expand their definitions of useful knowledge for research and practice. To that end, harvesters' observations and recommendations about the sustainability of rest-rotation management of salal harvest areas were supported by the experimental results, and were offered to forest managers as a key management recommendation of the Salal Project. The participatory approach to the study of salal harvest impacts will potentially result in positive outcomes both for policies of NFTP harvest permitting and access, and for management of NTFPs by public land management agencies on the Olympic Peninsula. Ballard presented the results of the sustainability study to the Forest Service District Manager, the Washington State Department of Natural Resources land managers and foresters, and private timber company personnel. The results included recommendations for permitting and management changes based on the results of the salal harvest experiment and on input from harvesters in the Association. Because official forest managers lack information on salal harvesting and its impacts, both the ecological and permitting recommendations should contribute to better forest management practices and improve harvester livelihoods in the region. For example, public and private land managers were surprised by the harvesters' extensive knowledge of timber management practices and how they affect understory species. In many cases, the land managers had assumed that harvesters either did not know about sustainable management practices and forest ecology or did not care, resulting in the exclusion of harvesters from participating in management or research. As the research and management activities of the Association have become better known, several private and public land managers changed their attitude toward the harvester organization and began negotiations about exclusive resource access in exchange for monitoring and research by harvesters.

Changes in the Practice of Science   It would be incorrect to suggest that the Salal Project is leading to a sea change in the practice of forest ecology. Nonetheless, it is true that as a result of the Salal Project, university and natural resource agency ecologists learned that a marginalized group without formal education are very important knowledge producers. These conventional scientists recognize that the combination of harvesters' and Ballard's knowledge and methods resulted in new ecological knowledge, methodological innovations, and the development of improved management practices and policies. And they have begun to incorporate harvesters as resource monitors in other projects. Meanwhile, Ballard has begun planting more seeds of her methodological innovations in other similar projects.

Participatory Plant Breeding[12]

Participatory plant breeding (PPB) is plant breeding research that starts from a user perspective and involves farmers as well as professional scientists in major roles within the research process.[13] For the simple reason that women, particularly in sub-Saharan Africa, often do most of the subsistence farming and are generally considered experts in plant and seed selection, PPB often centrally involves women and hinges on making their knowledge visible and integrated with conventional scientists' contributions.

From 1988 through July 1993 (shortly before the Rwandan genocide), the Institut des Sciences Agronomiques du Rwanda (ISAR) and the Centro Internacional de Agricultura Tropical (CIAT) conducted research on participatory bean breeding to test anthropologist Louise Sperling's hypothesis that women's knowledge was important to agricultural research and that farmers could collaborate in plant breeding research much earlier in the process. The premise was not that "poor women farmers knew more than scientists" (who were overwhelmingly male) but rather that "female expertise was highly specialized, crucial for increasing plant breeding impact, and complemented select strengths of formal scientists." While the research was subsequently documented by the Gender Program of the Consultative Group on International Agricultural Research (Sperling and Berkowitz 1994), it was institutionally supported by a regional network of African scientists from Rwanda, Burundi, and Congo—again, a group of mostly classic (conventional) agricultural male researchers.

The Production Context   Beans are a major crop in Rwandan agriculture, grown by 95 percent of farmers and providing an estimated 65 percent of the protein and 32 percent of the total caloric intake. They are considered the "meat" of the Rwanda countryside and, if a family could, it would serve beans three times a day (Sperling and Munyaneza 1995). For the most part, women do all the work in growing beans (selecting seeds, weeding, sowing, and harvesting), and beans are considered to be a woman's crop—one associated with considerable expertise (Sperling and Berkowitz 1994). Bean diversity is exceptionally high in Rwanda with about 1,300 types sown in a country the size of Switzerland (see Sperling 2001 for details). Women dynamically use this diversity. They generally grow mixes rather than single bean types in order to cope with variability of soil, moisture, pests, and other factors affecting yields—and adjust their blends as production conditions shift. Hence farmer experimentation is both lively and directed, and one Rwanda woman alone may test 75–100 varieties in a lifetime (Sperling and Scheidegger 1995). The expertise of Rwandan bean farmers presented an unusual collaborative opportunity, but the constraints of the research system also served to spur more participatory designs. Surveys in the late 1980s showed that "only 10 percent of the roughly 50 bean varieties tested on farms in the previous decade were still being grown—and with most in sharp decline" (Sperling et al. 1993, 510). Given that farmers grow mixtures and can easily add a new variety to the 20–30 they already sow, such an adoption rate was deemed "modest" even by the most optimistic of scientists.

Experimental Design   The formal plant breeding program was held largely responsible for such results. Under the conventional model, professional breeders start with roughly 250 potential varieties and screen them mostly for yield (on station), with disease resistance being a secondary consideration. Farmer participation, if there is any, comes for the last season or two (in a ten to sixteen season process), and at that time, just before final release, the "choice" is whittled down to just two to five varieties (Sperling 1992). In the research project at hand, Sperling sought to arrange a collaboration that (1) brought farmer expertise in early, before useful varieties were discarded and that (2) exposed women to a wide diversity so as to share decision-making criteria. The issue went beyond "what" women selected to "why" the selection—and strategic discussions among women farmers and male breeders subsequently shaped breeding processes for years to come.

In Phase I (1988–1990) of the research, the women bean experts selected among fifteen varieties in on-station trials two to four seasons before normal on-farm testing. In Phase 2 (1990–1993) the timeline was moved back to five to seven seasons before routine on-farm testing and women bean experts evaluated on-station trials normally containing about eighty lines, but with varieties filtered out for unusual disease susceptibility.[14] In both phases, varieties selected by experts from on-station trials were then taken back to farmers' own rural areas, where subsequent "on-farm testing" was managed in community plots or across a range of individual farms. Such "decentralized" testing—early—became a central feature of subsequent PPB work in the region as (1) it ensured the screening of varieties under truly realistic (predictive!) conditions, (2) communities shared the expenses of on-site screening, and (3) widespread farmer evaluation became the driving force for spurring the better varieties forward quickly.

Technical Results   *Criteria*: Traditionally, professional plant breeders have focused on increasing grain yield and resistance to disease, insects, and other pests. Varieties that meet these criteria may nonetheless not be adopted because they do not meet the requirements of farmers.[15] Women farmers use a wider range of criteria than breeders for selecting varieties—and in a number of well-defined realms. In terms of environment, Rwanda women look at how varieties tolerate common climatic stress such as drought and rain. Agronomically, they assess how the different beans will perform under conditions where they are actually planted: for example, on poorer soils, when they were intercropped, or when they were planted under dense banana stands. Women, of course, look at post-harvest use: how fast the beans cook, how long they last before spoiling, and whether the texture is firm and rich (that is, like meat). Finally, routine crops may be used for nonroutine purposes—and women in Rwanda scrutinize bean leaves for "lack of toughness." Bean leaves, as a condiment, add flavor to sweet potatoes and are critical for filling the "hunger period"—long after sowing and well before harvest. The point is that these range of concerns are not "optional" and that most of the traits are not anticipated in the formal breeding selection procedure.

Technical Results: New Varieties, Diversity, and Production   The result of plant breeders collaborating with women bean experts and incorporating their knowledge into the breeding research was spectacular. Longer-term follow-up showed that the number of varieties (21) adopted from the first two-year period matched the total number released over the previous twenty-five years (Sperling et al. 1993). From Phase II, which consisted of community-managed trials, twenty-six varieties were selected for home testing during the first two seasons alone (Sperling and Berkowitz 1994). While such diversity gains are key for stabilizing production and for identifying varieties that might meet quite different user preferences, the yield advantages really caught plant breeders' eyes. Over four different seasons, the farmers' selections outyielded their own local mixtures 64–89 percent of the time. The production increases were also remarkable, with increases of up to 38 percent. Formal breeder selections, in the same region over a comparable two-year period, showed negative or insignificant production increases. As Sperling notes:

> Even though farmers' selections . . . had to satisfy a range of . . . [criteria], they still performed better than varieties breeders chose with respect to yield, the scientists' primary criterion. (Sperling et al. 1993, 515)

Changes in the Practice of Science   The Rwandan bean PPB project demonstrated key points in regard to the practice of plant breeding. First, it showed that real technical gains can be achieved through direct collaboration (and knowledge sharing) with farmer experts, in this case women. Plant criteria essential for farmers are brought to the fore, productions gains are achieved, and variety diversity is promoted. Second, early farmer partnership also improved research cost-effectiveness. Adoptable varieties were identified many seasons sooner, testing was decentralized to realistic conditions, and—by implication—failure rates of the nonadopted or discarded varieties dropped sharply. Third, the experience led to a fundamental reconceptualization of the division of labor in plant breeding that builds on partners' respective strengths. Formal plant breeders have a unique ability to generate new bean types (that is, "genetic variability") quickly and on a wide scale. They also have skills to detect a range of stresses, which might be "invisible" to farmers, such as susceptibility to select plant diseases and soil pathogens. Farmers, in turn, definitely have the edge in targeting for their local agroecological conditions and (quite complicated) socioeconomic needs. Hence, the Rwandan experience suggests that formal breeders might focus on providing local experts (often, women) with a range of potentially useful germplasm—that meets broad client needs and that has been screened to reduce risk. Farmers should then take the lead in managing these wide variety pools: testing, evaluating, discarding, or diffusing.

Utilitarian Feminism: Improving Research Outcomes   Feminist analysis of women's participation in research and development processes distinguishes between functional/utilitarian effects and empowering effects. In the former, women's participation enhances the success of the activity, focusing particularly on its efficiency and effectiveness (for example, makes the work less expensive or results in more productive technology identification). In the latter, women themselves benefit from the participation because it increases their own decision-making roles, their skills, and, at times, their status and even independence (that is, empowers them).

In reflecting on the scope of these changes in the practice of science, we might characterize this first set of PPB gains as "functional" or "utilitarian" ones. The project showed (not least to the breeders involved in the research)[16] that the collaboration of formal plant breeders and women experts can lead to the mutual acceleration of each other's processes, resulting in the production of better varieties in less time—and resulting in the definition of a more targeted, and "on the mark" set of breeding goals. Thus, in the Rwandan case, women farmers helped improve the quality of science. Looking through a feminist lens: bringing women into a central technical role, recognizing their specialized expertise, and additionally incorporating their unique needs and wants (that is, precise variety criteria) led to enhanced scientific quality and on-the-ground gains.

The subsequent adoption of these methods by breeders of many other crops: sorghum, teff, rice, and cassava, to name a few (R. Buruchara, R. Kirkby, personal communication, 2006), suggests that such "utilitarian feminism" can find a niche in even some of the more classic or conventional of scientific arenas. In the intervening ten years, the Rwandan experience has also helped spur plant breeding changes in the wider East, Central, and Southern Bean Research Networks. As of mid-2005, 50 percent of the plant breeders (twenty-seven out of a total of fifty-three) employ aspects of participatory approaches in their routine variety selection and breeding practice, with all also embracing elements of utilitarian feminism.

Empowering Feminism? Changes in the Recognition of Knowledge   Beyond strictly utilitarian advances, some of the enduring and more enabling changes can be traced as shifts in the way that farmer and, often, female expertise is recognized in official channels. In some countries, farmer evaluation is now deemed obligatory, not optional, for official variety release, and in places like Ethiopia (where fuel wood is scarce) long cooking time, a characteristic highlighted by women farmers, now means a death knell for even the most productive of varieties. Longer-term breeding collaborations are also changing the ways that breeders acknowledge their farmer (and often female) counterparts. Farmer names are increasingly being used to baptize the joint plant-breeder farmer creations (for example, "Ushindi"/"Victory" and "Hujuti"/"You don't regret" out of Arusha, Tanzania; or "Mulwanisa"/ "tolerant to harsh conditions" and "Muzahura"/"restoration" from Southern Uganda [F. Ngulu, A. Namayanja, personal communication, 2005]). In rarer cases, where individual (versus community) contributions can be recognized, women farmers may also figure centrally in the breeder spotlight, such as the pearl millet population baptized the "Maria Kaharero Composite (MKC)" developed in Namibia (Monyo et al. 1977). And the ultimate accolade, jointly developed varieties are increasingly put forward for formal variety release with some sites publicly recognizing the "jointness" and labeling them as "products of joint farmer and formal plant breeder research collaboration."

Empowering Feminism? Changes in Social Processes   To reflect on whether there were other empowering effects of this PPB work (that is, elements of empowering feminism), one might briefly go back to the context in which it first unfolded. In Rwanda, the central role of women to family security is well recognized. So the proverb goes: "If someone has a better wife, he has a better home than you" [*Ukurusha umugore akurusha urugo*]. Women, in practice, however, are divorced from most power structures. The saying "Women have no race" [*Umugore ntagira ubwoko*] describes the concrete reality that their position in society derives from their relationship to significant male others: their fathers, their husbands, their brothers—whatever the case may be (Sperling and Scheidegger 1995). Women don't even have basic control over

FIGURE 5.1 Mrs. Sarswoti Adhikari from Begnas Village, Nepal, crossing rice in her home field. Women in many regions of the world are recognized for their specialized expertise in plant and seed selection and management. Courtesy of B. Sthapit, Bioversity International.

their bodies: in a country where rape is rampant and HIV/AIDS rates among the highest in world, women are jailed, for life, if they abort. In terms of PPB, women experts, even to visit on-station trials, had to get permission from their husbands first.

Given such a setting, the fledgling steps spurred by PPB appear somewhat remarkable. Women involved as "experts" increasingly expressed public confidence in their own, very specialized abilities: "We are researchers," they explained, and publicly took accountability for the quality of their work ("Since we selected these varieties ourselves, we have no one to cry to if they do not do well"). Through time, women organized in clusters, not only to better share varieties but to debate their respective research results. Larger groups then formed to produce seed commercially and to capture the first profits that come when new varieties are put in circulation. In countries beyond Rwanda such as Ethiopia and Uganda, PPB work has catalyzed the development of new trading and even new export niches, with women traders occasionally reaping the first windfall gains. All of these "empowering elements" (developing professional confidence, forming research groups, developing self-controlled economic enterprises) emerged from a PPB program whose primary rationales and goals were overtly functional or utilitarian. This example has shown that participatory research can bring technical gains and institutional change, and (slowly) shift the way that one set of experts sees, interacts with, and evaluates another set of experts. It can also bring utilitarian advances to women and even result in select changes that are at least tinged with elements of empowerment.

There is still plenty of room for further change. While breeders with PPB experience are convinced it is valuable, many breeders (including women) without such experience will cheerfully tell you that "only plant breeders have that special eye that can recognize a good variety" or that "I get my knowledge of what to breed for from life experience and the Internet."[17] And participatory research in the terrestrial environmental sciences can fall short of feminist goals in much the same way in the social sciences, namely fail to bring about meaningful change through the research. Participatory research can be a rousing success from the scientific standpoint and even from the practical standpoint without creating, for example, an improved livelihood or standard of living.[18] Further, as Katz (1994, 71) notes, frequently the academy does not recognize "applied grounded work despite successes on the ground."[19]

Conclusion

We have seen that gender analysis and feminist methods have affected the content and practice of the terrestrial environmental sciences. Both case studies involve participatory methods. The participatory plant breeding study had roots in long-standing gender analyses of agriculture (such as those discussed above) that had identified women as bean experts. Both demonstrate that it is often not possible to do good scientific research in human-dominated ecosystems, particularly if that research is to be policy or practice relevant, without reference to the social systems and the knowledges in which the research is embedded. These case studies also demonstrate that even if the change they bring is initially around the edges of mainstream science, its effects can be profound.

Notes to Chapter 5

1. Evidence of human habitation in "pristine wilderness" often goes unrecognized although humans leave biogeochemical signatures on the landscape that affect contemporary ecological processes. Sanford et al. (1985) found charcoal indicating historical human settlement (and therefore influence) in areas of the Amazon thought never to have been inhabited. See also Horn and Sanford (1992).

2. The prejudice against women was, however, still alive and well. One blurb on the back cover of the 1970 paperback edition states, "Although this book was not written as propaganda for the women's liberation movement, it is the most rational argument for female equality I have ever read" (Boserup 1970, back cover).

3. Percy's decision to introduce the amendment was the result of the vigorous efforts of feminists concerned about women in development, including Virginia Allan, Clara Beyer, Arvonne Fraser, Mildred Marcy, Carmen Maymi, and Irene Tinker (Tinker 2004).

4. Although beyond the scope of this chapter, it is important to note that Agarwal (1995) makes a compelling argument against making sharp distinctions between indigenous and scientific knowledge.

5. Historical examples of the importance of women's scientific knowledge include, among many, the contributions of a poor enslaved woman to the botany of Linnaeus (Grove 1995) and women's knowledge (eventually suppressed) of abortifacients used by enslaved women to avoid bearing children who would also be enslaved (Schiebinger 2004).

6. The rosy periwinkle (*Catharansus roseus*) used in traditional (not necessarily women's) medicine in Madagascar and adapted by conventional scientists for use against Hodgkin's disease and childhood leukemia is an example of this pathway. This raises issues of biopiracy that are addressed in Posey and Dutfield (1996) and http://www.etcgroup.org/main.asp.

7. Introductions to participatory research can be found in Minkler and Wallerstein (2003), Wilmsen (2005), and http://nature.berkeley.edu/community_forestry/Community/bibliographies.htm.

8. This assumes that the researcher and her research are truly participatory. In their critique of participatory practices Cooke and Kothari (2001) point out that participation is sometimes nothing more than a performance, a Potemkin participation, if you will. Such practices are obviously not feminist.

9. Further details on this research can be found in Ballard (2004), Ballard and Huntsinger (2006), Ballard and Fortmann (2007), and Kerns et al. (2003).

10. Ballard's research team included three women harvesters, but the knowledge in question was not gendered.

11. Plants growing under the main tree canopy in a forest comprise the understory. Stand conditions are structural and environmental characteristics of a particular stand of trees.

12. Thoughtful analyses of participatory plant breeding more generally can be found in Sperling et al. (2001) and Witcombe et al. (2005). For further details on the

Rwandan research, see Sperling et al. (1993), Sperling (1996), and Sperling and Scheidegger (1995).

13. Other key "users" might include processors and grain traders. Involving these
groups is particularly important if farmers are to improve their livelihoods through
value-added products and sales.

14. Because Phase I taught formal plant breeders that farmers can "see" a good
deal—including yield, in Phase II the division of research labor was refined and
breeders, or more precisely the pathologist, Kenyan Robin Buruchara, focused on
what farmers could not generally "see"—diseases. Hence the pool of 80 varieties was
sorted down to 79, 41, and 43 lines in 1990, 1991, and 1992 respectively to allow farmers
wide choice in "risk-reduced" germplasm pools.

15. Written and oral accounts of plant breeding are filled with stories of breeders'
varieties that don't cook well (Apodaca 1952), don't taste right, have poor grain quality
(Witcombe et al. 2005), or achieve grain productivity at the cost of productivity in another part of the plant (such as leaves or stalks), which is used as part of the livelihood
strategy (Kirkby 1981). Hecht (1999) has comprehensively sketched out some 54 criteria
that women (and often the poor) may use in evaluating crops.

16. One of the scientists involved in this project said that when he was initially
introduced to participatory approaches, he was very concerned that he was going to
have to waste his time working with farmers and never achieve any useful scientific
results. He therefore set up his own and parallel on-station trials so as to be on the
"safe side" and not lose a season. In the course of so doing he discovered that his work
with the farmers was much more productive by making him avoid evaluating "use-
less" technologies that farmers were never going to be interested in. From then on, he
says, he would never go back to the traditional method.

17. For obvious reasons neither these breeders nor their institutions have been
identified.

18. A conversation with Sally Humphries helped to clarify this point. This is addressed in a forthcoming book (*Participatory Research on Conservation and Rural
Livelihoods: Doing Science Together*, Blackwell) that Louise Fortmann is preparing in
collaboration with local research teams and professional researchers, Heidi Ballard,
Sally Humphries, Jonathan Long, Nontokozo Nemarundwe, and Eva Wollenberg.

19. For example, a scientist once mentioned "the feeling of letting the university
down" because his work, which had saved 3 million people from devastating disease
and brought land into production that fed 17 million people, "wasn't really research."

6 Feminist Perspectives on Geographic Information Systems

Implications for Geographic Research

Mei-Po Kwan

T HE TERM *geographic information systems (GIS)* refers to a collection of technologies for the storage, management, analysis, and mapping of geographic data. Initially developed in the early 1960s, GIS found widespread application in a variety of contexts and became a major subfield in geography in the past decade or so. Despite the phenomenal growth of GIS and their wide applications, the gendered understandings of these technologies and their implications for feminist geographic research have remained largely unexamined until recent years. In the field of geography, for instance, advocates and critics of GIS understood these technologies mainly as a tool for positivist and empiricist science in the 1990s. This understanding of GIS has made it difficult for geographers to think about GIS as a tool for enhancing our understanding of women's lived experiences. It was also difficult to imagine any role for feminist perspectives in shaping the development and use of GIS (Kwan 2002a, 2002b).

Feminist geographers have been critical of the use of vision or visualizations in GIS practices. Liz Bondi and Mona Domosh (1992, 202–203) assert that the promise of GIS to produce singular representations from myriad interconnected variables represents "a god's eye view" that entails "the distancing of a unitary self from the object of vision." They argue that GIS's "emphasis on vision as the sense that bestows on the perceiver a unitary and apparently external position" demotes other senses more closely associated with women (Bondi and Domosh 1992, 203). Reflecting on the use of satellite images,

Dianne Rocheleau (1995, 463) argues, "when the gaze begins from space, and when the gaze-from-space is uninformed by the logic of gendered livelihoods and landscapes, then the erasure of women's place in the mapped spaces is all but certain." These criticisms not only highlight the objectifying power of GIS-based visualizations, they also call into question the suitability of GIS for feminist research. If the vision enabled by GIS is incorrigibly disembodied and masculinist, as these feminist critics have argued, the use of GIS will only serve to perpetuate the objectifying gaze of a masculinist master subject.

In light of these critiques, the use of vision and visualization as an important means of knowledge production in GIS is therefore a major concern for feminist geographers. Before exploring how these issues may be addressed, it is important to recognize the historical and social context of the critique of vision, and to avoid "an ahistorical condemnation" (Nash 1996, 151) of all visualizations as objectifying or masculinist. As Catherine Nash (1996, 153) argues, "There is no inherently bad or good looking." For Gillian Rose (2001, 9), the dominant visuality (or scopic regime) is neither inevitable nor uncontested. As she suggests, "There are different ways of seeing the world, and the critical task is to differentiate between the social effects of those different visions." Given that objectification can also occur through other means, such as the use of language, the problem is less the use of vision or GIS-based visualizations per se than the failure to recognize that vision is always partial and embodied and to acknowledge the risk of privileging sight above the other senses—or as Donna Haraway (1991, 195) puts it, "only the god-trick is forbidden."

Feminist theorists help re-vision the types of vision that power GIS in three distinct ways. First, GIS can be reclaimed from its abstract, disembodied practice of modern technoscience through re-corporealizing all vision as embodied and situated (Nash 1996; Rose 2001). Haraway (1991, 199, 195) advocates "feminist visualizations" grounded in "the view from a body . . . versus the view from above, from nowhere, from simplicity." Jennifer Light (1995) also suggests proactive redefining of technology that entails the creative act of re-envisioning its potential use. Julien Murphy (1989, 107) proposes a "feminist seeing" that "confronts and moves beyond the distance, destruction, and desire that permeate the look of oppression." Feminist geographers can therefore engage in the appropriation of the power of GIS's visual technologies and "participate in revisualizing worlds turned upside down in earth-transforming challenges to the views of the masters" (Haraway 1991, 192).

Recent works on alternative practices in critical, feminist, and postcolonial cartography provide significant insights that may help inform the development of alternative GIS visual practices (for example, Harley 1992; Nash 1994; Huffman 1997; Sparke 1998). The purpose of these alternative cartographic practices is to re-present the world in ways that give voice to underprivileged social groups (Nash 1994; Sparke 1998). At the level of practice, Rose (2001) provides guidelines for critical visual methodologies—including content analysis, discourse analysis, and psychoanalysis—in GIS and focuses on the central question of how to retain a critical awareness of one's positionality with respect to research participants, the research project, and the knowledge produced. She identifies three sites where I argue this can be done: (1) the site of production where we reflect on our meaning-making visual practices; (2) the site of the image itself where we examine the exclusions, silences, and marginalizing power of our representations; and (3) the site of reception where we consider how our images encourage particular ways of looking, and how meaning may be contested or renegotiated by various audiences (Kwan 2002a).

Second, GIS-based visual practices can be developed for representing gendered spaces. Feminist cultural and art critics have argued that women tend to represent spaces and construct spectator positions differently from men (for example, Doane 1982; Pollock 1988; Stacey 1988; Broude and Garrard 1994; Neumaier 1995; Rose 1995). In an analysis of the scene location and spatial ordering in the Impressionist paintings of Berthe Morisot and Mary Cassatt, Griselda Pollock (1988, 56) concludes that "they make visible aspects of working-class women's labour within the bourgeois home" and that their spaces are characterized by proximity and compression instead of vast spaces where the viewer's position is hard to infer. Rose (1995) also examines how the work of three women artists (Jenny Holzer, Barbara Kruger, and Cindy Sherman) offers ways of seeing that are constructed not through voyeurism but through intimacy and care. Feminist geographers using GIS methods can experiment with creating new visual practices, especially those that can better represent gendered spaces and help construct innovative spectator positions.

Third, historical studies of the experiences of women travelers hint at the possibility of a more reflexive mode of visualizing geographic data (Blunt 1994). In her discussion of the experiences of Victorian women explorers, for instance, Domosh (1991) alludes to the possibility of a feminine way of seeing based on the understanding that women travelers often had different goals, routes, and destinations from those of men's while traveling in foreign lands. Further, these women often spoke of the empowerment they felt when they were exploring. Thus, "even the exploitative appropriation of European exploration was not without the possibilities for developing other kinds of connections" (Bondi and Domosh 1992, 211). Based on these accounts, and given that the use of GIS technologies and methods often involves the exploration of cartographic images and high-dimensional graphics in a GIS's cyberspatial environment, it seems that different kinds of interactions between the GIS user and GIS technology are possible. This hints at the contestability of the GIS user-technology relations that can be a basis for creating alternative GIS visual practices for feminist research.

My experience in viewing a three-dimensional (3D) image of the World Trade Center site on the Web after the September 11, 2001, attack may help illustrate this point. The image was created from elevation data collected by a plane flying at 5,000 feet above the site using light detection and ranging (LIDAR) technology. The 3D topographic image shows the remains of the World Trade Center building structures and the craters that drop 30 feet below street level at the site. Although the text accompanying the image marveled at the technological achievement and usefulness of LIDAR technology in this context (which I fully acknowledge), I was instead overwhelmed by a deep sense of grief that led me to ponder on the meaning of such a tragic incident for the victims, for those who were affected, and for myself as a feminist geographer and GIS user and researcher. My reaction was a result not only of viewing the image but also of reading numerous chilling stories told by people from their personal experience of the calamity (including media reports, photos, and news on the Web, and messages on several electronic discussion lists). These data vividly wove together a tragic story that is evocative of critical reflections and emotions. These reactions suggest that GIS users can interact with GIS-created images in a relatively embodied manner, and GIS-based visualizations are not necessarily devoid of context or meaning. When complemented by contextual information on the ground and at micro-scale (for example, stories about the lived experiences of individuals), GIS visualizations can establish important connections between large-scale phenomena (for example, urban restructuring) and the everyday lives of individuals (for example, Pavlovskaya 2002).

GIS as Method in Feminist Geographic Research

As I have argued earlier, the purpose of using GIS in feminist geographic research is not to discover universal truth or law-like generalizations about the world, but to understand the gendered experience of individuals across multiple axes of difference. It aims at illuminating those aspects of every-day life that can be meaningfully depicted using GIS methods. As major GIS data models were designed to handle digital spatial data and many of the core functionalities of GIS are developed for analyzing quantitative information, earlier debate on the role of quantitative methods in feminist geographic re-search is still highly relevant (for example, Mattingly and Falconer-Al-Hindi 1995). For instance, GIS methods can be used to reveal "the broad contours of difference and similarity that vary not only with gender but also with race, ethnicity, class, and place" (McLafferty 1995, 438). They can be used to support arguments in political discourse for initiating progressive social and political change, and indicate research areas that urgently require attention and sug-gest directions for in-depth qualitative research. GIS methods can also help discover the gender biases in conventional quantitative methods. Further, as GIS is capable of displaying and overlaying many layers of data, it can be used to reveal the spatial context, depict spatial connections, and hint at the com-plex social relationships among people and places (Kwan 2002b). The strength of GIS methods is in helping the user or researcher to identify complex rela-tionships across geographical scales. Besides these conventional uses of GIS in feminist research, I describe in what follows five other ways that are congenial to poststructuralist feminist perspectives.

(1) Linking Geographical Contexts with Women's Everyday Lives

As geographic data of urban environments at fine spatial scales (for example, at the parcel or building level) can be assembled and incorporated into a GIS, it is possible to link the trajectories of women's everyday lives (including ac-tivities locations and travel routes) with their geographical context at various spatial scales. This would allow a mode of analysis that is more sensitive to scale and context when compared to conventional methods. Further, when in-dividual-level data are available, GIS methods can be attentive to the diversity and differences among individuals. An example is Hanson's (Hanson et al. 1997) study on the impact of local context on women's labor market outcome in Worcester, Massachusetts. The study examines whether the proximity to home of a large number of jobs in female-dominated occupations increases the probability that a woman will work in a gender-typed occupation. It com-puted the number of jobs in female-dominated occupations locally available to each woman using a person-specific spatial interpolation method and a job search space defined by a realistic estimate of the distance traveled to work for each woman. Using this GIS method, Hanson and colleagues (1997) were able to avoid the problem of using overgeneralized census data while conducting their analysis at the individual level. The study concludes that local employment context is important for part-time workers with a college education and young children at home. It illustrates that significant questions in feminist research can be addressed by developing and using innovative GIS methods that incorporate the geographical context into the analysis.

(2) Supporting Women's Activism Through GIS-Based Research

As GIS is increasingly used in the public decision-making process, especially in the context of urban planning, an important area where GIS can play a role in feminist research is empowering women's activist groups in local politics. Several ways in which feminist GIS users and researchers can play a role in supporting women's local activism include (a) assembling, codifying, and coalescing women's local knowledges and experiences; (b) performing GIS analysis that women's activist groups do not have the skills or resources to undertake; (c) preparing data and analytical results to facilitate the articulation of the course of women's activist groups; and (d) disseminating results to assist the formation of a collective consciousness that enhances the effectiveness of women's activist groups in the political arena. A good example is a community-initiated GIS project at Hunter College that aims at understanding the spatial tendency and potential environmental causes of breast cancer in the community of West Islip on Long Island, New York (McLafferty 2002). The project uses data collected by a group of women activists through door-to-door surveys to answer specific questions arising from their fears and concerns. For these women, as McLafferty (2002, 265) stresses, "mapping and GIS became important tools for acquiring knowledge outside the realm of daily experience and for connecting their personal experience of health and illness to a wider social and political agenda."

(3) Using Qualitative Data to Construct Cartographic Narratives

GIS can also be used as a representational medium in qualitative research. Despite the fact that GIS can handle only digital information and has limitations for representing the diverse and complex experiences of women's everyday lives, the recent development of digital technologies has greatly expanded the kind of information GIS can deal with. Qualitative data such as digital photos, voice clips, and video clips can be linked to or incorporated into GIS. In addition, subjects' handwriting, hand-drawn maps, and other sketches collected through ethnographic methods can also be incorporated into GIS. The use of

GIS therefore does not necessarily preclude the use of contextual qualitative information of subjects or locales. For example, in a multisite study of low-income and welfare recipient families and their children, family ethnographic field notes are linked with neighborhood field notes and other contextual data in GIS (Matthews et al. 2005). The integration of GIS and ethnography has allowed project researchers to visualize and better understand the complexity of the lives of low-income families and the strategies they adopt in negotiating the welfare system. GIS has also been used in the construction of biographical narratives. An example is the Ligon history project that was initiated to preserve the history, culture, and memory of an inner-city high school (Ligon High) in Raleigh, North Carolina (Alibrandi et al. 2000). Besides documenting the African American perspective of life during Ligon High School's pre-Civil Rights and Civil Rights eras, GIS was used in the project to create a series of historical *life maps* that describe the biography of an alumnus.

(4) Mapping Women's Life Paths in Space-Time

Despite recent advances in GIS technology and research, current GIS data models still have serious limitations for representing entities as complex and fluid as gendered spaces and bodies. But believing that GIS methods can be a helpful visual device for illuminating gender spaces and women's movement in space-time, I propose two directions for addressing GIS's limitations in this context. First, the lines representing women's life paths in space-time in GIS can be reimagined as *body inscriptions*—inscriptions of oppressive power relations on women's everyday spatiality, and inscriptions of gendered spatiality in space-time (Laws 1997). As Elizabeth Grosz (1992, 242) argues, "bodies reinscribe and project themselves onto their sociocultural environment so that this environment both produces and reflects the form and interests of the body." The geometry of women's life paths and the processes of identity formation and women's experiences of places are mutually constitutive. The movement of women's bodies in space-time is also an active element in the production of gendered spaces (Spain 1992; Nead 1997). Through this reimagining, the lines representing women's life paths in space-time are no longer abstract lines in the transparent Cartesian space of GIS. Instead, they are the material expressions of women's corporeality and embodied subjectivities—a mapping of their bodies onto space-time that emanates from their prediscursive practices of everyday life (Pile and Thrift 1995). In this light, I argue that feminist geographers can *appropriate* GIS methods for illuminating women's spatiality, while recognizing the apparent privilege given to the materiality of the body by GIS methods.

Extending the representational capabilities of current GIS is another direction for overcoming some of its limitations for representing gendered spaces and bodies. For instance, I have mapped movements of women's bodies in space-time as continuous trajectories using 3D GIS in a series of studies (Kwan 2000; Kwan and Lee 2004). The *body maps* I produced look similar to the space-time aquarium developed by time geographers—where women's body movements are portrayed as life paths in a 3D space. An example is provided in Figure 6.1, which shows the daily space-time paths of the African American women in a sample of households in Portland, Oregon (Figure 6.2 provides a more detailed view of an area close to downtown Portland). Geovisualizations performed using this method indicate that not only do the homes and workplaces of these African American women concentrate in a small area of the entire metropolitan region, but their activities locations are much more spatially restricted when compared to all other gender or ethnic groups (compare their space-time paths with those of the Asian American men in the sample shown in Figure 6.3; Kwan 2002b). The restricted spatiality of African American women in the study area suggests that urban space can be racialized in a manner that goes beyond what the socioeconomic processes in the housing and job markets can fully explain. In another

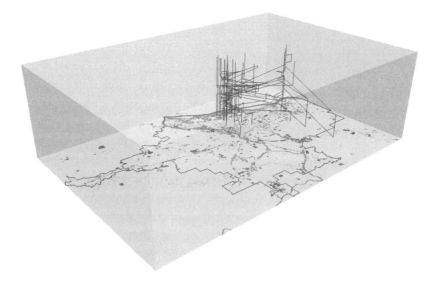

FIGURE 6.1 The space-time paths of a sample of African American women in Portland, Oregon. Source: Kwan 2002b. With permission, Blackwell Publishing, Ltd.

FIGURE 6.2 A detailed view of an area close to downtown Portland, Oregon. Source: Kwan 2002b. Feminist visualization: Re-envisioning GIS as a method in feminist geographic research. *Annals of the Association of American Geographers* 92:645–662. With permission, Blackwell Publishing, Ltd.

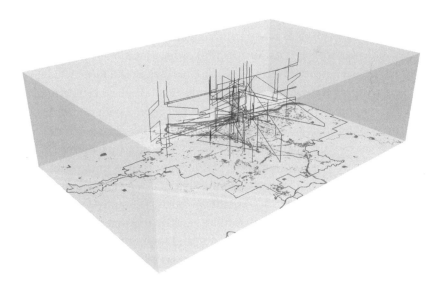

FIGURE 6.3 The space-time paths of a sample of Asian American men in Portland, Oregon.

study, I constructed cartographic narratives with 3D GIS to tell stories about women's experience of the urban environment using both quantitative and qualitative data collected through in-depth interviews (Kwan 2007a, 2007b). This particular study suggests that many representational possibilities of GIS remain unexplored to date.

(5) Revealing the Gender Biases of Conventional Quantitative Methods

As many quantitative methods in geography are based on the abstract logic of spatial organization and assumptions that ignore the complexities of life situations among different individuals, analytical results can deviate considerably from what people actually experience in their everyday lives. Since GIS can take into account certain complexities of an urban environment (for example, variations in facility opening hours and the ease of travel in different locales and at different times of the day) and incorporate some behavioral attributes of individuals into dedicated geocomputational algorithms, GIS methods can better approximate real-world behavior and can be used to reveal the gender biases in conventional quantitative methods. In a project that examines the impact of women's space-time constraint on their employment status and access to urban opportunities in Columbus, Ohio, I argue that conventional accessibility measures ignore the sequential unfolding of people's daily lives in space and time and the restrictive effect of fixed activities on their access to urban opportunities in a particular day (fixed activities are activities, such as work, whose location or timing is difficult to change). Instead of using conventional measures, I formulated three GIS-based space-time accessibility measures that take these factors into account. Using the activity diary data I collected from a sample of individuals in Columbus, Ohio, the results reveal considerable spatial variations in women's accessibility patterns, while men's accessibility patterns mainly follow the spatial distribution of the urban opportunities in the study area. The results from using conventional measures, however, do not indicate this kind of gender difference in accessibility patterns. The study concludes that GIS-based space-time measures are more sensitive to women's life situations when compared to conventional measures, and that conventional accessibility measures suffer from an inherent gender bias and therefore are not suitable for studying women's accessibility. As these conclusions would not have been possible without using GIS, applying GIS methods in feminist research has potential for revealing the gender biases in conventional concepts and quantitative methods in geography.

Conclusion

Although GIS and feminist geography may have the potential to enrich each other, they have remained two separate worlds to date (Hanson 2002; Mc-Lafferty 2002). Despite their limitations, GIS methods can play a role in addressing certain issues in feminist geographic research. Through revisiting earlier critiques of GIS and hinting at some possibilities for alternative practices, I propose a different kind of critical engagement with GIS—one that seeks to re-envision and re-present GIS as a feminist practice, and one that is actively involved in the creation of GIS practices informed by feminist epistemologies and politics. Recent writings of feminist theorists and methodological debates in feminist geography provide important guidelines in grounding GIS practices in feminist epistemologies and research methodologies. They suggest that feminist GIS users and researchers need to acknowledge and deal with the limitations of GIS methods, the power relations GIS entails, the difficulty of practicing reflexivity, and the ethical or moral implications of the knowledge produced. The question is perhaps less on the possibility of feminist GIS practices than on how this potentiality can be realized.

At the level of practice, there is an urgent need to go beyond the conventional understanding of GIS as largely a quantitative practice and to recognize the potential of such realization for disrupting the rigid distinction between quantitative and qualitative methods in geographic research (Kwan 2004). As I have argued elsewhere (Kwan 2002a), GIS can be a site for deconstructing the dualist understanding of geographical methods (as either quantitative or qualitative) and for enacting *feminist visualization*—the material practice of critical visual methods in feminist geography. Further, as Schuurman (2002) and I (Kwan 2002b) have argued, an important element in feminist critiques of science and vision has been lost in the critical discourse on GIS in the last decade or so. In this chapter, I employ feminist theory to create a new understanding and use of GIS in ways similar to how feminists in primatology and developmental biology have changed their fields through using gender analysis to enable new observations and attenuate androcentric biases. My work can therefore be situated in the larger context of recent feminist critique of twentieth-century science and technology, which is summarized nicely in Creager, Lunbeck, and Schiebinger (2001). For the contemporary social and natural sciences, much can be gained through teasing out the implications of Haraway's question, "Can cyborgs, or binary oppositions, or technological vision hint at ways that the things many feminists have feared most can and must be refigured and put back to work for life and not death?" Haraway has not only provided a trenchant critique of modern technoscience and visual technologies, she has also emphasized through her *cyborg manifesto* that feminists can reclaim the vision and power of modern technoscience (GIS technologies included) and participate in "earth-transforming challenges to the views of the masters" (Haraway 1991, 4, 192).

7 Stem Cells, Women, and the New Gender and Science

Charis Thompson

WHEN FORMER Harvard University President Lawrence Summers gave his speech on January 14, 2005, to the NBER (National Bureau of Economic Research) Conference on Diversifying the Science & Engineering Workforce, higher education entered a new phase of the politics of gender and science. This new phase of the politics of gender and science had three key characteristics that in some ways set the parameters of this collection. The first was that the debate about women in science was relaunched at a time when the resounding feminist critique of Summers's speech would get heard as coming from a position critical of science as usual, but as essentially *on the side of science.* Compared to the federal government under George W. Bush, which has wavered in terms of its support for science in general, the debate about women and minorities in science shows up for what it really is, namely, a debate about getting the best science we can have rather than as an anti-science critique. This is excellent news.[1] The second characteristic was that enough had happened legislatively and in terms of appointments of key women scientists to leadership positions in recent years to ensure that participants in the debate would get a hearing. Again, excellent news. And finally, Summers's comments not only raised eugenic specters of gendered and racialized aptitude but did so in a way that appeared entirely to ignore a vast body of scholarship in gender and science. A pressing new task for the politics of gender and science became to understand why this scholarship had not entered mainstream debate.

Summers' comments were shocking, but it is important to understand why. His comments themselves and the national conversation they revived revealed a situation that has long beset the academic field of gender and science: On the one hand, the field incorporates a rich body of scholarship, encompassing work on women and minorities in the sciences and engineering; the sciences of gender; the gender of science; and the intersectional (with race, class, nation) postcolonial, transnational comparative, and historical studies of all of the above (see Keller and Longino 1996; Schiebinger 1999; Creager et al. 2001; Lederman and Bartsch 2001; Mayberry et al. 2001; Wyer 2001). On the other hand, the policy arm of the field has been more or less limited to the politically pressing but theoretically and empirically anemic question of the (under)representation of women and minorities in science. The underrepresentation of women debate has its own argumentative chicken and egg dynamic, which sustains its successive salvoes and seems to make the debate relatively impermeable to the richness of scholarship in gender and science just mentioned. As is common in arguments about underrepresentation, one side puts most of the causality in the agents/victims, women in this case, and so espouses a naturalistic explanation. The temptation to naturalize achievement is common, and this side of the debate is usually a "winner's" position. The other puts the blame primarily on cultural processes, advocating a social structural explanation for underrepresentation. Frequently writing from disciplines, positions, and demographics of less power, it has been hard until recently for those on the social side even to have a seat at the policy table of science. Further impoverishing policy, both sides commonly ignore the evidence that nature and nurture play interacting roles. Now, more than ever, scholars of gender and science need to bring the richness of the field of gender and science into policy to break away from this impasse. The new politics of gender and science suggests that the timing is right to do so, and this book is part of that endeavor.

The renewed national attention paid to gender and science provided the context for a phone call and email I received in the same month as Summers's speech. An analysis of a strand of gender and science revealed by this phone call contributes to the aims of this chapter and this volume to widen the policy debate about underrepresentation of women in science. In the phone call I was informed that I had been nominated to a committee, the California Advisory Committee on Stem Cells, mandated by California Senate Bill 322 (SB 322). This committee was to be the successor to the similarly named California Advisory Committee on Cloning, which had met when research cloning and stem cell research were first made legal in California in 2002. The Department of Health Services (DHS) physician who called me told me that my name had been put forward as someone who would bring to the committee expertise in issues in human stem cell research that affect women (see Thompson 2005). I would, in effect, be representing the interests of women, whatever that might mean. In November 2004, Californians had voted by what amounted to a landslide in a bipartisan liberal democracy, 59–41 percent, in favor of the California Research and Cures Act, or Proposition 71. Proposition 71 broke with federal restrictions on the funding of embryonic stem cell research, establishing a state constitutional right to conduct stem cell research and authorizing the sale of $3 billion of state bonds over ten years to fund all stages of research and development of stem cell therapies. Proposition 71 also established a new state agency, the California Institute of Regenerative Medicine (CIRM). Proposition 71 mandated that CIRM would have its own standards-setting committees and procedures so the job of the SB 322 committee was unclear; some thought it had been rendered obsolete or redundant and would be left to sunset with the senate bill itself in January 2007. Others felt that the new stem cell initiative could do with some independent oversight and that this committee might provide that.

From what I subsequently discovered, it appears that I was nominated as a replacement for a prominent women's health activist who sat on the earlier cloning committee, on the grounds that I was more positively disposed than she to stem cell research and the stem cell initiative (although I had not signed up to support the proposition, primarily out of concerns about health care priorities and disparities) and thus less controversial than she and other possible candidates representing women's health activism. The terms of SB 322 had originally required that the new committee meet and report in 2005. The names of the committee nominees were submitted to the governor's office in January 2005. After a shake-up at DHS, a committee was appointed six months after the work was supposed to have been completed, putting into question the role of the committee in guiding an agency that had already met and widely consulted with all sorts of people (including me) for over a year. The new committee finally met on February 24, 2006, just before the hearing of the next round of litigation by pro-life groups against CIRM on Monday, February 27, and as Senator Deborah Ortiz was in the midst of submitting a new bill amending the terms of Proposition 71, and a mere handful of days after the resignation of President Summers from the presidency of Harvard.

Campuses and other research institutions across California, not to mention private donors, geared up for the state stem cell effort. I was appointed the director of the Project in Stem Cells and Society at the University of California, Berkeley, part of our nascent Stem Cell Center, and helped write our first stem cell training grant, including in our proposal the only social scientist graduate students to be funded under the initiative to date. I was also appointed to our campus stem cell research oversight committee and the equivalent committee at the hospital that is our clinical partner. Meanwhile, the new personnel at the Department of Health Services failed to inform me that I (perhaps for good reason) had not been included in the new incarnation of the California Advisory Committee. The public notice of the meeting on the DHS website listed the members not by name but by category, and while scientists, lawyers, medical ethicists, and religious leaders had been retained as categories deserving of representation, women's advocacy had been dropped. I received a call before the meeting from a representative of a women's health advocacy group who also was not aware until the last minute that the position of an advocate for women's concerns had been dropped from the committee, and whose members, by the short notice of the meeting, were mostly unable to contribute even to the public comment session.

I attended the first meeting as a member of the public and made a Public Comment on the topics about which I had originally been asked to contribute as a committee member. The meeting was the opposite of a committee chastened by a lack of consultation with women, minorities, and the public more broadly. No one seemed clear on what the point of the committee was despite repeated attempts to articulate just that, and much of the discussion was not only redundant given CIRM's year-long deliberations on similar topics, but less inclusive, less collaborative, and much less well informed than CIRM's procedures and personnel had become.[2] The sitting committee, predominantly elderly, white, and male, received a knowledgeable tutorial on federal versus CIRM stem cell guidelines from preeminent pro-stem cell research lawyer and consultant to CIRM, Alta Charo, leaving the comical situation that the agency supposedly being guided at the outset by SB 322 committee's recommendations was teaching the SB 322 committee the basics of the regulatory situation on the ground.

This chapter sets itself a thought experiment in incorporating different strands of scholarship in the gender and science literature: What if one were to take my original charge for the advisory committee seriously, and ask what it might mean to pay attention to the needs of a group called "women," which doesn't present as a group at all, let alone a unified interest group, as regards stem cell research? How could one represent (or whatever the right relationship might be) women's views and lives in regard to stem cell research state wide, in the context of renewed concern about women and science? In the rest of this chapter, I draw on my research, teaching, and committee service, primarily in the California context, to address these questions. I discuss issues in stem cell research that are emerging as "women's issues" and ask which women they affect and how they might best be navigated. I also consider issues of major significance to women but that run the risk of disappearing in the debate because the current framing of the stem cell debate leaves them out of the picture. By no means an exhaustive list of women's issues, I consider the following, all in relation to class and race as well as to gender:

Are women represented among stem cell researchers and biotech innovators?

Why aren't abortion politics a women's issue in the stem cell debate?

Why has egg donation arisen as the premier women's issue in stem cell research when it has had a very different valence in reproductive technologies?

Did authorizing the expenditure of an additional $3 billion, or approximately $6 billion after interest, of state funds on stem cell research adequately represent women's health care priorities?

What are the special women's roles, particularly as patients, caregivers, and mothers, in patient activism and disability rights and why are they heard less than would be expected?

What are the women's issues at stake in women's opposition to stem cell research?

I end where I began, with reflections on the role of scholars of gender and science in bringing these kinds of concerns into policy debates so that they have a chance of guiding research and affecting civic life in this area.

Involving Women in Stem Cell Science

Coming directly off the Summers affair, the top concern about women and stem cell research might have been to make sure that women were recipients of their fair share of state-funded stem cell training grants and biotechnology research and development (R&D). In fact, though, in California since the passage of Proposition 71, this issue has hardly been raised. By contrast, the minority advocacy agency, Greenlining, and the terms of CIRM grants themselves (rightly, in my opinion) made attracting underrepresented minorities into stem cell science a priority. Why women have not organized around this issue is not entirely clear to me, but in part it must be that the life sciences, if not the biotech industry, already attract a reasonable number of women scientists, and that prominent women scientists are already in the field, even if they are not the national spokespeople for stem cell science. By and large, though, the "women in science" contingent has been surprisingly quiet in the stem cell debate. Women scientists serving on stem cell committees have by and large not identified themselves as experts with a particular interest in supporting women in stem cell science or as committee members with special insight into the issue that has slowly emerged as the signature women's issue in the stem cell debate, the question of compensation for egg donors. Perhaps their reticence derives from a concern to be taken primarily as scientists, rather than as women scientists (a reasonable concern), but it does seem that these voices would bring moral authority to the debate. It would be powerful to see California's women stem cell scientists collectively address issues that affect different women, perhaps through a statement to the press, or through CIRM itself.

Abortion Politics

Abortion politics lurk behind debates about human stem cell science in many countries, both secular and religious, often dictating its legality and conditions of work, restricting public and private R&D funding and future markets, and pitting religion against science. In the United States much of the political power of opposition to abortion comes from evangelical Protestantism, not Catholicism, as is more common elsewhere. Nonetheless the United States is typical in that religious opposition to abortion extends to human embryonic stem cell research. The reasoning behind this is that embryos are thought to be destroyed in the process of extracting stem cell lines from blastocysts.[3] If embryos have the moral status of a person, then human embryonic stem cell research is murder. The United States is atypical in that its two-party majoritarian democracy has state-level as well as federal-level governing structures. This means that states can be Democratic when the federal government is Republican, and vice versa, leading to the possibility of state sovereignty, as in the case of passage of Proposition 71. Since President Bush's announcement of August 2001, human embryonic stem cell research could only be funded by federal funds (from the National Institutes of Health or the National Science Foundation, for example) if the research was done using one of the approved or so-called presidential lines of embryonic stem cells that had already been derived and immortalized thus prohibiting additional federally sponsored embryo destruction.[4] The passage of Proposition 71, on the other hand, not only promised public funds for "progenitor," or embryonic stem cell derivation and research but made carrying out this research *a constitutional right* by amending the state constitution. As mentioned at the beginning of this chapter, this California exceptionalism needs to be understood against a backdrop of opposing the federal government's "anti-science" position, as well as in a more nationalist vein of "not falling behind" other countries in this area of science and biomedicine.

Abortion politics, then, are central to human stem cell research, and nowhere more so than in the United States. And yet, is abortion a women's issue in the field of stem cell research? Paradoxically, even though women have abortions, and even though protecting the right to a legal and safe abortion, known as "a woman's right to choose," has been the signature political issue for pro-choice women for over a quarter of a century, the slide from embryonic stem cell research to abortion and vice versa does not seem to have been as straightforward for the "pro-choice" side as it has been for the "pro-life" side. Women who oppose abortion also commonly oppose stem cell research because it destroys embryos, not because of women's reproductive health or women's autonomy.[5] The political movement to bring to term leftover embryos from infertility treatments has importantly invoked right-to-life women as the literal and symbolic mothers/wombs willing and capable of preventing the "genocide" represented by destroying the unused embryos, bringing anti-abortion back to gender and family politics. Embryonic stem cell lines do not exist until after the embryo-like entity is sacrificed, however. This means that once stem cells are in question there is no longer any embryo that a right-to-life mother could bring to term. Anti-abortion, then, is still the major impediment to embryonic stem cell research and yet it is not really a "women's issue," even for right-to-life women, except indirectly.

Many women who support stem cell research also support legal abortion and vice versa, but it does not appear logically to follow, at least in California, as two parts of the same moral framing in the way that those who oppose abortion also tend to oppose stem cell research. There are, as far as I can tell, three main reasons why not all pro-choice women have been supporters of embryonic stem cell research and Proposition 71. The main reason is that many women, especially feminists, continue to be major participants in articulating opposition to reproductive and genetic technologies on different grounds from those of right-to-lifers, as described in the final section below. Part of this thinking is that many pro-choice women worry about the special risks to women in embryonic stem cell research, in particular, egg donation (on which more below). A second reason is that a major appeal of stem cell research is its promise of cures for disability and disease. The right to abortion gains part of its legitimacy from cases of "therapeutic abortion" for disability and disease. New conversations about disability rights and its tense relations with interventions to alleviate disability through stem cell research threaten this relatively unexamined pillar of the U.S. abortion rationale. A third reason that some women's pro-choice views do not always translate into pro-stem cell views comes from a desire to protect reproductive privacy. Many pro-choice women and men have fought for a gradual extension of reproductive and sexual privacy protections over the years, allowing such categories as single women, gay and lesbian lovers and parents, mixed race couples, and people with disabilities to reproduce and have access to reproductive technologies free from state intervention and discrimination in their private lives. The intensely public issues involved in stem cell research regulation risk undermining these hard-won trends in reproductive privacy. It is easy to see, then, that while support for abortion and support for carrying out stem cell research often go together, some pro-choice women consider embryonic stem cell research to occupy a different moral realm from abortion.

Despite the fundamental role of abortion politics in stem cell research and the gendered nature of abortion itself, "a woman's right to choose" does not effortlessly encompass support for stem cell research, and the latter is thus not prima facie a "women's issue" on either side of the abortion debate. The question remains as to whether abortion politics in the stem cell debate *should* be a women's issue. In other words, is representing women in the stem cell debate about picking up and arguing the threads that somehow emerge as women's issues, or is it at least as much about trying to figure out what women ought to have a say in? Drawing from my fieldwork, the latter might involve the following: articulating pro-life women's concern to distinguish among stem cell lines so that they can access stem cell lines and eventually cures for themselves and their families that did not involve embryonic stem cells. New research suggests that so-called adult stem cells have much more potential to differentiate into the body's different tissue types than was previously believed so this is more feasible than it was once thought to be. Funding adult stem cell research specifically to allow pro-life citizens access to stem cell therapies would lead to good labeling, tracking, and accounting practice, and might facilitate international standardization and end up improving stem cell science. A general truth here is that opposition can often be operationalized into standards of care that *improve* rather than *impede* research, as long as they are internalized as procedure rather than externalized as political barriers to research (a point that the British stem cell effort has taken to heart, but also a point that echoes in a microcosm the argument of this chapter that critique should be about improving not impeding science).

Pro-choice women's concerns about women's experience could also be insisted on. Drawing again from my fieldwork, a mother who has undergone pre-implantation genetic diagnosis and has leftover embryos that have or are carriers for a fatal disease might well be a compelling witness to the value of those embryos for research and the problems associated with attempting to bring them to term. Pro-choice women articulate both the differences between the right to reproductive privacy including safe legal abortion and the right to conduct stem cell research, making sure that the unique role of a woman's body in the two cases be kept in mind. And again, one could drive policy and practice in ways that are designed to mitigate rather than exacerbate other concerns that some pro-choice women have expressed toward stem cell research, such as resistance to eugenics and cloning, and concerns about the health disparity implications of the research. This, too, would probably lead to better not worse research and care. Pro-choicers could learn from pro-lifers about dangers for disability rights implicit in prenatal diagnostic procedures and therapeutic abortion, and pro-lifers could learn from pro-choicers about the extraordinary trials and suffering that they and their loved ones have endured and that prenatal diagnosis and stem cell research have the potential to alleviate. Certainly the different roles gender can play in the link between stem cell and abortion politics should be studied and appreciated.

Women's Bodies as Substrates for Research: The Egg Donation Issue
For a range of interesting reasons, protection of potential egg donors has become a signature ethical concern in the politics of stem cell research in California and elsewhere, and has emerged as *the* women's issue. It is one of the

few ethical issues that has garnered bipartisan support. Fueled by the South Korean stem cell scandal, it is also functioning as a chip in a game of national and individual rivalries over supremacy in stem cell research, as if protection of egg donors were *ab initio* a universal ethical standard in barely emerging national and transnational regulatory and trade regimes for human stem cell research. Women's health advocates, including Judy Norsigian of the *Boston Women's Health Book Collective* (1999), have played a role in bringing this issue to the fore. Despite how overdetermined this concern for women's bodies now seems, it is in fact somewhat surprising given the state of affairs in other organ and tissue donation, and in egg donation as it has been routinely practiced for assisted reproductive technologies.

Oocytes have been removed from the bodies of women for their own and others' reproduction for a quarter of a century in the United States with very little outcry about donor protection. As I argued in my book, *Making Parents: The Ontological Choreography of Reproductive Technologies* (Thompson 2005), reproductive technologies in the United States have penetrated popular culture (movies, TV shows, books, magazines, and so on), but nonetheless remained more or less private in three essential ways that make them radically different from the human stem cell research arena.[6] The medical organization that represents health care providers in the area, the American Society for Reproductive Medicine, has staved off most kinds of regulation by collaborating with the Centers for Disease Control and with the major patient activist umbrella organization, RESOLVE, in a data collection effort in which results of all reproductive technology procedures are reported and monitored each year. This allows physicians to carry out experimental protocols and to use in-house patient protection mechanisms out of the eye of abortion foes. This also allows physicians to proceed relatively free of governmental regulation that might otherwise require animal trials or other procedures that would dramatically slow down implementation of new drug regimes and protocols (animal models are of little use as reproductive endocrinology, even among primates, differs radically).

Patient activists, too, have had a strong interest in keeping reproductive technologies private. They invoke legal traditions advocating reproductive privacy. On the one hand, the presumption of privacy allows patients to enter into reproductive technology treatment free from scrutiny about their fitness as parents that adoptive parents must face.[7] And on the other hand, the presumption of privacy allows patients to discuss their choices under the rubric of family building. The political right wing in general wants families to be free from government intervention as much as the political left wants reproductive privacy, and so the commonly used language of "family building" works in a bipartisan manner to keep reproductive technologies legal and relatively free from regulation. This rubric shields them from the type of anti-abortion pressure that might have emerged if the technologies had been debated in the policy public sphere in the way that stem cell research is being debated. Patients just as much as practitioners are wary about being too closely aligned with public conversations about gamete manipulation in vitro, and so have distanced their well-established reproductive practices from stem cell research, despite the identical procedures of egg procurement. Drug companies, too, have benefited greatly from this lack of public scrutiny of reproductive technologies. Whereas many corporations have not dared to invest in human embryonic stem cell research, drug companies have found fertility drugs to be very profitable, and innovation—for example, recombinant versions of the drugs used for ovarian hyperstimulation—has been lucrative.

Although egg donation in reproductive technologies hits the news regularly, egg donor protection has not been a major aspect of comment or censure. Overwhelmingly, it is the price for eggs from certain kinds of donors that has been the subject of debate and outcry. A middle-class student attending an elite university who gets $30,000 for donating her eggs is not usually considered a victim of coercion or particularly in need of public oversight. Instead the focus tends to turn to the eugenic folk biological implications of paying for "good-looking young woman with high SATs and leadership skills." Occasionally, the dangers of repeat donation come up, but usually for sperm donors, not for egg donors, and usually because of incest risk, not because of the negative health effects of repeat donation. Worries take the form: Did Jane unwittingly marry her half brother because of the overuse of a single donor's sperm? Is it incest if a daughter donates an egg to her mother and stepfather for them to have a child?

From the start of reproductive technologies, feminist and anti-racist voices have been raised about the potential for exploitation along class, race, and national lines with both egg donation and gestational surrogacy; these critiques are not concerned with the exploitation of women as a class, but rather with the exploitation of some women by other women and men and by the fertility industry. From time to time a woman suffering severe ovarian hyperstimulation might hit the news headlines, but she is more likely to garner sympathy if she is a woman providing eggs for her own treatment than if she is a donor. The stockpiling of unused embryos, some of which come from fertilized donor eggs, has become a major point of focus in the United States of anti-abortion groups. But again, this has to do with abortion concerns noted above and does not arise from the politics of egg donation per se or concerns for protecting donors. Public attention in reproductive technologies derives from the general media except in a handful of states where there have been political campaigns to enact insurance coverage mandates for the procedures. Media attention to reproductive technology related problems has been post hoc and largely devoted to the exposé-of-disaster genre rather than fostering the type of preemptive public debate that has surrounded stem cell egg donation.

Ethical committees of the American Society for Reproductive Medicine and others, working largely out of the public eye, have long upheld the need to hold down payments to egg donors and have issued guidelines on acceptable payments that in their minds do not represent "undue inducement to donors" and do not inflate the vulgar eugenics of fertility clinics that do not restrict payments to donors. Practitioners of reproductive technologies also commonly acknowledge the potential for coercion in other than economic forms; it can arise in particular over family or friendship donations, just as much as in cases where eggs are paid for, stemming from a desire or sense of obligation to donate to family or friends. It is worth noting that this kind of pressure is considered exemplary in some appeals for donation—for example, blood or bone marrow—but has to be offset by the added risk to the donor of egg donation (as it does in kidney donation, for example), and by the kinship complications and risks of incest of gametes used in reproductive technologies. Egg donation guidelines from the American Society for Reproductive Medicine also spell out donation kinship limits so as to avoid incest.

While low-income women are considered to be at risk for exploitation in egg donation for IVF (in vitro fertilization), this is tempered by the fact that the market for IVF tends to pay less for eggs from women of lower socio-economic status, and to favor students. This stands in contrast to gestational surrogacy and to procurement for stem cell research. Surrogates and donors for research are assumed to pattern in ways characteristic of the domestic and transnational division of labor in general, because the market is not dictated by recipient choice of donors with desirable traits, but rather according to the need for work. Immigration status as well as money can be major incentives. Low-income women for whom any kind of reimbursement represents a significant improvement in circumstances, as well as undocumented aliens are often especially ready to take on caring and other domestic labor under the INS radar. The access to health care and to various kinds of medical attention, albeit for donation purposes, is recognized as another possible incentive. In short, even in the policy realm, and even where concerns about coercion seem to coincide, the debates around egg donation for reproductive technology are very different from those around egg donation for stem cell research. This difference indicates what a jump it was to make egg donor protection the major women's issue of stem cell research.

Consider also the landscape of policy around organ and tissue donation, which makes it clear that it was not self-evident that the particular aspects of egg donation that have garnered the most attention would have done so. Many body parts and products can be gifted or sold apart from the body of which they were once part (for example, organs, hair, blood, sperm, eggs); many can be sold, although not always by the donor (for example, blood, sperm, eggs, some organs); many are used for medical diagnostic procedures (for example, urine, feces, blood, embryos); many are used in industry to generate value-added products for forensics, security, wig making, medical or fertility treatment, and so on (for example, teeth, blood, fingernails, skin, hair, urine, eggs); many are rarely and only with difficulty designated as waste (for example, cadavers, organs, eggs, embryos) while others are often waste (for example, blood, sperm) and others are usually waste, and their management as such requires an enormous infrastructure worldwide (for example, urine, feces, hair); several involve considerable short- or long-term risk to the donor (for example, living donor organ donation, skin, eggs) while many normally do not involve much risk (for example, post-mortem organ donation, hair, blood, sperm, urine, fingernails); many are sometimes sacred and sometimes profane (for example, organs in a dead body, which are usually sacred and their taking would be a desecration, but which can be extracted under the right consent and medical conditions; hair, which is sacred to members of some religions and profane to others; embryos); some can only be donated by certain members of the population and not others (for example, matched tissue, sperm, eggs). Each part of the body has a different history and pragmatics of alienability that itself varies from one part of the world to another.[8]

As can be seen by the partial list above, there is no a priori reason to model human oocytes on one body part or product rather than another, and in general eggs have characteristics that are shared, but in different combinations, by different body parts. In addition, the donation or sale of body parts and products always faces, but to varying degrees, questions about the voluntarism or coercion of the donation or sale; questions about the beneficiaries of the value-added economy of the body part; the risk of biological, social, or transnational segmentation and stratification of the donor and recipient pools; the urgency or moral appeal of the donation or sale; and whether the body part donation or sale is part of a preexisting bureaucracy and whether that bureaucracy is seen as having legitimacy. Again, these things are not unique to egg donation, although they have surfaced in the stem cell debate in a particularly public manner generally uncharacteristic of other body parts.

Human embryonic stem cell research currently requires the procurement of human eggs or of human embryos, although it may soon be possible to reverse engineer some adult stem cells. Embryos can be procured from IVF facilities, with the right consents and the right capabilities. They can also be made in the lab by combining in vitro gametes, which requires prior procurement of eggs and sperm, or by parthenogenesis of an egg. Or, eggs can be enucleated and fused with the nuclear DNA from a somatic cell to make a clonal blastocyst, in the procedure known as research cloning, or somatic cell nuclear transfer (SCNT), which was used to create Dolly, the cloned sheep. Human embryonic stem cell lines are derived from the inner cell mass of early embryos or blastocysts, and each of these ways can lead to blastocysts. The second and third procedures need a supply of fresh eggs, although the UK is currently embroiled in a national debate about the feasibility of using enucleated nonhuman eggs in combination with human somatic cell DNA for SCNT. SCNT holds particular promise because it can potentially produce stem cell lines that are genetically almost identical to the person providing the somatic cell and nuclear DNA, which, if it is the patient him- or herself, will guarantee an almost perfect tissue match and reduce the problems associated with tissue rejection that plague organ donation. It is also the most controversial, being the procedure that the South Korean team lied about having achieved. If human embryonic stem cell research is to advance rapidly, so the argument goes, a steady supply of eggs will be needed. Thus, egg donation is essential to the research, but not part of either stem cell treatment or clinical trials of therapies. Ethical procedures and informed consent are thus hard to model on any preexisting tissue or organ donation, including egg donation in reproductive technologies.

In California, Proposition 71 has banned payment to egg donors, and Senator Ortiz sponsored a bill that further restricted compensation to women who donate eggs for stem cell research to ensure that coercion is not involved. What are the arguments that lurk around the question of paying for eggs that have suddenly come to the fore? One line of thinking has it that if donors are compensated, it amounts to paying for eggs, which is perilously close to paying for babies. There is overwhelming consensus that paying for babies (the goal for eggs in reproductive technologies is to make babies, but not in stem cell research, unless the embryo from which the stem cells are extracted is seen as a baby) should be prohibited because it amounts to trafficking in human beings, and trafficking in human beings is slavery. Paying for eggs seems also to mean that eggs are commodified. The anti-commodification argument, as long as it is not spelled out too clearly, has broad support across the political spectrum. This is one reason for the surprising unity around egg donor protection that has emerged in the time since the passage of Proposition 71. The different objections to treating eggs as a commodity include (1) that eggs and embryos are sufficiently people-like, or inextricably connected to and thus not completely alienable from people, and people are never commodities; treating humans like commodities implies treating them as instrumental, rather than as means unto themselves; (2) commodifying eggs introduces market dynamics that can make the world's most vulnerable subject to coercion by rent-seeking parties and encourage trafficking in eggs; (3) that there is an ethos of a gift economy in tissue and organ donation that aims to provide cures, such as stem cell research, and to commodify eggs would be to subvert the emotions and motivations of patients and donors alike.

Is all payment commodification? There are many examples legally recognized as such and informally honored as such where it would be a stretch at best to say that paying for something is the same as commodifying it in the sense of the critiques above. Thus, if Ms. X pays her mother to take care of her toddler at home three days a week, most people would probably say she is respecting her mother's labor by paying her, not commodifying her mother's relationship with her grandchild. Similarly, there are many examples of things that are not entirely commodified despite being paid for, such as the use of people's names, or licensing techniques that are patented; license fees are paid for use, but the innovation, or the individual-referring name does not leave its original owner. Modeling egg donation on either of these kinds of things would work relatively well in averting the critiques of commodification. The other option is resolutely to enforce that it is the effort or expense of donation that is compensated, and not the eggs themselves.

Refusing payment for egg donation has a consequence that it prohibits the donor from acquiring any profit derived from their eggs, while those who commercialize cell lines derived from the eggs are free to profit (see, for example, Thompson 2007; Landecker 2000). If companies, and even individual researchers at public universities, can profit from state investment in stem cell research, is it fair that egg donors themselves cannot? The argument against commodification of persons has it roots in many religious traditions as well as in Kantian ethics, which enjoin one never to treat humans as instrumental means to an end but always as things unto themselves. This also lies behind the first principle of post-Belmont biomedical ethics, namely, the autonomy of the person. Similarly, it has roots in nineteenth-century social theory, including Marxism, where to be commodified—that is to be bought and sold in a market—is considered to be a way in which one is alienated from one's humanity. Putting a price on one's head, or one's soul, runs afoul of the prohibition on "pricing the priceless" captured in the credit card advertisements. Here, of course, it is not the person who is being instrumentalized or commodified (unless, again, one believes that the clonal and reproductive embryos involved in stem cell research are persons, but in that case one has moved away from egg donors themselves).

To be concerned about commodifying eggs because that would rob women of their essential human dignity, one has to believe that body parts should be treated in significant ways as persons. Those on the left who worry about commodification tend to get some of the moral heft of their concerns from these meta-ethical concerns, but have more practical problems in mind. Usually they are worried on the one hand that the commodification of body parts signals the end of our human future, threatening a fundamental condition of humanity, the valuing of people in and of themselves, not because of their instrumental or other use value. On the other hand, and with very good cause given some organ donation markets, anxiety about commodification is part and parcel of anxiety about coercion. From Indira Gandhi's state-sponsored vasectomy campaign in the 1970s to more and less well-substantiated accounts of the kidnapping of street children for organ donation in Brazil and elsewhere, trafficking in human tissue is a real danger when there is a market for body parts. If there is a market for eggs, or any other human tissue, there is no end to the lengths that unscrupulous third parties will go to attain those eggs.

This kind of traffic is incredibly hard to police because it preys on the most vulnerable people in society and tends to be part of an informal or illegal economy. The economic calculus is simple: when a person is worth little or nothing in society, any value attached to their organs or body tissue is value-added. Harvesting eggs, if the eggs themselves, rather than the act of donation, are paid for, makes economic sense even if it sacrifices the donor, in the most desperate of circumstances.

While the protection of egg donors is extremely important (I have been advocating for strict protections, particularly around potential long-term effects on donors of ovarian hyperstimulation) and clearly is an issue of great importance to women as a class, we should be wary of taking the current framing as the only way to view the topic. Bearing in mind how different other donations and sales are, and how different egg donation is in assisted reproductive technologies, it is important to be able to ask other kinds of questions that might give answers that are just as important for the well-being of women. For example, it is equally important to be able to ask which kinds of tissue or organ living donation for which purpose is oocyte donation like, and what lessons can be learned from donor protection in each of these cases? When is something waste, a gift, a commodity, a research substrate, or a combination of these, and how can we move beyond the gift/commodity dichotomy for the research situation? What are bioethical regimes in other countries and what can be learned from them, and is the "ethics of egg donation" at risk of being a way of imposing a particular bioethical regime on other countries that gives countries with regulation based on human subjects protection an unfair head start, and perhaps set up transnational dynamics that will themselves lead to a transnational and inequitable egg trade? Which groups can or do donate, with which motivations? Are barriers to donation—for example, being in the right information networks to be aware of the option of donating, or having expenses covered—substantial? How much do research imperatives require demographic variety in the donor population, and what recruitment practices will address this? In particular, is it necessary to have representation of all socioeconomic strata and ethnoracial groups among egg donors for non-SCNT stem cell line derivation on the off chance that this correlates with tissue match criteria, in terms of the likelihood of every California citizen of finding a good tissue match in a stem cell bank? For disease modeling, rather than therapy delivery, how important is it to get eggs from all groups of women in society? Do levels of reimbursement discriminate against one group or another in ways that affect either the research imperatives or the health and safety of donors? Just as it is essential not to over-induce any groups of women to donate, how do you make sure that enough women from all groups participate in egg donation? How can long- and short-term health and safety concerns best be met, both for donors undergoing ovarian hyperstimulation and surgery, for technicians working with the eggs, for the eggs themselves, and for recipients of donated eggs? How can psychological expectations of cures be tempered without suppressing support for a hopeful technology, so that undue pressure is not put on family members to engage in altruistic donation? Egg donation, as a women's issue, really should go far beyond the question of whether or not to pay for eggs.

Health Care Burden: Access, Affordability, Priorities

In some ways, the question of health care priorities, access, and affordability is the exact opposite of the egg donation issue. Access and affordability for stem cell therapies themselves are being addressed in the California debate since the passage of Proposition 71, but health care priorities more generally have hardly been raised at all in public discussion. In my fieldwork I have asked several women a version of the following question: "Does authorizing the expenditure of an additional $3 billion, or approximately $6 billion after interest, of state funds on stem cell research adequately represent your own, or women's health care priorities?" So far, no one has answered that it does, even if they are strongly in favor of stem cell research. The most common response is that if it had been up to them to spend $3 billion on health care it would have gone toward insuring the uninsured and on providing primary care and preventive medicine for all. Women tend to see themselves as especially responsible for their own and their families' health care and to worry about its availability.

Debating stem cell research from the point of view of its place in the allocation of scarce health care resources requires a rather different perspective that is not easy to sustain when the question at hand is the implementation of regulations and policies for an already enacted stem cell bill. One woman told me that "stem cell research is like gay marriage" in her congregation—the pastor asked his congregants one Sunday to stand if they thought that prohibiting gay marriage was a serious issue. One woman stood up. He then asked who thought access to basic health care was a serious issue and the whole congregation surged to its feet. That, she said, represented her views on stem cell research—not only is it less important by far than basic health care, but she assumed that it would not affect her African American community as they would be so unlikely to be the beneficiaries of high-tech interventions like stem cell therapies. On the one hand, then, there is a readily identified primary health care burden on women that makes them question whether this is a good use of funds, and a sense among some women that stem cell research doesn't apply to them or their families. On the other hand, though, whether or not women say they would have spent health care money this way, many women articulate support for spending on stem cell research because of the promise of respite from chronic diseases and debilitating conditions. Care for the seriously disabled, both one's own kin and those women tend as paid work, is still a heavily gendered domain, so women disproportionately witness the suffering that some conditions can bring as well as disproportionately endure the sometimes harsh conditions of being a caregiver. Addressing all these concerns and bringing the debate about stem cell research back into a broader discussion of health care priorities and access and affordability is a major women's issue, and yet it is barely articulated in the current conversation.

Women, Patient Activism, and Oppositional "Moral Pioneers"
Following on from the last point about women's caregiving roles in relation to disability, it is essential to bring to light the role of women as patient activists and as oppositional activists. Women have been extremely influential as patient activists on their own behalf, and have also come to exemplify what Rayna Rapp (1999) has called "moral pioneers" with respect to their efforts to get treatments for their sick and disabled children. To forgo consideration and debate of women's roles as patient activists in stem cell research would be to completely ignore the gender dimensions of the very biopolitical and biosocial movements that led to the passage of Proposition 71. The "direct democracy" aspect of a bond issue, and its success through its so-called "heartstrings appeal," depended deeply on family and care relations and dedicated parental activism as well as on patients acting through their disease groups on their group's behalf.

Another way in which women have been and remain prominent moral pioneers in the stem cell debate and that needs taking into account concerns their role as spokespeople in opposition to stem cell research on feminist, antiracist, and disability activist grounds. Women activists have been key players in articulating gateway fears associated with tampering with germ lines, and with chimerical research. They have pointed out the way that stem cell research could play into the hands of older or still existing eugenic platforms, and even bring back race science. They have acted for the protection of egg donors, and for responsible and just policies for access and affordability that will prevent some women's bodies being the pharmaceutical chest for the world's wealthiest. Women have also been important in supporting disability rights and pointing to the risk that stem cell research, as it is frequently represented, seeks to find cures for everything, and as such casts everything deemed a deviation from normal as in need of a cure. Disability rights spokespeople recognize both the importance of finding cures but also the fundamental risks of casting everything as in need of curing, instead of putting pressure on the world to accommodate a little better to different embodiments, and to celebrate the different realities of those with disabilities. In California, the staff of the Center for Genetics and Society have been exemplary and relentless in providing challenges to the all too ready assumptions with which we assume that scientific progress is good for us all, let alone good for (all) women.

Gender and Science, and the New Politics of Science

I started this chapter by suggesting that the time is right, given the political climate toward science and the renewed debate about women in science and engineering prompted by Summers's comments, to bring the full richness of scholarship around gender and science into the policy arena, and to use it in turn to inform remedies to the continued underrepresentation of women and minorities in science and engineering. Specifically, I took up a thought experiment that this suggestion prompted, namely, taking a particular emerging field of science and thinking about its gendered role in society. How might women and minorities take part in but also legislate and use a particular branch of science and technology were gender and race and class and globalization to be taken seriously? What ways of thinking and matters of concern linger in particular debates and how can they be sources of progress in participation and distributive justice rather than barriers to both?

In the body of the chapter I discussed the kinds of concerns for the domain of stem cell research that this might enable us to bring to bear on public debate and policy. This approach demands an intersectional view of gender, where gender is seen as always in dynamic formation with other relevant cat-

egories of personhood such as race and class and immigration status and political and religious affiliation. It also requires that the category of "women"
be taken not as an a priori category but as something that is sometimes invoked personally, politically, bureaucratically, and so on, and sometimes not,
in ways that can be equally salient for gender scholarship; "women" is also
sometimes anything but unitary and sometimes a unifying class or category.
This perspective also requires that gender and science scholarship that addresses policy-relevant issues not separate the question of women's representation or otherwise in science from other questions about science in society.
Gender and science scholars must open up ways of informing policy while
bringing the richness of the field in the past and present to that task. There are
always questions about the gendering of science itself, and about the sciences
of gender, about scientists and users, and about the governance of science, and
they cannot be separated from the question of the numbers and well-being of
women in science. Addressing the multiplicity of "women's issues" in a given
scientific field would likely make the field more attractive to women and make
women more attractive to those recruiting in the field in question. The stem
cell debate stands as a significant site to begin to bring gender and science
scholarship to bear directly within the new politics of science.

Notes to Chapter 7

1. The Bush government and its allies (apart from fundamentalist opposition to
evolution) have been science denying in the fields of tobacco and global warming and
science opposing in the field of human embryonic stem cell research.

2. Advocates and activists who had been working with CIRM included Greenlining, a minority advocacy agency; the Center for Genetics and Society, a group
concerned among other things with halting cloning, protecting women's reproductive rights, and civic accountability; the Pro-Choice Alliance Against Proposition 71;
HOOO, or Hands Off Our Ovaries; and various other groups calling for more public
accountability and for tougher conflict of interest laws—were altogether absent on
the SB 322 roster. Also missing were theological and other voices opposed to stem cell
research on the basis of the moral status of the embryo.

3. There are debates about this—some maintain that an embryo need not be sacrificed for stem cells to be extracted, for example, if a single cell is biopsied and cul-
tured from a two-four cell embryo, and others maintain that embryos are not created
and so not destroyed by somatic cell nuclear transfer procedures (research cloning)
because there is no sperm, no procreative intent, no implantation, no meiosis, and no
fertilization.

4. HR 810, an effort to overturn the 2001 decision in favor of permitting human embryonic stem cell derivation using leftover embryos from fertility treatment, fell just short of the two-thirds majority to survive a presidential veto; a similar House bill fared better but still fell short, on January 11, 2007, after the Democratic gains of November 2006.

5. Some pro-life women also resist stem cell research because of the possible ill effects on women of such procedures as egg donation.

6. Note, too, that women mostly carried out activism and scholarship around reproductive technologies, while stem cell activism and scholarship is more masculinized.

7. Most recently, China has begun requiring that U.S. adoptive parents meet body mass index criteria before they are allowed to adopt, adding fatness to heterosexual, coupled, monied, and age norms that have long characterized the adoption picture.

8. There is a robust and ever growing literature on procurement and provenance, egg donation, selling, and trafficking in body parts, tissue economies, medical tourism, and stratified reproduction, on which this section draws. See, for example, Andrews, L., and Nelkin, D. 2001. *Body Bazaar: The Market for Human Tissue in the Biotechnology Age.* New York: Crown; Franklin, S., and Roberts, C. 2006. *Born and Made: An Ethnography of Pre-implantation Genetic Diagnosis.* Princeton, NJ: Princeton University Press; Konrad, M. 2005. *Nameless Relations: Anonymity, Melanesia, and Reproductive Gift Exchange Between British Ova Donors and Recipients.* Oxford: Berghahn; Lock, M. 2001. *Twice Dead: Organ Transplants and the Reinvention of Death.* Berkeley: University of California Press; Reardon, J. 2004. *Race to the Finish: Identity and Governance in an Age of Genomics,* Princeton, NJ: Princeton University Press; Roberts, D. 2003. *Shattered Bonds: The Color of Child Welfare,* New York: Basic Books; Scheper-Hughes, N., and Wacquant, L. eds. 2002. *Commodifying Bodies.* Thousand Oaks, CA: Sage; Spar, D. 2006. *The Baby Business: How Money, Science, and Politics Drive the Commerce of Conception.* Cambridge, MA: Harvard Business School Press; Strathern, M. 2005. *Kinship, Law and the Unexpected: Relatives are Always a Surprise.* Cambridge, UK: Cambridge University Press; Waldby, C., and Mitchell, R. 2006. *Tissue Economies: Blood, Organs, and Cell Lines in Late Capitalism.* Durham, NC: Duke University Press.

8 If You Meet the Expectations of Women, You Exceed the Expectations of Men

How Volvo Designed a Car for Women Customers and Made World Headlines

Tatiana Butovitsch Temm

T HE IDEA OF BUILDING A CAR responding to the needs and wishes of women was born among women at the Volvo Car Corporation. It was an idea that initially swam upstream.

It all started in October 2001, when Martha Barletta, a Chicago-based marketing-to-women expert, came to Gothenburg, Sweden, for a seminar on how to better cater to women customers. Why focus on designing for women? Volvo Car's customer statistics show that more than 53 percent of buyers in the United States are women, and even in Europe women who buy cars in the premium segment are a fast-growing group. Listening to what the customers want is a sound business decision. After the seminar, in the doorway, the idea was born. What if only women made the entire car—what would it look like?

The idea for a car created by women expanded as more women engineers at Volvo got involved and contributed their expertise and insights. In June 2002, the group had a chance to present their ideas to Hans-Olov Olsson, at the time president and CEO of Volvo Car Corporation. The week preceding the meeting with Olsson, the group contacted Anna Rosén, a young automobile exterior designer who had just started working with Volvo. Would she like to join the project, and could she make a first sketch over the weekend? She answered yes and yes, and Olsson saw that the car the team had in mind would be sleek and sporty, not cute and pink. The project was approved and given a budget for a preliminary study.

In late December 2002, the Volvo Car management team gave the order to make a concept car for the Geneva Motor Show just fourteen months away. The "Your Concept Car" (YCC) project revved up. All manufacturers in the auto industry make concept cars. They are suggestions to the market—ways to find out whether new ideas are practical or to tell the market that your cars are technologically advanced. They are never intended for production. Neither was the YCC.

The YCC project now had a budget and a time frame. The core group found more team members and started the difficult job of selecting which of the numerous ideas would or could fit into the car, and which ones would have to wait for another concept car later on.

Our team had a thesis: if you meet the expectations of women, you exceed the expectations of men. In other words, the car should include women without excluding men. Market research showed that this thesis not only sounds good but also can be relied on. When we looked at the car market sorted by gender, we saw that among consumers looking for budget cars, women and men differ greatly in what they want in their cars. For consumers in the mid-price range, the difference between men and women is somewhat smaller. In the premium segment, however, a woman who purchases a car wants everything that a man wants when it comes to performance, style, quality, and status. But then she wants more; she has a longer wish list. And that makes her the most demanding of all customers. If we focused on the most demanding customer, we would also please the ones who are slightly less demanding—in our case, the men in the premium segment.

To help us choose what should go into the car, we invented a target customer and called her Eve. At that moment she had the characteristics shown in Figure 8.1.

The car would give Eve what she needed *this very second*. The things she did not need right away would have to wait. The YCC project team did not specifically consider child and pregnancy safety. This decision was discussed a lot in the group, and in the end the consensus was to leave this theme for another concept car. One objective was to distance the project from the stereotype that women all come equipped with babies. Regardless of gender, the parent phase is a rather short one in the life of a car owner. The Volvo fleet offers plenty of excellent family cars for the baby years; the YCC is for the other 40 or so years you drive your car. Still, most women in the YCC team are mothers of young

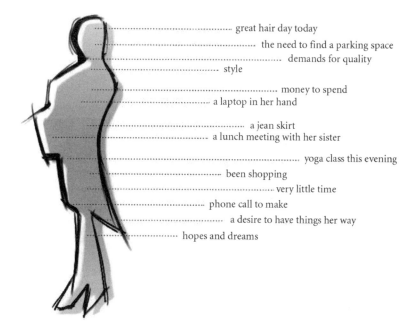

great hair day today

the need to find a parking space

demands for quality

style

money to spend

a laptop in her hand

a jean skirt

a lunch meeting with her sister

yoga class this evening

been shopping

very little time

phone call to make

a desire to have things her way

hopes and dreams

FIGURE 8.1 Guiding document: the target customer at one moment in time. All images in this chapter courtesy of Volvo Cars Corporation.

children, and all of us would love to drive our kids to school or daycare in a YCC. And of course all standard Volvo child safety equipment fits in the car.

We chose to concentrate on the areas where we saw that the expectations of the women in the premium segment were clearly higher than those of the men in that segment (marked in Figure 8.2):

- Good overall visibility
- Good handling and maneuverability
- Interior convenience, easy-to-reach controls, and easy-to-read dials
- Ease of entry to and exit from vehicle
- Ease of parking

From the outset, we knew what problems we had to solve, but not how we could solve them. That was our task for the ensuing fourteen months. What we did know was that we wanted the car to be stunning and that in no case would we "paint it pink" or opt for makeup and flowery solutions.

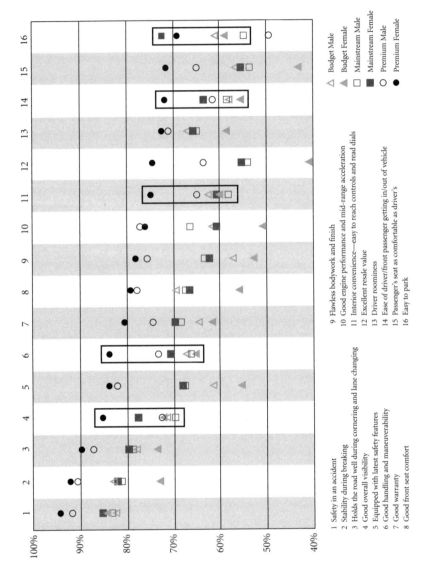

1 Safety in an accident
2 Stability during breaking
3 Holds the road well during cornering and lane changing
4 Good overall visibility
5 Equipped with latest safety features
6 Good handling and maneuverability
7 Good warranty
8 Good front seat comfort

9 Flawless bodywork and finish
10 Good engine performance and mid-range acceleration
11 Interior convenience—easy to reach controls and read dials
12 Excellent resale value
13 Driver roominess
14 Ease of driver/front passenger getting in/out of vehicle
15 Passenger's seat as comfortable as driver's
16 Easy to park

△ Budget Male
▲ Budget Female
□ Mainstream Male
■ Mainstream Female
○ Premium Male
● Premium Female

FIGURE 8.2 Needs and desires from a gender and market segment perspective.

YCC: The Car

Exterior Design

The exterior designer, Anna Rosén, had a tough task. Apart from making a car that is stunning and practical at the same time, she was to ensure that the driver could see where the car ended, regardless of her size. Many shorter drivers of today's cars cannot see where the hood ends, making parking difficult. Rosén solved this problem by inverting the traditional Volvo V in the hood and raising the fenders. In that way, she got a front end that resembles a classic sports car, and at the same time, the front corners are clearly visible from the driver's seat (see Figure 8.3).

In the back, the rear window ends where the car ends, so that drivers can judge their position easily. Moreover, the door opening is very large, as the B-pillar (between the back window and the side window) is moved back, giving the driver a good over-the-shoulder view when changing lanes (see Figure 8.4).

Our market research also showed that women, especially in North America, tend to claim that they choose SUVs because the driver sits higher and gets a better overview of traffic. So the YCC has a variable chassis height. The car can ride low and sporty on the highway, but the driver can raise the chassis 60 mm to get into a high mode in city traffic. This feature was added purely to increase visibility for the driver.

The YCC also has a bumper that wraps around most of the car to emphasize its functionality. By contrast, most of today's cars try to conceal the bumper's function by painting it the same color as the car.

Entry

The YCC is equipped with an auto-opening system. When the key is pressed, it sends a signal to the car to open the door. The car will pick up the signal when the key is near the wheel housing and then automatically open the door. The auto-opening system makes it easy to put bags and other luggage in through the wide door opening without first setting them on the ground in order to open the car door.

The project designers opted for a wide door opening from the beginning. But a wide opening requires a large, heavy door. A conventional door encounters difficulties because of both the size and strength of the hinges and the free space the door requires to open. After intense discussions, we reached a consensus: for the YCC, the only way was up. The car was equipped with

FIGURE 8.3 Front end designed for increased visibility.

FIGURE 8.4 Side and back designed for increased visibility.

gull-wing doors. Conventional gull-wing doors give a car an albatross-like wingspan, complicating parking. The YCC's doors are cut horizontally, so the bottom part, or the sill, rotates out of the way, and the rest of the door opens out only about two feet from the side of the car. The rotating sills also make it easier to get in and out of the car, as there is no high sill to climb over. Moreover, the side that turns out is a clean surface, so that winter grime from the car doesn't end up on your clothing (see Figure 8.5).

When the door opens, the chassis moves to its highest position, making it easier to get in and out. At the same time, the driver's seat moves as far back as possible and the steering wheel goes as far forward as it can. This flexibility gives the driver plenty of room to get into and out of the car.

Ergovision

When the driver puts the key in the ignition, the YCC recommends a seating position that is based on her (or his) body proportions. At the Volvo retailer, the drivers are scanned, and their proportions are stored electronically in their personal keys. The car then adjusts the seat, the steering wheel, the pedals, the head restraint, and the safety belt outlet to ensure that each driver has the best possible view and that all controls are within reach.

FIGURE 8.5 A big door opening for easy entry and exit.

If you'd rather lean farther back or sit more upright, you can change your position and store it in the key. The lenticular hologram on the A-pillar will tell you if you have adjusted yourself out of the optimum line of vision. We named this combination of ergonomics and vision Ergovision. We believe that one can't live without the other.

For a long time, vision has been a problem for shorter people, who have been forced to choose between seeing well and not reaching the pedals comfortably, or reaching the pedals and not seeing much at all. Some short drivers sit with their chest close to the steering wheel—a dangerous solution should the airbag release.

Ergovision increases safety. Well over 90 percent of all the impressions we get when we drive come through our eyes. Drivers have a better chance of avoiding accidents if they can see well (see Figure 8.6).

Front Storage

Storage solutions are not only about where to put your purse. They are also about where we put our keys, coins, mobile phones, shopping bags, and all the

FIGURE 8.6 A hologram on the A-pillar (top left) helps the driver see where to find the best possible vision.

other things most of us carry around in our cars. The most common place to store a mobile phone in a car today is in a cup holder!

We believe that the best place to store things you want close at hand is between the front seats. In many cars, that space is occupied by a gear shift and a parking brake. We moved these things. The parking brake is electronic, and the driver changes gears behind the steering wheel as in a race car. The area between the front seats is freed up for storage. In the YCC, we put a trash bin in the very front, in addition to shallow storage for keys and coins and mobile phones (and two cup holders). The shallow tray slides back to reveal a deep storage compartment that easily accommodates a laptop or a normal-sized purse (see Figure 8.7). There are two deep compartments like this, should you have both a purse and a laptop. In the back, a cool box can be reached from the driver's seat.

Back Seat Storage

Most people we know carry a bag in the backseat more often than a passenger. If that is how people use cars, why don't we make them accordingly? In

FIGURE 8.7 An abundance of storage between the front seats.

the YCC, the backseat is made for storage by default and for passengers when needed. Cinema-style seats ensure plenty of space for storage, but they turn into fully functional passenger seats when folded down (see Figure 8.8).

The Hallway

The hinges of gull-wing doors are in the roof, leaving the doorjambs available for storage. We called this storage area the hallway, for things you need when the doors are open. Here you can find a flashlight (one that is always charged, because it's connected to the car's electrical system), a first aid kit, an umbrella, and a lockable compartment where you can keep things you'd like to hide when you leave the car. Even if someone smashes the side window, he or she can't take items hidden in the structure of the car (see Figure 8.9).

Interior Design

The team had a strong desire to show Scandinavian design in the YCC, because Volvo is a Swedish car brand. For interior designer Cynthia Charwick, Scandinavian design means space and grace. She made the instrument panel S-shaped for more passenger space. The seats look like they are floating, because the support structure is hidden underneath. Along the entire interior, light tubes in the console split lines give the entire car an ambient light. Ventilation concealed in the ceiling split lines gently diffuses air throughout the whole interior (see Figure 8.10).

In the YCC, even the instrumentation is cleaned up. Gone is the "visual pollution" of meters you don't really need for driving, such as engine temperature meter, oil pressure meter, or tachometer (rev counter). What remains is what you need to know to drive efficiently: How fast am I driving? How far can I go before I need to fill up the fuel tank? How do I find my way (answered by a turn-by-turn navigational system)?

Color and Trim

For Maria Uggla, the color and trim designer, Scandinavian design means light colors and honest materials. She wanted to give the YCC the feeling of a living room rather than a cockpit. She brought living room materials into the car, and she made sure all edges are visible, so you can see that they are genuine. The YCC has bleached laminated oak on all horizontal surfaces and brushed aluminum on all functional surfaces where you interact with the car. The seats are thick saddle leather. Wool felt upholsters the rear, and parts of the interior are made of a glossy semitransparent plastic foil that does not try to imitate anything else—it is beautiful in its own right (see Figure 8.11).

FIGURE 8.8 The fold-down cinema-style backseat is made for storage by default and passengers when needed.

FIGURE 8.9 Storage in the doorjambs.

FIGURE 8.10 The interior is designed to give a feeling of space and grace.

FIGURE 8.11 Honest materials such as wood, leather, aluminum, and wool.

Today's cars come with very limited interior colors. Most are beige, grey, or black. Customers hesitate to buy bright colors, fearing that the resale value of the car will sink. In order to increase the customer's options for personalizing the car, the YCC has exchangeable seat pads that can be swapped in two minutes. This easy customization introduced both new colors and new materials into the cars. For the car's debut, Maria Uggla made eight different seat pads. Each comes with a detachable and washable soft woolen carpet that won't scuff the back of your shoes.

If you don't like pale yellow car seats with embroidered flowers, you can choose classic leather. Woven leather with rubber details might appeal to the sporty driver. Cool linen for summer? Red wool for Christmas? The choice is yours (see Figure 8.12).

Maintenance

Time is precious for all of us, not least for our target customer. Everyone has more fun things to do than to take care of a car. Therefore, the YCC is designed for minimal maintenance.

The paint is EasyClean, which means that it contains some Teflon that

FIGURE 8.12 The seat pads are exchangeable.

makes it work like a nonstick fry pan. Dirt and grime slide off easily. The tires are "run-flat," so you can drive to a gas station even after a puncture.

Most owners and drivers of premium cars open the hood only in order to fill up the windshield-washer fluid. Our team thought the hood was a rather oversized hatch for such a small operation. In the YCC the windshield-washer filling point is moved to the outside of the car, right behind the driver's door, next to the fuel filling point. To make it even easier to use, these filling points have been made capless like those in race cars (see Figure 8.13).

The YCC does not have a hood you can open. Just as in old sports cars, the entire front part comes off for access to the engine. Modern engines are all about electronics; there is very little, if anything, that a layperson (either man or woman) can do there. Because the hood cannot be opened, the entire engine bay can be repacked for easier access by auto mechanics. And we save a few dollars that can be spent on the inside of the car, on things the driver sees and uses every day.

The YCC also books its own service appointments. This can be done in a number of ways; the easiest is to use the car's integrated telephone. The system can send a text message to a garage the owner has chosen, saying, "I need service, could you please ring my owner and make an appointment?" The car's diagnostic system could be hooked up to the same telephone, notifying the garage of which service needs to be done, which spare parts are required,

FIGURE 8.13 Windscreen washer filling point is right behind the driver's door.

and whether the car needs a specialized mechanic. This system will save time for both the customer and the garage.

Parking

"Easy to park" was at the very top of our customers' wish list. We directed much thought and effort toward meeting this need. We were certain we'd get a lot of jokes and snide comments about "women who can't park," so we asked our research department to carry out a study. They asked a number of women and men in several countries about (1) their parking habits and (2) their feelings about parallel parking.

We found out (generalizing heavily) that the typical man drives from his known parking space at home to his known parking space at work and back again. He parks in two places that he knows by heart. In contrast, the typical woman also shops, visits friends, and drives children to various activities. She parks almost twice as often as the typical man, quite frequently in unfamiliar parking spaces. That is why we think parking looms large for women drivers.

The survey respondents were also asked how they liked parallel parking. Half of the women said that they had no problems with it. The other half said that they did not like it, but they could park parallel if they had to (in Europe, it is compulsory to learn parallel parking for your driver's license). The vast majority of the men surveyed said that they did not mind parallel parking.

In the last part of the study, subjects were filmed parallel parking a car. This exercise showed that half of the women did not have any problem; they just parked. The other half had to work hard to park, going back and forth several times. They got there in the end, and they were very careful. Half of the men also had no problems. The other half had to work hard to get the car where they wanted it. The main difference was that the men were not quite as careful—one man from Spain exclaimed, "I have no problem, I park by the ears" (meaning that he will hear the crunch when he hits the car in front or behind).

Some critics argued that including a parking aid is patronizing and therefore sexist. The YCC team does not agree. One cannot draw the conclusion that women designers included a parking aid because women can't park. If so, using the same logic, one could say that men designed the automatic gearbox because they can't change gears (an argument that can be applied to any other practical invention made by men). The YCC team sees the parking aid purely as a convenience feature. I use it as I use a dishwasher—because it is convenient not because I don't know how to wash my dishes by hand. Other car brands offer similar parking aids, and we don't hear a whisper about these being sexist or patronizing.

For head-in parking, the YCC's gull-wing doors require only two feet of free space. And the doors have sensors, so the driver will not have to guess whether space is adequate. For parallel parking, the YCC is equipped with a sensor to measure the available space. Drivers who would like some extra help simply press the "park" button on the steering wheel, and the car guides the steering. The driver operates the accelerator and brake, but the car does the steering by itself. No one need know that the Easy to Park system was used, so the car makes its driver look good, a very important feature of a car.

Power

The YCC is a concept car and therefore has no engine. It is prepared for both engine and transmission. Performance is important for our customers, but so is the environment. We prepared the YCC for a 215 bhp (brake horsepower, a measure of engine power) PZEV turbo engine. PZEV (Partly Zero Emission Vehicle) means that the nitrogen oxide emissions are so low that the car could be sold in the Green states of the United States, such as California.

We equipped it with a 60 Integrated Starter-Generator, which makes the YCC a hybrid. One of the benefits of an Integrated Starter-Generator is that the engine doesn't idle at traffic lights—it stops totally, thus consuming less fuel and producing fewer emissions. When the driver touches the accelerator again, the engine starts immediately. We chose a six-speed Geartronic transmission so that the car is an automatic by default but can be shifted manually when the driver wishes. The transmission is also equipped with Powershift (dual wet clutches) to lower the fuel consumption even further. Our overall aim has been "as much power as possible with as little environmental impact as possible with known techniques."

YCC: The Team

The YCC has nine mothers. These nine women made all the decisions about the car. They all came from different functions within the company and did not know each other at the beginning (see Figure 8.14).

The YCC team and their functions:

Camilla Palmertz: Project manager

Eva-Lisa Andersson: Project manager

FIGURE 8.14 From left to right: Maria Widell Christiansen, Eva-Lisa Andersson, Elna Holmberg, Maria Uggla, Camilla Palmertz, Cynthia Charwick, Anna Rosén, Lena Ekelund, and Tatiana Butovitsch Temm.

Elna Holmberg: Technical project manager

Lena Ekelund: Deputy technical project manager

Tatiana Butovitsch Temm: Communications manager

Maria Widell Christiansen: Project manager, design

Anna Rosén: Exterior designer

Cynthia Charwick: Interior designer

Maria Uggla: Color and trim designer

But of course we did not make the car alone. Some 140 people at Volvo were involved in the making of YCC. Not all at once—a lot of designers were active in the beginning and a lot of model makers at the end. About half of them were men, so clearly men were not excluded.

The project managers had a secondary goal of showing that there are a great number of very capable women in the industry. One way of demonstrating their abilities was asking sponsors and suppliers to appoint women project managers for the YCC. Most of them did.

YCC: The Reactions

In late February 2004, the YCC was ready. The surface was polished, the tires were blackened, and the YCC team was photographed and prepared for the launch. The stage was set at the international Motor Show in Geneva, Switzerland—one of the most important motor shows in the world, and one where many concept cars have been launched. Switzerland also has the advantage of having no car manufacturers of its own.

When the time came for the press conference, the Volvo stand was full of journalists. So were the neighboring stands and even the ones beyond. Everyone was very curious (and perhaps skeptical) to see what a car made by women would look like. During the two press days in Geneva, the hype was enormous. Each of the nine team members gave an interview every 30 minutes, in total some 200 interviews. Some of the media representatives came to Switzerland just for the YCC presentation; they do not normally cover motor shows.

The initial publicity was carefully measured. The first six weeks generated around 1,700 press clippings from major markets. Of these articles, 2 percent were negative (a large share of those came from letters to the editor in Volvo's hometown paper, *Göteborgs-Posten*). The remaining 98 percent of the world's media were neutral, positive, or very positive (see Figure 8.15).

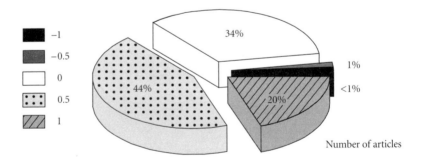

FIGURE 8.15 Reactions from the initial wave of publicity: all countries; full articles. The overall assessment of the articles about the YCC is based on a five-point scale from +1 (clearly favorable to Volvo) to −1 (clearly unfavorable to Volvo).

TABLE 8.1 Most-wanted features.

Five most popular features of the YCC—women	Five most popular features of the YCC—men
1. Storage compartments between the front seats	1. EasyClean paintwork
2. Run-flat tires	2. Storage compartments between the front seats
3. EasyClean paintwork	3. Run-flat tires
4. Windshield-washer filling point at the side of the car	4. Windshield-washer filling point at the side of the car
5. Doors that open automatically	5. Lockable storage in the doorjambs

Since then, the YCC world tour has taken the car to some thirty cities, many outside Europe, including New York, Los Angeles, Sydney, Tokyo, and Shanghai. During the world tour, the audiences have been asked what YCC features they would like to have in their future cars. So far, we have collected 3,000 responses. The top-five list, split by gender, reveals more or less the same features, only in different order (Table 8.1).

Our findings suggest that our original thesis was right: If you meet the expectations of women, you exceed the expectations of men.

9 Are Photons Gendered?

Women in Physics and Astronomy

C. Megan Urry

T HE GOAL OF SCIENCE in general is, like the specific case of archaeology, to dig up and report truths about nature. The fundamental processes of nature exist independent of scientists, and physical laws describing nature can be discovered and explicated by scientists. In archaeology and many other branches of science, interpretation and reported "facts" can be influenced by the gender (and other qualities) of the scientists doing the work. In contrast, for physics and astronomy, although there is some freedom in the choice of what problems to undertake, there is little freedom in—and certainly no gender-related influence on—the results of experiments or the interpretation of observations of the natural world.

Figure 9.1 shows an image of two galaxies close enough together that gravity of each on the other pulls stars into long, mouse-like "tidal tails." The image was taken with a sensitive camera on the Hubble Space Telescope (several images were taken in light at different wavelengths and then recombined for an approximately real-color result). These images are beautiful, and men and women might even react differently to them (in my experience, women are more likely to speak of beauty in astronomy), but the light reaching the Hubble, and the reaction to that light of the CCD detectors in the Hubble Advanced Camera for Surveys, are unaffected by Earth, life on Earth, or the gender of anyone on Earth involved in the observation.

To put it bluntly, gender does not affect results in physics, astronomy, or mathematics. In shorthand, *photons have no gender.* Newton suggested

FIGURE 9.1 A Hubble Space Telescope image of two galaxies close enough together that gravity of each on the other pulls stars into long, mouse-like "tidal tails."
SOURCE: NASA, H. Ford (JHU), G. Illingworth (UCSC/LO), M. Clampin (STScI), G. Hartig (STScI), the ACS Science Team, and ESA, reprinted by permission of Holland Ford.

400 years ago that $F = ma$ (Force equals mass times acceleration, Newton's Second Law of Motion). This physical law relating force to motion is clearly independent of the gender of the person asking or answering the question about an object's motion, or indeed of the nature of the object. Stars emit light because of energy generated by nuclear fusion at their cores; no part of this process has gender or is influenced by gender. The expansion of the universe is accelerating because of something we call "dark energy"—not because the gender of the scientists studying it has any influence. Planets form out of tiny grains of dust that agglomerate into rocks that collide and form solid bodies. These inorganic processes occurred long before there *was* gender, long before the formation of the first cell, much less anything we could call male or female. Indeed, most of the light from stars in galaxies throughout the universe was emitted long before life developed on Earth. The laws of physics simply know no gender. What gets studied has little or no relation to gender, with possible exceptions in applied areas. Here physics and astronomy and mathematics are very different from, say, archaeology or anthropology or biology, where gender is part of what is being studied.

My research is not on gender analysis; it is on supermassive black holes in distant galaxies. Years in astrophysics have taught me that, while the substance of physics and astronomy is not affected by gender, the culture of these fields owes much to the fact that they are dominated by male scientists. In an effort to understand the world in which I work—and more importantly, to devise ways to make it more hospitable to women scientists—I have become an enthusiastic (if amateur) student of all things related to women in science. This chapter is a report of my experiences as an astrophysicist and an attempt to describe the gendered culture (see also Urry 2005). I begin with the statistics on women in physics and astronomy, then describe the cultural dissonance often experienced by women in science.

Women in Physics and Astronomy

Astronomy, physics, and mathematics enjoy a long tradition of accomplished women: Laura Bassi, Maria Gaetana Agnesi, Caroline Herschel, Emilie du Châtelet, Sophia Kovalevskaya, and Mary Somerville, to name a few (Alic 1986; Koblitz 1983; Schiebinger 1989; Zinsser and Hayes 2006). Still, over the centuries there were not as many women scientists as their male counterparts, and they were probably handicapped in their pursuit of science, especially because science—perhaps unlike art or music—advances collectively. The individual scientist must be steeped in existing knowledge to move forward, to explain the new or unusual. (In art, one could start from nothing—from no knowledge—and still make profoundly important contributions.) Sophie Germain, a brilliant mathematician in early nineteenth-century France, is a good example of how brilliance can be stifled in the face of exclusion from the academy (Alic 1986).

Despite this rich history of extraordinary women, there are relatively few women in physics and astronomy today. A new study published by the American Institute of Physics (Ivie and Ray 2005) offers the latest data on the limited participation of women in these fields. The percentage of women getting PhDs in physics has hovered between 10 and 15 percent for the past 15 years, with a recent upward spike to 18 percent in 2003. The percentage of women physics (astronomy) faculty has also risen, from 6 percent (9 percent) ten years ago to roughly 10 percent (14 percent) today (Urry 2000; Ivie and Ray 2005). Women faculty are concentrated in the younger ranks, where it appears women assistant professors are being hired in numbers commensurate with (or even slightly above) the rate at which women PhDs were produced five to ten years earlier. Ten years ago, many physics departments had no women at all on their faculty. Today fewer than a quarter lack any women—clearly progress in the right direction—yet it is still unusual to have more than one or two women in a particular department. Many students never see a female professor, much less one with children or a visible family life. (Roughly half the women in physics and astronomy do not have children.) The representation of women continues to increase but physics is not attracting women at the same rate as other quantitative fields, such as mathematics or engineering (Ivie and Ray 2005).

The Culture of Physics

If the science of physics itself is gender free, the style of physics has everything to do with gender. The physics culture in the United States can be summed up in a simple metaphor: chest beating. To succeed as a physicist, one must not only do good work but also aggressively promote one's ideas and accomplishments. Part of self-promotion is a precise calibration and articulation of where one stands relative to other physicists (that is, how far above). Comfort with this hierarchical approach and unself-conscious elitism is essential for success.

The provost of a large state university recently offered a succinct summary of what physicists are like (though he is an economist, his father was a physicist, so he has some expertise), which I paraphrase: Physicists think they are smarter than everyone else; they imagine that once they shine the light of their superior intellect on whatever problem is at hand, the solution will be found; they don't trust anyone else's work on a problem, and must be persuaded with great effort of its correctness; and they believe absolutely in a meritocracy, such that the best people will become full professors of physics in the top institutions. This captures in a nutshell the elitist culture of physics.

One small anecdote may illustrate the hubris driving this culture. Last fall I organized a half-day strategic planning meeting for members of our physics department, involving a professional facilitator (who was not a scientist). The idea was to discuss future directions in astrophysics, and my goals were two: to form a consensus and to educate other groups in the department about what we were doing. One of my (male) physics colleagues responded negatively to this approach. (He is, by the way, a generally supportive colleague who respects my abilities.) In his opinion, a leader (me) should just decide what to do, then march in and announce the plan, marshal the troops, and hand them their marching orders. If necessary, I suppose one persuades the reluctant with some combination of argument, forcefulness, intimidation, and stubbornness. My approach—discussion leading to consensus—was perceived as too tentative to be effective. It seemed "weak." It was, he said, "not how we do things in physics." It probably didn't help that the discussion was led by a non-scientist (zero credibility to start). As it turned out, the session was extremely successful, and even the skeptical came away enthusiastic about the process and the outcome. I like to think there was education of more than one kind that day.

Actually, many men don't seem to know how to hold a discussion. Their view of a "discussion" is that they state their opinion. They apparently don't feel an obligation to respond to anyone else's arguments, or to explain why they don't agree. There is no give and take. They simply opine, and after that it's a matter of muscle of one kind or another. For years I was puzzled by pseudo-discussions of this kind—I thought the men were deliberately ignoring one another, and I couldn't understand why they would choose to be so rude. Only after many years did I realize that they probably didn't think they needed to respond. The notion of an exchange of information followed by a moderation of one's position was simply foreign to them.

For women raised to be polite and deferential, the physics culture is not a natural home. Listening carefully to others—or worse, moderating one's position in response to what one hears—can be interpreted as a sign of weakness. Moreover, the physics persona is inherently boastful. Many science departments have a daily ritual called science coffee or science tea, where colleagues gather to discuss the latest news in the field. It is an excellent and important opportunity to think about science and to generate new ideas. But it also serves as a brag session—"look at what my lab's just done!"—and for me, it took years to respond appropriately to the simple question, "What are you working on?" The social response, ingrained since childhood, is "Not much, how about you?" The correct response for a scientist is, "Let me tell you about this fabulous work we are doing . . . I just invented the wheel, and now I am working on warp-speed travel."

The constant need to boast takes its toll. Surveying physics departments (as part of a site visit program administered by the American Physical Society's Committee on the Status of Women in Physics, or CSWP), we find that differences in job satisfaction and ambition between men and women in physics increase with seniority. Undergraduates who have chosen physics as a major are almost uniformly enthusiastic about physics and their departments (although, disturbingly, women undergraduates report sexist remarks or lack of respect from their male peers). First- and second-year graduates are similar—they acknowledge the stress and pressure in classes and qualifying exams, and talk about how hard the work is, but this does not seem to affect their enthusiasm. Fifth- and sixth-year graduate students are another story. The men report varying degrees of success but relatively few cases of burnout. In contrast, many senior women graduate students are sick of physics, think they made the wrong career choice, deeply doubt their abilities, and are less ambitious for the future. In some cases, where we have independent evidence of their career progress, their self-assessments are clearly too harsh: They are actually accomplished, respected scientists. Somehow the climate has beaten them down and made them feel out of place (Urry 2005).

Constant discouragement eventually undermines ability. Women students who have been thoroughly discouraged—through lack of mentoring or attention—become convinced they don't have what it take to be top physicists. I have no doubt (though I cannot prove it) that were these women in a better environment, free of doubt and fear and constant challenge, their ideas would flower, and they would become outstanding researchers. Instead, they drain their energy trying to maintain a façade of invulnerability and superiority.

These women function much like *Star Trek*'s spaceship *Enterprise*, which has an impenetrable force field that can repel alien attacks. Maintaining this force field takes considerable energy so it must be used sparingly. Women in fields that are heavily male-dominated construct force fields to repel daily attacks from the alien culture in which they must operate. For women graduate students, their energy supplies are depleted as incoming missiles find their marks and do their damage.

Some researchers have chalked up the attrition of women at these levels to women's special role in reproduction. Specifically, senior graduate students and postdocs are at the age where women often want to start families. A disproportionate number of women leave the profession before taking on a ladder-faculty position; some take on part-time or lecturer positions. Mary Ann Mason has suggested that having babies early can impede career progress, and she has shown that those who interrupt their careers do not reach the same levels of success as full-time academics (Mason and Goulden 2002, 2004). Many see this as an affirmative choice of family over career—let's call it the "opting out" choice. But another interpretation is equally possible: that after enduring a chilly professional climate for five to seven years, women see raising a family as an attractive alternative to a full-time tenure-track position in that same uninviting climate. In other words, they are really "pushed out" rather than opting out—it is a "choice" strongly influenced by environment. Pushing in the same direction is the fact that, in today's world, turning to full-time childcare is highly praised, seemingly more so with increasing levels of education and professional accomplishment of the mother. That is, the more a woman has advanced in her career prior to full-time motherhood, the greater the apparent value of her sacrifice and thus the societal pat on the back. It is little wonder that the opting-out "choice" is an attractive one compared to a perpetual struggle to assert one's abilities.

Women faculty also grow more discouraged as they move up the ladder, according to the CSWP site surveys. Junior faculty—those who successfully made it through graduate school and postdoctoral positions (often thanks to strong support from a mentor)—may spend little time thinking about their status as women in a male-dominated field. But senior women faculty in physics departments have often encountered serious problems, such as lack of respect, not being appointed to important committees (for example, a search committee in their own research specialty), too high a teaching burden, too little space or other resources, or unfairly being held responsible for all things female (affirmative action, mentoring undergraduate women, representing the department on diversity issues, etc.)—all of which saps precious energy from research. Some are very angry, disaffected, and even bitter, and it is not uncommon for them to be disconnected from their departments. With such a high emotional burden and relative lack of support, some women faculty may be performing below their high potential. A number have moved into university administration, partly because they are in demand for their people and technical skills, but also because they are escaping the unpleasant cultures and aggressive people in their departments.

The Culture of Winning—and Leaving

Physics professors (and other academics) are usually rewarded for being pushy, arrogant prima donnas. To a physicist, arrogance signals competence—to be deferential signals inferiority. In my twenty-five years in astrophysics, I have seen people push their way onto the author lists of papers they had little to do with; invite speakers to conferences with more of an eye toward their quid pro quo potential than their scientific excellence; criticize competitors to gain an edge; and put themselves forward for recognition, salary increases, prizes, invited talks, without doing the same for younger colleagues. These people would rather advance themselves than mentor others. Men who are highly aggressive, intrusive, peremptory, and obnoxious still enjoy the confidence and respect of their colleagues. Women with even a fraction of the same toughness are characterized as "difficult" (there are other words for this) and demoted or told to play nice. Madeline Heilman (Heilman et al. 2004) shows in a simple set of experiments that despite comparable records, women are generally seen as less competent than men, though equally friendly and likeable. If externally validated (the way one might be with, say, an offer from another university), women will then be judged competent but hostile and difficult. Apparently, women can be competent or likeable, but not both.

Psychology experiments like Heilman's are convincing because they control the input parameters and can be repeated many times. In real life, gender-based discrimination is rarely so clear. Yet over a twenty-five year career span, one starts to see patterns. Young men are talked about as superstars, while young women are described as "very good." I used to believe these assessments—until I compared hard data like publication record, citations, number of invited talks, number of proposals accepted, and success in attracting funding. It turned out that women colleagues whose abilities were dismissed often had a much stronger record of accomplishment. A quantitative study of applications for a prestigious Swedish postdoctoral fellowship in medicine showed that female applicants had to have considerably better records than male applicants in order to be awarded a fellowship (Wennerås and Wold 1997). Let me offer just one example I witnessed personally at a previous institution. A female junior professor was given a very negative first review (held two years after joining the faculty), despite her extremely interesting research, and was advised by senior faculty to step down from the faculty ranks to a less prestigious research staff position because, they claimed, her science was simply not strong enough. Happily, she ignored this advice and became a leader in her field in just a few years, with many high-impact papers and key scientific contributions. She was even tenured a bit early. This story turned out well because this particular woman was tough enough to overcome a fairly harsh critical assessment, but her response was unusual—many in her position would have followed the advice and had their promising careers derailed.

In my own career, there have been a number of startling occasions when I discovered people had underestimated my abilities or achievements. At one point I was serving on the highest-level advisory committee in NASA's Office of Space Science (responsible for carrying out NASA's missions in astrophysics, space and solar physics, and planetary science). To my knowledge only one other of the hundred or so colleagues at my institution had ever been invited to serve on this committee; I considered it an honor and a sign of my high standing in my field. On returning home after each meeting of the committee, over a period of three years, I briefed my local colleagues formally, at faculty meetings, about the issues discussed, many of which were highly relevant to our work as an institution. Nevertheless, my institutional leadership never informed or consulted me about serious issues that were routinely discussed by the NASA committee. When I asked why not, I was told, "Oh, we forgot you were on that committee." On another occasion, when I mentioned I hoped to move to another even more selective advisory committee, I was told that was "awfully ambitious"—clearly they did not have a very high opinion of me. Despite this lack of confidence, six months later I was appointed to that committee, and as far as I know, I remain the only member of that institution ever to have served on that committee.

Episodes where I recognized that people were underestimating me were rare. (That they are disproportionately represented in this account is to respect the privacy of others to whom similar things have happened.) I think I was (mercifully) oblivious to my own situation. It was easier to see what was happening to other women around me. One woman manager was bullied by another manager who constantly questioned her decisions, her budgets, and her portfolio, yet he never countenanced similar scrutiny of his division. When she complained to their mutual boss about the constant interference, she was told she was "depressed" and should seek professional help. Other women were passed over for promotion, or demoted at the first sign of trouble, while male managers with well-known flaws or demonstrated incompetence were rarely replaced. After a while, it was possible to see a pattern of women being marginalized and their contributions minimized.

Men being tenured, for example, always had strong advocates to help push them through, while women often lacked advocates and were less likely to be tenured. It did not help that women arguing in favor of other women were discounted, almost as in Saudi Arabian jurisprudence, where the word of a woman is worth less than the word of a man. (When a woman argues against another woman, however, her word is worth several times that of a man.) For a few outstanding men and women scientists, tenure can be a sure thing, but for most, the case could go either way, and it goes the way that strong voices argue for. One true sign of equality will be when women of moderate ability advance as easily as do men of moderate ability.

At one time, when my previous institution was desperate for science leadership and a more productive, more cohesive science staff, I started a large multiwavelength astronomical survey project that took advantage of our institutional strengths and the breadth of talent on our scientific staff. Eventually, with important leadership from others as well, this project, called GOODS (for Great Observatories Origins Deep Survey, because it uses NASA's great space observatories: the Hubble Space Telescope, the Spitzer Infrared Telescope, and the Chandra X-ray Observatory), brought in millions of dollars in research support. More to the point, the GOODS project has been a great success scientifically, yielding important results on black hole growth and galaxy formation. Yet my role in this proposal remains little known or acknowledged. One of the senior colleagues with whom I had worked very closely on GOODS told me I lacked ability as a leader, and specifically would not be a strong candidate for an open position in science leadership. He apparently did not see GOODS as science leadership, nor did he see another of my accomplishments (the successful overhaul of one of our most important institutional activities) as a sign of leadership. He questioned my scientific abilities and hesitated to support my promotion to full professor—until, that is, Yale University offered me a full professorship. Then I got the promotion and a 30 percent raise—sufficient, I was told, to place me "above the bozos." (After a few days it dawned that I had been paid considerably less than the "bozos" for a long time!)

This man was not overtly biased nor would I call him sexist in any stereotypical sense. He worked well with a number of female colleagues and consciously tried to make sure men and women were treated equally. He had a very refreshing way of insisting that everyone in a discussion have a chance to express a view. I expect he would consider himself a feminist. Rather, our styles were different and he probably interpreted me through the prism of his own personality. For example, because I was polite and deferential, he mistakenly concluded I was not strong and competent. He could see that I was not like him. If someone like him acted like I did, it must signal being beneath others—rather like a dog rolling belly up rather than bristling its fur and growling. Since he would not behave that way unless indeed he saw himself as less able, he assumed my behavior meant I was less able. He also listened to people who had ranked me lower on the scientific totem pole, for whatever reason. His assessment could not have been based on objective data—I had more papers, more citations, more students, more postdocs, more funding, and had done seminal work in more areas than almost any of my colleagues. His judgment derived from the fact that the denizens of a dominant culture rarely think to examine their unconscious attitudes (why should they? why would it even occur to them?), which strongly influence how they evaluate others (see Valian 1998).

In the context of the Stanford meeting on gender and science, it is interesting to note shared cultural resonances. Meg Conkey noted in her talk (this volume) that archeologists are thrilled by finding the "earliest," "first," or "oldest." I felt an instant recognition. Superlatives seem to be a common feature of male-dominated cultures. In physics, the coin of the realm is how "fundamental" the result is. In astrophysics, we revere the most distant galaxies, the deepest images, the widest surveys, the earliest photons, the oldest stars, the most luminous gamma-ray bursts, the fastest pulsars, the most massive black holes. Make no mistake—these are indeed extraordinarily interesting things! But the values attached are essentially arbitrary. To paraphrase (and slightly distort) Virginia Woolf's observation, Tolstoy is celebrated as a *great* writer because he wrote about war (and love), while Jane Austen who wrote only about love is merely a *good* writer (Woolf 1929). (Woolf essentially agreed with this ranking but said Austen would have been a better writer had she had a wider experience of the world.) In the end, these rankings are all choices. What is important is decided by the dominant culture.

Hyper-aggressive science culture is outdated and counterproductive. In the past, science was done largely by individual scientists, working alone, and chest beating was probably a winning strategy. But in recent years, as the tools of research have gotten more complicated, projects have gotten bigger, and extensive cooperation among scientists has become increasingly important. Nowadays, teams of hundreds or even thousands of physicists collaborate to build orbiting space telescopes, huge underground particle accelerators, and detectors that are the size of small buildings and cost as much as the annual budgets of small countries. In this environment, teamwork is far more productive than chest beating. Indeed, chest beating and the I-have-to-be-the-leader-or-I-won't-get-my-Nobel-prize neediness of some top (usually male) scientists is counterproductive. Women (at least as they are usually socialized in the United States) are demonstrably better at teamwork than most men (ditto caveat). A few years ago, a survey of women and men in the business world found that women were better than men at 46 of the 47 desirable traits for a manager. So in principle, women should be better suited to lead big science projects. But the culture of physics has not yet adjusted to the new reality.

Women Are Voting with Their Feet

The elitist, hierarchical climate of science contributes to the gender imbalance in participation in science. Where arrogance and elitism are the most unbridled, you find the fewest women: physics (compared to chemistry, for example); cosmology (the hottest subfield of astrophysics); theory (more prestigious than experiment, assumed to attract the smartest people). Farther afield, there is surgery (the elite subspecialty in medicine; read Elsa Walsh's portrayal of breast surgeon Alison Estabrook in *Divided Lives* [1995] for a picture of that culture), orchestra conducting (Zubin Mehta, while music director of the New York Philharmonic Orchestra, announced that women did not have the temperament to be outstanding musicians; his view is widely shared by musicians in the Vienna Symphony and the Munich Philharmonic; see Osborne's [1994] discussion about bassoonist Abbie Conant), chefs in premier restaurants—I could go on and on. More elite means more male, and vice versa. Many women are uncomfortable with the inherently boastful style that is the standard in physics. Some think it is reality—that you truly have to be the best in the world—while others see it as posturing. In either case, the culture definitely drives women away.

So too does the near-monastic devotion with which one is supposed to approach one's work. Women talk to me all the time about their concerns about "having a life" along with doing science—I can remember only one man ever raising the topic. Science is supposed to be a calling, it seems, a religious calling. (After all, modern universities evolved from the monastic culture of medieval Europe.) This kind of all-consuming culture creates barriers against women in physics and astronomy. By the way, though, the eighty-hour workweek is a myth. All of us put in that kind of work (or more) for selected periods but my male colleagues definitely have lives. They ski, sail, play hockey, race in marathons, climb mountains, travel, have parties, raise families—and, most of the time, they are not doing physics in the shower.

A more welcoming, less competitive, more cooperative culture is markedly more attractive to women. Programs that recognize this—for example, the Computer Science program at Carnegie Mellon University (http://women.cs.cmu.edu/) or the BEST (Building Engineering and Science Talent) initiative (http://www.bestworkforce.org/)—have dramatically increased the number of women participants. For a country with declining levels of science and technology expertise, and increasing political difficulty in importing that expertise from other countries, the prospect of a flood of women scientists ought to be extremely attractive. In theory we know how to attract women to science—and just as importantly, how to avoid repelling them—but changing culture is proving very difficult.

The "Male" Versus "Female" Debate

Some call traits like objectivity and rationality "male" and argue that science is a male construct. Science also involves discussion, interaction, consensus, teamwork, intuition, creativity, and curiosity—traits that are called "feminine" so it could as easily be called a feminine construct. As it happens, I do not believe in those gender assignments, and more importantly, science is too complex a process, too multifaceted an intellectual pursuit, to be perceived as gendered in those terms.

I do make an important distinction between science—the knowledge base, the fundamental laws of physics or biology, for example—and its applications, which can certainly be gender related. To make this concrete, consider the example of computer science. There is no question that the use of information technology, the design of computer interfaces, and software design and implementation, are affected strongly by the gender of the participants. But the underlying mathematical basis for computer science—essentially, binary (base 2) mathematics—has no gender. Computer chips are combinations of logic "gates" that ask input data streams questions like "and" or "or." The combination of a 0 and 1, or 1 and 1, or 0 and 0, offers no choice to such gates. The answers are what they are, 0 or 1, completely deterministic. No influx or exodus of women will change that.

Some might argue that the choice to use a binary-based logic for computing was influenced by men, not unlike the argument (to my mind, absurd) that mathematics is a "male" science that would look different if created by women. (N.B. Women such as Ada Lovelace and Grace Hopper were important contributors to the early development of computing.) Whether the choice of binary logic was gendered depends on what the alternative bases for computing might be. Since these have not been fully developed, we cannot yet answer this question. But just to take an example, you could imagine a computing system based not on binary decisions but three-way decisions. Instead of "yes-no," one could design logic gates that decide "less-equal-more" or equivalently, −1, 0, 1. I am not a computer scientist—perhaps such systems have been developed to some extent. Perhaps some gender theorists have an opinion as to whether three-way logic is more feminine than binary logic. Or there might be more radical departures, for example, biological computing (allowing cellular functions to work collectively in a deterministic way). Until those alternatives are clear, however, one cannot judge the gendered nature of the present systems. Just because mostly men do it does not make it male.

Women and the Future of Science

The attrition of women from physics occurs not because science is too rational or too objective. Universally, I have found that the women who do physics enjoy those aspects of it. This is true also for many women who leave the field. They enjoy the math, the certainty, the inevitability of the path from question to answer—all of this appeals to women as much as to men. (It may have little appeal for many men and many women; only a small fraction of American students are interested in science and technology by the time they reach high school. However, the numbers of girls and boys studying physics is similar at the high school level, then drops dramatically during undergraduate years [Ivie and Ray 2005].) Women do not avoid physics because it is "male."

Instead the attrition of women is greater because of the unpleasant climate created by the (currently mostly male) practitioners of science—the emphasis on competition, the elitist style of speech and thought, the constant challenge to prove oneself repeatedly, and to defend not only the accuracy of one's work but its relevance, its importance, its prestige. The elitist, competitive, hierarchical environment of modern science in the United States is unappealing to many women raised in American society. It puts a premium on the chest-beating, macho style ("I was in the lab until 3 A.M., how about you?" "I stayed 'til 4 and was back by 7!"), and it devalues cooperation and mutual learning.

The presence of more women in physics will change the atmosphere of physics departments. This is clearly demonstrated by a comparison of physics and astronomy, which have very similar demands in terms of skills (mathematical and technical abilities), yet astronomy offers a much more comfortable environment for women, and in turn it attracts more women. Right now there is an explosion of women at the entry end—nearly half the astronomy majors nationally are women, and 60 percent of the youngest cohort of membership in the American Astronomical Society (ages 18–25 years) are women (Marvel forthcoming). Women speakers at professional meetings are common, the national society has many women officers, and respect for women colleagues comes more readily than in physics. The problems are not solved in astronomy, but the culture is perceptibly more comfortable than in physics, so it feels as if it is only a matter of time. In physics, one feels fundamental transformation is still needed.

The bulk of the work of transforming culture is educating one's colleagues. Change in most universities happens at the departmental level, so getting colleagues on board—or at least a few powerful colleagues—is an essential step. Toward that end, we organized two conferences on Women in Astronomy, the first in 1992 in Baltimore. We were poorly educated ourselves at that point, and the meeting taught us a lot. Afterward, we wrote the Baltimore Charter (Urry et al. 1993), a sort of manifesto for change, which was disseminated widely among astronomy departments and in other branches of physics. In the ensuing decade we made a lot of progress. In 2003, in Pasadena, we held the second conference on Women in Astronomy, and developed a much bolder, detailed, and comprehensive set of recommendations, which have been endorsed by the American Astronomical Society (http://www.aas.org/cswa). At Yale we have two women faculty in astronomy, one recently tenured, and have hired three women as junior faculty in physics. The president, the provost, and the deans of the college and of the graduate school are all eager to make further hires of women. The Women Faculty Forum at Yale (an association of women faculty across the university) is becoming a powerful tool for change. We simply have to work harder to make change happen.

10 "A Very Scholarly Intervention"

Recruiting Women Faculty in Science and Engineering

Danielle LaVaque-Manty and Abigail J. Stewart

I N AN INSIGHTFUL ANALYSIS of the National Science Foundation's ADVANCE program, Susan Sturm (2006) argues that

A key aspect of ADVANCE's strategy involves the development of a new role that has proven to be pivotal in enabling systemic change. . . . Because of their core function of mobilizing change at the intersection of different systems, we have called these individuals "organizational catalysts." Organizational catalysts are individuals who operate at the convergence of different domains and levels of activity. Their role involves connecting and leveraging knowledge, ongoing strategic relationships and collaborations, and forms of accountability across systems.

Sturm's analysis helped us understand that when the University of Michigan ADVANCE program created a faculty committee called Strategies and Tactics for Recruiting to Improve Diversity and Excellence (STRIDE),[1] we in fact created both a collective "organizational catalyst" and a set of individual catalysts, or change agents (see also Sturm forthcoming a and b). In this chapter we hope to illustrate both the process of internal change that committee members experienced, and the connection between that process and their role on campus as faculty change agents.

Of course the larger context of UM's STRIDE committee is crucial in ways we cannot measure, but must recognize. In 2001, the National Science Foundation (NSF) created a new program called ADVANCE, designed to cultivate a series of experiments in institutional transformation, nationwide, that might help to change a system littered with barriers to the success of women faculty in science and engineering. ADVANCE offered universities several million dollars and five-year time horizons to develop creative approaches to improving their institutional climates and their recruitment and retention of women. When the University of Michigan received funding, along with eight other institutions in the first round,[2] it initiated many concurrent ADVANCE interventions, including grants to departments wishing to try their own experiments in improving climate, recruitment, or retention; grants to individual women scientists and engineers to foster their projects and careers; a university-wide network that provides women science and engineering faculty with opportunities to socialize, attend workshops on leadership and negotiation, and mentor one another; and a theatre troupe that promotes facilitated discussion of difficult climate issues in faculty groups. This list is not exhaustive but should give a sense of the range of activities that may be supporting and catalyzing the university community's ability to absorb STRIDE's message.[3]

Nevertheless, since its inception in 2002, STRIDE has certainly been a major factor in the increased hiring of women faculty in science and engineering at Michigan, the transformation of committee members' understanding of gender, and the addition of new elements in the campus discourse about gender. In 2005, recognizing STRIDE's accomplishments, the university administration chose to institutionalize it, committing funds until at least 2011, not only to maintain the group but also to expand its purview to departments outside of science and engineering.[4] Although it is important to point to STRIDE's positive impact, it is not without critics and detractors. STRIDE has sought and taken seriously feedback about all of its efforts, often altering its presentations in response to that feedback. For example, in response to one presentation, one critic wrote, "Our faculty felt accused of being sexist. The presenters urged us to adopt a goal of having the same proportion of women among professors as there are among PhDs granted in our field nationwide. No additional argument for the feasibility of this goal was presented. None of us thought the issue was that simple." STRIDE normally does not advocate any particular target goal, but when asked, they do often suggest this sort of approach to goal setting. However, they have increasingly recognized that for some fields that goal seems quite remote and unattainable, so they have developed alternative strategies for discussing the issue of goals. At the same time, some critics and detractors oppose STRIDE's very focus and purpose, and STRIDE members recognize that in these cases they must respectfully disagree and continue to represent their perspective as well as they can.

Because STRIDE has always been an experiment, the Michigan AD-VANCE project's principal investigator (PI) and steering committee had no way of guessing at the outset how effective it would eventually become. In fact, they began with no specific criteria for selecting its members, much less any definite sense of what the committee would actually do once it had been formed. Thus, while we write with the purpose of encouraging others to consider interventions similar to STRIDE, we want to be clear about the fact that STRIDE is the result of an evolutionary process, that its particular structure, practices, and priorities are contingent, and that the insights and recommendations in this chapter have been developed through trial and error and are meant to serve more as a well of ideas than as a blueprint. In what follows, we draw on STRIDE's organizational history, hiring data collected by the University of Michigan, survey data collected by the ADVANCE project's evaluation staff, and interviews conducted with STRIDE members in September 2002, December 2003, and January 2006 to construct a narrative of the committee's development and evolution.[5]

Development of STRIDE

The original group of STRIDE members included eight distinguished full professors in science and engineering, recruited by the project's principal investigator, Abigail Stewart, early in 2002.[6] They were nominated by the deans of their colleges, who regarded them as having high credibility with their fellow faculty members and who believed they cared about issues of diversity in science. The idea behind the creation of STRIDE was that in order to recruit more women faculty in science and engineering at Michigan, faculty would have to believe that cultivating "the pipeline" alone (increasing the participation of women students at the beginning of the science career) would not solve the problem of the low participation of women scientists and engineers at the highest levels of academia. Faculty would need to believe that it was also important to recognize and address the "leaky pipeline" problem—the fact that at every transition point, from college through postdoctoral fellowships and faculty appointments, women leave academic science and engineering at a higher rate than men (Valian 1998; Etzkowitz et al. 2000; Long 2001). Finally, they would need to believe that hiring more women was not only desirable, but possible. It seemed likely that scientists would be most receptive to learning about these phenomena and concepts like gender, evaluation bias, and other ideas they might otherwise deem unimportant or "political," if the ideas were presented by colleagues whom they already respected as research-ers and as individuals. Because women might be perceived to be partial with respect to gender equity issues, five of the original eight committee members were men.

Prior to convening STRIDE for the first time, the PI met with members of Harvard's Committee on Faculty Diversity to gather advice.[7] Several of the Harvard committee's recommendations became standard practice for STRIDE: acquiring sufficient staff support for committee activities; engaging in regular communication with deans; having multiple members meet with search committees; including both men and women in every meeting if pos-sible; and being ready, with data, to talk about the demographics in each field. Other aspects of their approach (for example, a focus on informal meetings outside of official settings) seemed better adapted to Harvard's local culture than to Michigan's. We believe that other institutions should be able to adapt STRIDE's practices to suit their local conditions, reconfiguring as needed, just as we adapted what we learned from Harvard's committee.

UM's PI is a social scientist with faculty appointments in psychology and women's studies. Before the members of STRIDE came to their first meeting in April 2002, she provided them with reading material, including Virginia Valian's *Why So Slow? The Advancement of Women* (1998) and a packet of ar-ticles on gender and science. At the meeting, they watched a videotaped lec-ture Valian had given at Rice University (Valian 2001). They thus began their discussions about how to approach their colleagues about improving their re-cruitment and hiring practices with a pool of data and concepts that proved to be not only new but also intellectually interesting to them. In an interview conducted in 2002, one of the men on the committee noted that he had been "surprised by the number of studies that have been done on the nature of the bias, and where the bias comes from, against women in the sciences . . . there's been a lot of really, really good research that's been done, you know, these studies are fantastic." Another man, who joined the committee in 2004 and was interviewed in 2006, said, "Well, what I learned was that you can't put your finger on one main culprit, which explains . . . this angst that I've had . . . that, you know, there's a problem, but . . . who's to blame? Or . . . what's wrong in the system? And so to learn about all the different things that add up . . . is great."

The ability of this group of scientists and engineers to draw on social science knowledge and convey it to colleagues has turned out to be a key to STRIDE's success. In their early days, the committee members spent many hours not only learning about gender schemas (hypotheses about what men and women are like), and evaluation bias (the tendency shown by both men and women to overvalue men and undervalue women), but also debating how to present what they learned to a science and engineering audience they presumed would be skeptical. In their initial study they found Virginia Valian's work, which draws heavily on experimental psychology, consistently persuasive, and they believed their peers would, too. In addition, they found her self-presentation (as seen in the Rice videotape) authoritative and effective. Feeling insecure at first about presenting these concepts themselves, but having decided that the most efficient approach to intervening in the hiring process would be to present what they had learned about gender and science to faculty search committees and even entire departmental faculties, they created a Microsoft PowerPoint presentation into which they integrated clips from Valian's lecture, with her permission. To accompany the presentation and serve as a reference for search committees, STRIDE also created a recruitment handbook.[8]

Creating these materials required a substantial amount of discussion. STRIDE members had different intuitions not only about what would be most persuasive to recruitment committees but also about what would be the most effective tools to address bias or appeal to potential job candidates. Sometimes their differences in perspective tracked gender; for example, the men on the committee thought it would be helpful to let women candidates know that a department was eager to hire more women and was actively trying to improve its climate, while the women were wary of making women candidates feel that they were being recruited for their gender rather than for their scientific accomplishments. After several rounds of discussion, the committee finally came to consensus on recommending that departments "recruit women as scientists and not as women," or in other words, emphasize their interest in women candidates' academic work and not talk directly about gender issues unless candidates raised them first. Anecdotal evidence suggests that this approach helped at least one science department hire two extremely competitive women candidates who were being courted heavily elsewhere during STRIDE's first year, because they believed their scientific work would be valued more at Michigan than elsewhere.

During the first year or two of STRIDE's existence, the committee members became increasingly comfortable that they knew their material and could present it convincingly. Between September 2002 and April 2003, STRIDE made twenty-six presentations and distributed over 300 copies of the handbook. While this made a baseline of information available to a large number of faculty, STRIDE wished to cultivate a deeper understanding of the issues as well. During the summer of 2003, the committee created a program to develop additional colleagues who would have a fuller understanding of the issues and who might eventually become new members of STRIDE. They designed a 6-hour program (which took place in two half-days), based on their own past curriculum, to share what they had learned with selected colleagues. Because having specific tasks and problems to solve (for example, a presentation to design and a handbook to write) had given them concrete ways to apply new theoretical insights, they invited their colleagues to work on a project as well: helping to improve STRIDE's approach to departments and search committees. The new group named itself Friends and Allies of Science and Technology Equity in Recruiting (FASTER). STRIDE has since acquired two new members, one of whom attended FASTER in 2003.

By the end of its second year, STRIDE was confident enough to develop a new mode of engaging other faculty, one that was longer and more interactive and therefore less "safe" than the original lecture presentation. In addition, in fall 2004, the provost expressed an interest in having STRIDE offer its workshops to units outside of science and engineering. The group began to offer 2½-hour workshops to search committee chairs, including some from social science and humanities departments, during fall 2004. These workshops included brief presentations on six topics: (1) What is the problem? (2) Why diversity matters; (3) Unconscious bias in evaluation; (4) Recruitment strategies; (5) Dual career and family policies; (6) How family matters for evaluation bias. Abigail Stewart introduced the presentations, summarized key points at the end, and facilitated discussion of issues raised. This offered fuller coverage of each issue. A total of fifty-nine faculty heading or participating on search committees in the three largest colleges (the School of Medicine, the College of Engineering, and the College of Literature, Science, and the Arts) participated in the workshops in 2004.

UM ADVANCE's evaluation staff sent an online survey to the fifty-nine attendees. Twenty-three of the twenty-six respondents (88 percent) rated their workshop overall as very effective or somewhat effective; three attendees gave a neutral rating. There was relatively little variation in specific topic ratings, though the section on "unconscious bias in evaluation" received the most uniformly positive rating. No respondents reported a "not at all effective" rating for any topic. Another set of workshops, slightly redesigned, was held in fall 2005, with similar ratings.

There has been a marked increase in the hiring of women faculty in science and engineering since the creation of STRIDE. As we noted earlier, STRIDE is only one of many ADVANCE interventions currently operating at Michigan, but while many factors no doubt contributed to departments' willingness to hire more women, STRIDE is the intervention that most directly provides tools and ideas to aid in recruitment. Hence, we believe that the increase in women's hiring reflected in Table 10.1, which presents data for the three colleges that employ the largest number of scientists and engineers at Michigan during two "pre-STRIDE" years (AY 2001 and AY 2002) and three "post-STRIDE" years (AY 2003, AY 2004, and AY 2005), is substantially attributable to STRIDE. In the two pre-STRIDE years, ten women scientists and engineers were hired, or about five each year in absolute numbers (and 14 percent in percentage terms); in the three post-STRIDE years, forty-six women scientists and engineers were hired, or about fifteen each year (and 34 percent in percentage terms).

The university administration also believes that at least some portion of this hiring success is due to STRIDE. In addition to asking the committee to broaden its mission and work with departments beyond science and engineering, the president and provost announced in 2005 that although Michigan's NSF ADVANCE funding will terminate in December 2006, the university will continue to support STRIDE (and the ADVANCE program) until at least 2011. STRIDE-related expenses include not only staff support

TABLE 10.1 Men and women hired in natural science and engineering departments in three University of Michigan colleges.

	Pre-STRIDE				Post-STRIDE					
	AY2000–01		AY2001–02		AY2002–03		AY2003–04		AY2004–05	
	M	W	M	W	M	W	M	W	M	W
Number hired	41	6	22	4	32	19	19	12	37	15
Percent women	13		15		37		39		29	

and physical materials (handbooks, presentation equipment) but also sufficient compensation to committee members to allow them to support students or laboratory staff or to release themselves from some portion of their usual teaching load. Not only does this enable them to devote more time to STRIDE—a demanding committee that currently holds two 1½-hour meetings per month, in addition to providing presentations and workshops—it also signals the value of the committee's activities to the university.

Institutionalizing STRIDE

It is fair to say that many, if not all, members of STRIDE experienced a significant transformation in their understanding of academic science as a gendered system through their participation on the committee (Stewart et al. 2004; Stewart et al. 2007). As a result, they have become committed and articulate activists. They have also continued to gain knowledge and confidence over time; where they originally felt most comfortable talking about these issues in groups, so they could fill in the gaps for one another if they forgot any information or had difficulty expressing any ideas, they have now internalized what they've learned to such an extent that they routinely respond to questions and intervene spontaneously in situations outside the context of workshops and presentations. In an interview in 2006, one of the women said:

> STRIDE has had a big effect on me, I mean, in what I'm willing to talk about routinely, when I go to universities . . . This is new . . . it's just happened in the last year. . . . I say, "Well, I can give a research talk, but I also have this other talk that I can give about women in science and ADVANCE at Michigan and what we're doing." And so I'm much more willing to talk about it, not just at Michigan, but at places around the country.

One of the men noted that he often finds himself talking about gender and evaluation bias even in casual conversation:

> And I think every time you make somebody really aware . . . even coincidentally, I think it can make a big difference in the world because there's a cascading effect as that person influences other people. I mean, I know that making me aware has had a large effect, because I am always telling about what the literature is like in casual conversations, dental hygienists, whatever. . . . I'll talk to anybody about this. You know, it ranges from just random people to other participants at conferences, to reporters from the *New York Times*.

In interviews conducted in 2002 and 2003, several STRIDE members attributed their newfound activism to the "consciousness-raising" experience they shared in 2002. For example, one of the men said:

> The process that we went through worked so well. I don't know whether it was just the chemistry of the particular group, or whether the process could be replicated . . . the process being to identify a group of senior faculty, both men and women, in the sciences and engineering, who have shown some evidence of being concerned about these issues, but who clearly don't know all the literature. And I think every one of us on the committee now is like that. That is, we all had some previous commitment, but what we realized when we got together and started actually looking at the data and learning together was that we didn't understand, we didn't really know what was going on, we really were quite naive . . . that discovery process, I think, was so critical to building the passion that the current group has.

This might lead one to wonder not only whether such a discovery process could be replicated but also whether it would be difficult to sustain and institutionalize this group by adding new members over time. STRIDE will continue operating through at least 2011, and it is not reasonable to expect the original members to stay on the committee for ten years. So what happens next?

In fact, STRIDE has already added three new members, all of them men, since its inception. One was invited to join in 2003 and participated for a few months but ultimately chose not to stay. Two others joined in 2004 and remain enthusiastic participants. All three were interviewed in 2006.

The new member who chose not to stay on the committee had never seen a STRIDE presentation before joining and did not have a clear sense of what he was signing up to do, though he was "taken by the charge of the committee . . . [and] interested to learn more about what ADVANCE . . . was trying to do." He had been asked to join as a replacement for a member from his department who had retired from the university. Soon after his first few meetings with STRIDE, he left the country for a year on sabbatical, and by the time he returned, he had decided not to continue with the committee. In addition to signing on with STRIDE, he had also taken on another administrative role that he felt "more committed to in that [it] originated from [him]." In the end, he said, "I didn't leave because I didn't accept what STRIDE was trying to do, but I left because I felt that the time it would take to get up to speed and to deliver that message with conviction was just going to be more than I could afford."

The new members who stayed joined under very different circumstances. One had been through the FASTER sessions in summer 2003, and both had long-standing interests in gender and science. Both joined in December 2003 and were able to catch up on the reading the other members were already familiar with by the following summer, when most of the planning for the following academic year took place. They were thus able to play a role in making decisions for the upcoming season. They had a better sense of what they were agreeing to in the first place, experienced no extended interruption in their interaction with the rest of the group, and may have been helped by the fact that there were two of them starting at the same time. As one of these new members said, "[W]e both came, I think, with our own ideas and enthusiasm for doing something, and at the same time, since there were two of us, it was more comfortable to say, 'Hey, wait a minute, I don't remember that. I don't remember it because I wasn't here a year ago,' or something. And we both did that."

One said he had been eager to join in part because he had become familiar with some of the problems of gender and science while serving as an associate dean for his college, and he had a sense that STRIDE was a "positive, action-oriented" committee. He appreciated its style of operation, which he described as following "pure academic principles of engagement . . . It was clear that they wanted you to study, work, read, form opinions, validate or invalidate current approaches . . . to become educated."

The other new member was motivated to join in part by his observations about his graduate students' careers:

> Most of my graduate students have been women, and so, you know, I want to see them . . . succeed, and so to know that there are glass ceilings beyond the areas where I had direct impact, which is getting them trained . . . to me was just something I found very discouraging. And so the opportunity to actually participate in a program that could begin to . . . address and reverse those and actually get involved with trying to change those within the university, I . . . was . . . I mean, I jumped at that opportunity.

While this new member also noted that joining was "intimidating at first . . . having to bring myself up to speed with everything that they had read and discussed in the previous couple years," both described the group's atmosphere as being "welcoming."

The original members, when asked what it was like to integrate the newer members into their group, typically described the process as being quite smooth. Intriguingly, a couple of them were initially confused by the question. For example, one said, "Well . . . we haven't really integrated new members. Unless you're talking about [names the two new members]." At the time of this interview, the newer members had been part of the committee for two years, and the committee as a whole had been in place for three and a half years. This interviewee said, "I would say it has been seamless. In fact, when the [addition] took place, the committee was still fairly new. We barely knew each other." Another of the original members remembered adding one new member but thought that the other, whom he had already known in other contexts, had been part of the group from the very beginning.

Based on these experiences, STRIDE plans to integrate at least two new members at a time in the future, rather than bringing a new recruit in on his or her own. And though most of the current members would describe themselves as having been "open to" questions of gender rather than as having been actual activists prior to their engagement with STRIDE, in the future they will try to bring in new people who are actively interested in promoting diversity in the academic community. While this may cut down on the potential for transformative personal experience, it is likely to make for a smoother transition to a group that has developed a strong sense of shared values. FASTER serves as one pool of potential recruits; faculty who are willing to spend six hours attending FASTER sessions, and who seem to enjoy engaging with the material presented there, are also likely to find serving on STRIDE appealing.

STRIDE is likely to be adding at least two more new members in the near future, not only because initial members are likely to begin rotating off but also to accommodate the university's request that they work with departments beyond science and engineering. As they reach out to include broader audiences, they intend to invite representatives from a wider range of fields to join them. Not only do they think it is important to include people who are respected by the faculty in those fields on STRIDE, they also assume that they will benefit from having informants who can teach them about the relevant disciplinary cultures. Further, some of them are concerned that much of what they have to offer to science and engineering departments is knowledge they've learned from the social sciences, knowledge that may already be familiar to those in the social sciences and humanities. For example, one STRIDE member said, "I have to say it's also a little intimidating for me as a . . . scientist to be talking about what are fundamentally social science issues to people who come from the social sciences." Others, however, see it as an exciting opportunity:

> I might be the wrong person to ask about that, in the sense that . . . at [my college] I had worked for years . . . to extend what I do beyond [that] campus and into the undergraduate campus, with teaching, with committees, things like that. And because I personally like feeling part of a university community as a whole . . . for me personally, being part of a committee that involves [multiple colleges] and now down the road some additional departments, . . . it's refreshing and interesting. And so . . . I welcome it.

In response to a question about whether there is anything they wish STRIDE could add to what it already does, several members mentioned that they would like to be able to address recruitment and retention of underrepresented minorities more thoroughly than they currently do.[9] They also said they wish they could find more time to address climate issues that might not only improve retention of women faculty, but also make life better for faculty in general; consult more intensively with hiring committees throughout the recruitment season; find opportunities to reduce "leakage" of women postdocs and graduate students; work with the School of Education to help future K–12 teachers understand the role gender and evaluation bias might play in shaping the science and engineering pipeline; and be able to address issues of sexual orientation.

In contrast, in response to a question about whether there are any activities they would like to discontinue, none of them suggested dropping anything they currently do. All but two of the members said they feel they can continue to sustain the amount of time they've been putting into STRIDE for the near future, though most also plan to rotate off at some point before 2011. One member who felt less able to sustain his earlier pace has been on leave from the committee since becoming an associate dean in his college two years ago; another had recently become the chair of her department. Thus, both of them confronted increased administrative demands outside of STRIDE. Several members noted that it would probably be best to rotate members off the committee over time in order to bring in "new blood," create direct STRIDE connections to more departments, and allow the committee "to have the same effect on somebody else that it's had on me."

As noted earlier, STRIDE members receive modest compensation for their work, which helps free up a small portion of their time. While many committee members mentioned this as being a crucial infrastructural commitment, they also indicated that it is not primarily the compensation that motivates their high level of enthusiasm. Instead, one of the key components sustaining their willingness to participate is the sense of efficacy they get from STRIDE's successes. As one member said, "[W]hat's been really fulfilling is the fact that . . . we can come up with solutions . . . to make changes. And . . . now, after being there a couple years . . . if the early numbers continue . . . the way that they're going, it looks like they're a success. I mean, the trends are changing. And so . . . that's been great." Another said, "I think it's one of the most interesting committees that I've ever been on. . . . so my advice would be . . . if you are interested in making, or participating in a group that actually is making change, you should do this."

Another factor that contributes to their ongoing engagement is the intellectual satisfaction members get from the group's discussions. As one put it:

> [U]niversity committees frequently are sort of nothing but administration. And . . . the responsibility of doing something that's relatively onerous. This committee has been very different than that. It's intellectually very stimulating. You read original literature. Get to read things that I wouldn't normally read. And then have, you know, really, really intelligent people to discuss those things with. It's really a tremendous committee. It's a great committee. I really . . . I really enjoy it.

Another said:

> I would characterize STRIDE as, as a very . . . very scholarly intervention into the issue of climate and recruiting practices for women faculty. And people could debate what I mean by scholarly, but it's . . . based more on knowledge and understanding the complexity of the problem with not just an emotional response to a condition. I feel that I learn something every time I come to a meeting, or spend my homework time doing reading.

Recommendations to Others

As noted above, we have now conducted three rounds of interviews with members of STRIDE. Each time, we have asked them what recommendations they could offer to other universities wishing to create STRIDE-like interventions. In keeping with the theme that STRIDE's development has been an evolutionary process, we first offer a summary of their earliest list of recommendations—framed not as imperatives, but as statements about the characteristics that may have contributed to STRIDE's success. We have not addressed the basis for all of these here but have elaborated on them elsewhere (see Stewart et al. 2004). We follow the original list with new suggestions that emerged in the interviews conducted in 2006.

1. Having the request to serve on STRIDE come from a legitimated campuswide project embedded in a long-term process of change underscored its institutional importance.

2. Being compensated for time spent on the committee communicated the value to the institution of this service.

3. Being asked to serve for several years convinced committee members that plans were consistent with the scope of the goals.

4. Having access to social science expertise shored up committee members' confidence.

5. Having substantial staff support enabled the committee to achieve its goals in terms of access to the literature, to experts, and to implementation of its ideas (in documents, presentations, etc.).

6. Having the freedom to define and redefine its mission, message, and strategy gave the committee a strong sense of responsibility for its work.

7. Having representatives from the colleges with the largest number of scientists and engineers brought crucial cultural knowledge, examples, and experiences to the committee.

8. Including in the committee only respected scientists and engineers in their own fields—both men and women—gave it considerable credibility in the community.

9. Debating issues they disagreed about (like whether to emphasize Michigan's eagerness to improve things for women scientists and engineers), rather than avoiding conflict, built trust in each other and confidence in their message.

10. Meeting frequently allowed the committee to reflect on experiences both as a group and as individuals; this allowed a wide range of discussions about concrete examples and difficult conversations, and built up their skill at addressing many issues.

We noted above that as STRIDE members have gained confidence in their expertise about gender and science, they have begun to talk about these issues with a wider range of people, including those from other institutions. One recently visited a university with an ADVANCE project that had attempted to create a committee that would offer presentations like STRIDE's. However, an administrative unit within that university was already offering recruitment presentations and did not want to give up that role. This STRIDE member said, "I think what I would tell universities is you need to figure out how to provide the information and how to educate your community, but that you probably need to figure out what the best way to do it at your university is, because each university has a different set of constraints."

Another STRIDE member visited a different institution whose ADVANCE program was housed in a unit that was viewed as peripheral by some of its target audiences; it therefore had difficulty gaining the kind of access it required to succeed. This STRIDE member suggested that "if you're going to cater to science departments and engineers, you want to be where they are, not dictating to them . . . [from elsewhere]."

A third STRIDE member pointed out that while articles or chapters like this one may be a helpful source of inspiration, they are necessarily "archival" in nature. He recommended that other institutions "benchmark" against Michigan, by which he meant that they should gather information from us in real time, and at all relevant levels of administration, including, for example, provosts and presidents. Those administrators should then discuss pertinent issues with "their counterparts here. Because we all know that there are budget constraints. There are many good things to do. How did you pick it . . . how did this work? . . . Who do you engage in the faculty? How do you support them? How do you reward them? How do you define unique circumstances there versus Michigan?"

These comments lead us to offer the following additions to the list above:

11. Being aware of potential "turf" issues will help institutions identify the right kind of interventions; even if another group meets with search committees, perhaps STRIDE's "workshop" format (which is aimed at committee chairs from the entire institution) could be adapted to work. Or perhaps a completely different focus (on workshops for all faculty, or for all chairs) would be more successful. And meanwhile, of course, it is important to be sure that the people who *are* meeting with search committees have themselves been exposed to the same issues.

12. Locating an institutional change effort at the heart or center of the institution enables that effort to be viewed as both important and

"central." There are reasons to make trade-offs (for example, centrality may cost some measure of independence, or focus on a particular unit), but those trade-offs should be intentional, and may be more costly than anticipated.

13. Gathering up-to-date ideas and information from a range of institutional sources will make it easier to build on the experience of others without necessarily replicating that experience.

Finally, we ourselves learned from the STRIDE committee interviews how important it has been that the STRIDE process is an academic, scholarly process. Faculty not only enjoy learning and evaluating information, theories, and evidence, but those practices are at the core of their understanding of their academic roles and identities. If institutional change efforts are thoroughly grounded in that set of intellectual and collegial practices, they are much more likely to enable the sort of deeply personal commitment that is associated with becoming an ongoing organizational catalyst—on the STRIDE committee or elsewhere.

Notes to Chapter 10

1. STRIDE's acronym originally stood for "Science and Technology Recruiting to Improve Diversity and Excellence." However, the group's expanding mandate, as described in this chapter, required it to adopt a more disciplinarily inclusive label.

2. The other eight were Georgia Institute of Technology; Hunter College; New Mexico State University; University of California, Irvine; University of Colorado–Boulder; University of Puerto Rico–Humacao; University of Washington–Seattle; and University of Wisconsin–Madison.

3. More information about all activities undertaken by NSF ADVANCE at the University of Michigan is available online: http://sitemaker.umich.edu/advance.

4. This commitment was partially stimulated by recommendations for institutionalization made by the NSF-sponsored site visit committee; their report is also on the website: http://sitemaker.umich.edu/advance/files/sitevisit.pdf. The university subsequently announced that it would continue to fund other core components of its ADVANCE project as well.

5. We are grateful to STRIDE committee members for their seemingly endless goodwill, insight, and commitment. In addition, we depended in this chapter on the support and help of Janet Malley and Keith Rainwater, who collected and analyzed the evaluation data, and Cynthia Hudgins, who provides support to STRIDE.

6. The initial committee included Pamela Raymond and Michael Savageau from the School of Medicine; Anthony England and Martha Pollack from the College of Engineering; and Carol Fierke, Melvin Hochster, Samuel Mukasa, and John Vandermeer

from the College of Literature, Science, and the Arts. Michael Savageau retired from UM and the committee at the end of the first year. Joel Swanson from the School of Medicine participated during the beginning of 2003. Gary Huffnagle from the School of Medicine and Wayne Jones from the College of Engineering joined the committee in December 2003. Kathy Spindler from the School of Medicine and Charlie Brown from the College of Literature, Science, and the Arts joined in 2006, after this chapter had been completed.

7. See http://schwinger.harvard.edu/~georgi/women/cfd.html for information about Harvard's committee.

8. The PowerPoint presentation, recruitment handbook, and other materials developed by STRIDE are available online: http://sitemaker.umich.edu/advance/STRIDE.

9. In January 2007, STRIDE and the University of Michigan's Center for Institutional Diversity sponsored a UM conference on increasing racial and ethnic diversity among students and faculty in science and engineering on our campus.

11 Building Two-Way Streets to Implement Policies that Work for Gender and Science

Sue V. Rosser

I N HER INTRODUCTION to this volume, Londa Schiebinger gave a succinct and insightful analysis of three levels at which policies in federal agencies have impacted gender and science: (1) research support to increase the participation of women in science; (2) transformation of the structures of institutions to make them more accessible and friendly to women scientists; and (3) reconceptualization of research to include women and gender in its focus and analysis of results. She pointed out that most agencies, including the National Science Foundation (NSF) and the National Institutes of Health (NIH) have done quite well at level 1, and that NIH and some of the international agencies, such as the European Union (EU) have begun to focus on level 3, with explicit policies requiring gender and sex differences in focus and analyses (Schiebinger, this volume). In contrast, NSF has done little with level 3, but has begun, particularly through its ADVANCE initiative to work on level 2. Building two-way streets that allow cross-talk and sharing of policies between NSF and NIH might permit each to learn from the other about policies that work for gender and science in the area in which each has done pioneering work.

In this chapter, I will provide a brief history of women's programs at NSF, which documents the shift in NSF policies over time from a focus on level 1 to

Parts of this chapter were taken from Rosser and Lane (2002) and from Rosser and Chameau (2006).

level 2. Perhaps this history and a brief outline of the current ADVANCE program might provide a model for NIH and other agencies seeking to increase numbers of women in science and engineering through structural institutional transformation.

Level 1: Women's Programs at NSF in the 1980s

In 1945, Dr. Vannevar Bush's report—"Science: The Endless Frontier"—became the blueprint for the long-term U.S. national investment in scientific research and education through research universities, industry, and government that led to the establishment of the National Science Foundation. Almost four decades later, the Science and Technology Equal Opportunities Act of 1980 mandated that NSF collect and analyze data and report the status of women and minorities in the science and engineering professions to Congress on a biennial basis. In 1982, NSF published the first congressionally mandated reports documenting trends in the participation of women and minorities in science and engineering. These biennial reports on Women and Minorities in Science and Engineering, to which persons with disabilities were added in 1984 (NSF 2000, xii), provided data documenting that science and engineering have lower representations of men of color and of women compared to their respective proportions in the U.S. population overall.

These reports laid the statistical foundation for NSF officials to plan initiatives to address these underrepresentations. Programs such as Research Opportunities for Women and Visiting Professorships for Women (VPW) exemplify these initiatives. As Mary Clutter, assistant director of the NSF in charge of biological sciences, recounted in the evaluation of Professional Opportunities for Women in Research and Education (POWRE) Conference in 1998, the director of NSF established a Task Force on Programs for Women in the spring of 1989 with the charge of ascertaining the barriers to women's full participation in science and engineering and recommending changes in the foundation's existing programs to promote full participation (Clutter 1998, Appendix B).

The task force concluded the following:

1. Significant progress has been made in increasing the representation of women in the sciences.
2. Serious problems remain, preventing the recruitment, retention, and advancement of women in science and engineering.

3. These problems are more severe in some fields than in others, although advancement to senior ranks is a problem in all fields. (Clutter 1998, Appendix B)

The task force also made several specific recommendations, including expanding the level of effort in some existing programs at intervention points along the pipeline and establishing two new programs: one designed to enhance the graduate environment in academic institutions; the second designed to recognize and advance outstanding women faculty to the senior ranks (Clutter 1998, Appendix B).

NSF funded several initiatives targeting various segments of the science and engineering pipeline. Graduate fellowships for women provided an incentive for women graduate students to remain in graduate school and complete their PhD. These fellowships provided support for individual women and their research in science and engineering.

Career Advancement Awards (CAA), initiated in 1986, were superseded by Professional Opportunities for Women in Research and Education (POWRE) in fiscal year 1998. As the CAA name suggests, the award focused on advancing the careers of individual women by providing them funds to pursue their own research agenda. By targeting junior women, CAA used a combination of release from teaching and recognition of potential to make a significant research contribution, to place these women on a fast track to academic success in science or engineering research.

The task force also recommended that the NSF "incorporate the existing Research Opportunities for Women programs into Division-level strategic plans, but retain the Visiting Professorship as a Foundation-wide program" (Clutter 1998, Appendix B). Many of the divisions used a segment of the Research Planning Grant funds as discretionary add-ons, often called Research Planning Grants for Women. These grants targeted women scientists or engineers who had never held an NSF grant or who sought reentry after a career interruption.

Visiting Professorships for Women (VPW), established in late 1982, stood as the primary, foundation-wide initiative for women until POWRE succeeded it in 1997. VPW sought to retain women who already had faculty appointments in science and engineering by providing them with new equipment and supporting them at different, generally more prestigious institutions, where they had an opportunity to develop new research methodologies and collaborations. A 1994 evaluation of VPW documented the success of VPW, stating that an award often came "at a critical time for keeping the recipient active in research as opposed to other academic, non-research responsibilities" (SRI International 1994, 13).

Although support of research of individual women scientists and engineers served as the predominant focus for the VPW during most of its fourteen-year history, each VPW recipient was required to spend approximately 30 percent of her time and effort to attract and retain women scientists and engineers at the institutions she was visiting (SRI International 1994). As part of her "interactive activities that involve teaching, mentoring, and other student contacts" (SRI International 1994, 1), each awardee engaged in activities such as forming a Society of Women Engineers (SWE) chapter, establishing mentor networks among women graduate students, and teaching women in science courses jointly with women's studies programs. This division of 70 percent support for individual research and 30 percent to improve institutional infrastructure to attract and retain women in science and engineering signaled recognition that support of individual research alone might not be sufficient to increase the numbers of women scientists and engineers. The 30 percent underlined the dawning realization that steps needed to be taken at the institutional, as well as individual, level.

Level 2: Women's Programs in the Early 1990s

Although Faculty Awards for Women (FAW) held only one program solicitation, in 1990, FAW attempted to address a systemic problem—the dearth of women scientists and engineers in senior positions that the Task Force Report had identified. The initiative used the traditional approach of supporting the research projects of individual women faculty for a period of five years at the level of $50,000 per year, in its attempt to solve the systemic problem. Almost all of the hundred awardees achieved the primary stated goal of the program of achieving tenure. The controversy within the peer review panel surrounding the criteria for selection of the FAW awardees (reviewers could not come to consensus over whether individuals who showed potential, but appeared to need a boost, or those whose records indicated they were very likely to receive tenure even without the award, should receive higher priority) contributed to the termination of the program after one year. It was difficult to judge the efficacy of this program of support for research of individual investigators as an approach to systemic change, given that there was only one cohort of awardees.

Recognizing that a focus on efforts to target individuals in groups such as minorities and white women would not work as long as the system remained unchanged, the Directorate of Education and Human Resources at NSF began to focus on systemic initiatives. In addition to Statewide Systemic Initiatives (SSI), Urban Systemic Initiatives (USI), and Rural Systemic Initiatives (RSI), NSF established the Program for Women and Girls (PWG) in 1993 to explore comprehensive factors and climate issues that may systematically deter women from science and engineering. In addition to Dissemination Projects, PWG included two other initiatives for women and girls: Model Projects for Women and Girls (MPWG) encouraged "the design, implementation, evaluation and dissemination of innovative, short-term highly focused activities which will improve the access to and/or retention of females in SEM (science, engineering, and mathematics) education and careers" (NSF 1993, 7). Experimental Projects for Women and Girls (EPWG) encompassed large-scale projects requiring a consortial effort with multiple target populations. They aimed "to create positive and permanent changes in academic, social, and scientific climates (for classrooms, laboratories, departments, institutions/organizations) in order to allow the interest and aptitude women and girls display in SEM to flourish; and to add to the knowledge base about interactions between gender and the infrastructure of SEM which can provide direction for future efforts" (NSF 1993, 7).

The only individual research projects supported under the Program for Women and Girls were those where the research and evaluation of a curricular change, cocurricular program, or faculty development initiative fit the individual researcher's agenda. Although K–12 always constituted the centerpiece of PWG, undergraduates, graduate students, and even faculty served as primary targets of several projects at the beginning of PWG. After 1995–96, and particularly after VPW was incorporated into PWG in late 1995, eventually to be succeeded by the cross-directorate POWRE, PWG centered on K–16 exclusively. Transitioning through reincarnations as the Program for Gender Equity in Science, Mathematics, Engineering and Technology (PGE), and Gender Diversity in STEM Education (GDSE), the current program is called Research on Gender in Science and Engineering (GSE). GSE "seeks to broaden the participation of girls and women in all fields of science, technology, engineering, and mathematics (STEM) education by supporting research, dissemination of research, and extension services in education that will lead to a larger and more diverse domestic science and engineering workforce" (accessed June 23, 2005 from http://www.nsf.gov/funding/pgm/ehr).

Temporary Return to Level 1:
Initiatives in the Late 1990s: Origins of POWRE

After the 1996 VPW solicitation, NSF replaced VPW with Professional Opportunities for Women in Research and Education (POWRE), giving the first POWRE awards in fiscal year 1997. POWRE was conceived in the wake of the November 1994 Republican sweep of Congress where 62 percent of white males voted Republican (Edsall 1995). This resulted in cuts in federal spending, with programs that had gender or race as their central focus under particular scrutiny.

In response to statements suggesting that Republican lawmakers were studying whether federal affirmative action requirements should be dropped on the grounds that they discriminate against white men made by Senate Majority Leader Robert Dole on NBC's *Meet the Press* on February 5, 1995, President Clinton initiated his own review of affirmative action programs (Swoboda 1995, A1). In June 1995, the U.S. Supreme Court ruled in the *Adarand Constructors, Inc. v Pena* decision that "federal affirmative action programs that use racial and ethnic criteria as a basis for decision making are subject to strict judicial scrutiny" (in Kole 1995, 1). On July 19, after holding a press conference to reaffirm his commitment to affirmative action, President Clinton issued a memorandum for heads of executive departments and agencies to bring them in line with the Supreme Court decision. On July 20, 1995, the University of California Board of Regents voted to end special admissions programs; that decision was confirmed a year later by a citizen referendum. In 1996, a Texas circuit court ruling banned affirmative action in admissions and financial awards. In 1998, in a referendum, the citizens of the State of Washington prohibited any "preferential treatment on the basis of race, gender, national origin, or ethnicity." In July 2000, an administrative judge upheld Governor Jeb Bush's plan to end the consideration of race and gender in admissions in state colleges in Florida (Lauer 2000).

Although the NSF initiatives challenged in court focused on minority programs, specifically the Summer Science Camps and the Graduate Minority Fellowships, programs targeted exclusively for women principal investigators such as VPW, FAW, and CAA were thought to be in jeopardy. Since the MPWG and EPWG had some men as PIs and did not exclude boys and men from projects, while targeting girls and women, PWG was considered safe, with the exception of VPW. Since VPW had moved to PWG only in 1995,

POWRE replaced it after the 1996 solicitation; CAA and RPG were subsumed by POWRE in fiscal year 1998.

Rather than being housed in Education and Human Resources where PWG, VPW, FAW, and CAA had been housed, POWRE became a cross-directorate program, with objectives of providing visibility for, encouraging, and providing opportunities for further career advancement, professional growth, and increased prominence of women in engineering and in the disciplines of science supported by NSF (NSF 1997, 1). Despite threats against affirmative action, the approach to achieving these objectives came through individual research grants to support science and engineering research of individual women researchers. POWRE did not retain from VPW the concept of committing 30 percent of time devoted to infrastructure to attract and retain women in science and engineering.

NSF became aware of several factors that might mitigate against POWRE and its effectiveness almost immediately:

1. The request for proposals for POWRE had been put together very rapidly.

2. POWRE had been removed from the former site of VPW (EHR and HRD) because PWG was focusing increasingly on K–12; this meant that program officers from the research directorates, rather than from the Program for Women and Girls, were overseeing POWRE.

TABLE 11.1   Timeline of initiatives for women at NSF.

1945:	Vannevar Bush's Report: *Science: The Endless Frontier*
1950:	NSF established
1980:	Women in Science and Technology Equal Opportunity Act mandates that NSF collect and analyze data on the status of women and minorities in the engineering professions
1982:	First publication of *Women and Minorities in Science and Engineering* (beginning in 1984, *Persons with Disabilities* were included)
1982–1997:	Visiting Professorships for Women (VPW)
1986–1998:	Career Advancement Awards (CAA)
1990:	Faculty Awards for Women (FAW)
1993–present:	Program for Women and Girls (PWG)
1997–2000:	Professional Opportunities for Women in Research and Education (POWRE)
2001:	ADVANCE initiated

3. Moving POWRE to the research directorates, coupled with having 100 percent of the time and support going to the science and engineering research of individual investigators, went against a growing sentiment that support for institutional and systemic approaches, rather than support of the research of individual women scientists, would be required to increase the percentage of women at all levels in science and engineering.

As part of the background research for a workshop that NSF asked me to organize in 1998 between NSF program officers and scientists and engineers from the community to consider POWRE and successor programs, I posed the following four questions via email to the FY 1997 POWRE awardees:

1. What are the most significant issues, challenges, opportunities facing women scientists today as they plan their careers?
2. How does the laboratory climate (or its equivalent in your subdiscipline) impact on the careers of women scientists?
3. What do you like least or find most problematic about POWRE?
4. What do you like best or find most useful about POWRE?

The responses of the awardees proved so useful and interesting that I continued to pose the same four questions to the next three years (FY 1998, FY 1999, FY 2000) of POWRE awardees. Responses were obtained from the complete four-year cohort of POWRE awardees before POWRE was succeeded by ADVANCE in 2001 (NSF 2001b).

A thorough analysis of all questions, including the methodology, broader context, and details surrounding response rates to the email questionnaire, was published in *The Science Glass Ceiling* (Rosser 2004). "Balancing work with family responsibilities" stands out overwhelmingly as the major issue for women from all directorates and for awardees for all years in response to question 1. Although many women did not mention problems in either their laboratory or work environment related to gender issues, the largest number of responses to question 2 did suggest that to some degree their gender led to their being perceived as a problem, anomaly, or deviant in the laboratory/work environment. The findings about questions 3 and 4, along with the earlier findings on the other two questions offer insights about the historical context of the NSF funding outlined earlier and the new direction of the ADVANCE program considered later in this chapter.

The responses to question 3: What do you like least or find most problematic about POWRE? fell under three broad categories: (a) gender related, (b) content or parameters of POWRE itself, and (c) NSF administration of the program. Gender related includes responses where awardees indicated that targeting POWRE for women only was especially positive or negative. The greatest dissatisfaction, almost double that for category A and almost quadruple that for category C, centered on the content or parameters of POWRE itself, although a substantial percentage (17–24 percent) of respondents all four years found "no problems" with POWRE. Category B referred to conditions such as limits placed on time, funds, and site of research imposed in the program solicitation by NSF. Awardees expressed only minor dissatisfactions with NSF administration processes of review, bureaucracy, and information surrounding POWRE.

The responses to question 4: What do you like best or find most useful about POWRE? provided not only the mirror image responses to question 3, but they also revealed considerable information about the strengths of POWRE. Gender-related responses were positive and reflected opposite opinions from those who felt uncomfortable that POWRE was for women only. Despite the negative to ambivalent feelings expressed in response to question 3 about POWRE being "less prestigious" and "for women only," many respondents to question 4 liked the fact that POWRE "helps women who have had career interruptions." NSF administration of the program registered the lowest response; this may reflect a smoothly running bureaucracy, since when programs are administered well, the administration appears relatively invisible.

In contrast, the positive response to the content or parameters of POWRE itself reflected in response to question 4 was lower than the negative response to question 3. This may suggest that NSF's decision to terminate POWRE, and have ADVANCE succeed it, reflected an appropriate response to negative reactions to the content or parameters of POWRE itself. Many respondents indicated an appreciation because POWRE "opens the door for advancement/research opportunities," especially for difficult to fund "non-traditional research." Grouping responses 1 and 2 with "getting funding for various needs" and "foot in the door for other funding" illustrates the pressure POWRE awardees felt to obtain funding to support their research in times of tight resource constraints.

Some awardees expressed frustration with supporting research of individual investigators as a way to solve the problem of too few women scientists. They noted the importance of institutional approaches:

> I'm not sure how much sense it makes to try to foster women's participation in science and engineering through project-oriented programs. Probably, the lives of a few individual women (i.e., the grant recipients) will be made somewhat easier but it's hard to see how this significantly benefits women in the S&E professions in general. The development of networks among women scientists and engineers and programs to increase the visibility of women scientists and engineers within the S&E profession (such as the Research Professorship for Women program) would probably be of more general benefit than project-oriented awards. As far as I am aware, the POWRE program does not incorporate even the simplest attempt at networking, such as circulating a list of POWRE awardees. In addition, the limiting of project-oriented awards to any sub-group tends to carry the "second-class" taint. (Respondent 58)

The recommendation to take an institutional approach also emerged from the 1998 workshop of NSF program directors and scientists and engineers from the community:

> In keeping with its combined focus on research and education, NSF should develop long-term strategies to encourage institutional transformation regarding the culture of science and to increase gender and ethnic diversity among scientists for both faculty and students; targeted programs such as POWRE do not have sufficient resources to bring about institutional change, which must also be encouraged by all programs in each directorate. The short-term individual strategies, through POWRE, should facilitate women to participate fully in all of NSF's programs, with an aim of developing institutions into places where women scientists and engineers can succeed as well as men. Grants to individuals or to groups of investigators should be made with this goal in mind, as well as the goal of helping the grant recipients' careers. (Rosser and Zieseniss 1998, 9)

Level 2: Systemic Approaches Through ADVANCE

In fiscal year 2001, NSF launched the ADVANCE initiative to succeed POWRE. Initially funded at the level of $17 million, ADVANCE has two categories to include institutional, rather than individual, solutions to empower women to participate fully in science and technology. NSF encouraged institutional solutions, in addition to the individual solution permitted under the category of

Fellows Awards, because of "increasing recognition that the lack of women's full participation at the senior level of academe is often a systemic consequence of academic culture" (NSF 2001a, 2). Under ADVANCE, Institutional Transformation Awards, ranging up to $750,000 per year for up to five years, promote the increased participation and advancement of women; Leadership Awards recognize the work of outstanding organizations of individuals and enable them to sustain, intensify, and initiate new activity (NSF 2001a).

In October 2001, the first eight institutions receiving ADVANCE awards were announced (NSF 2001b): Georgia Tech, New Mexico State, University of California, Irvine, University of Colorado–Boulder, University of Michigan, University of Puerto Rico, University of Washington, and University of Wisconsin–Madison. Hunter College joined the first round of ADVANCE awardee institutions in early 2002.

In 2003, NSF announced ten second-round institutional transformation grants: Case Western Reserve, Columbia University, Kansas State University, University of Alabama–Birmingham, University of Maryland–Baltimore County, University of Montana, University of Rhode Island, University of Texas–El Paso, Utah State, and Virginia Tech. Late in 2006, NSF announced thirteen third round institutions: Brown, Cal Poly–Pomona, Cornell, Duke, Iowa State, Marshall University, New Jersey Institute of Technology, Rensselaer Polytechnic Institute, Rice, University of Arizona, University of Illinois–Chicago, University of Maryland–Eastern Shore, and University of North Carolina–Charlotte. ADVANCE promises to go beyond individual research projects of women scientists and engineers that initiatives such as POWRE, FAW, CAA, and VPW supported to solve problems with broader systemic and institutional roots such as balancing career and family.

To initiate the institutional transformation necessary to advance women to senior ranks and leadership positions, Georgia Tech's ADVANCE project included five major threads. These threads also exemplify the characteristics of many ADVANCE institutional projects.

1. Termed professorships to form a mentoring network:
One tenured woman full professor in each of four colleges with disciplines funded by NSF became the designated ADVANCE professor. The title and the funds of $60,000 per year for five years associated with the ADVANCE Professorship conferred the prestige and funds equivalent to those accrued by other endowed chairs at the institution. This sum also meant that $1.2 million of the $3.7 million grant went directly to support the ADVANCE professors in keeping

with the NSF notion that the ADVANCE grants should be substantial to recognize the importance of activities to build workforce infrastructure. Because
Georgia Tech is a research university, the PIs of the grant particularly recognized the necessity for ADVANCE professors to sustain their research productivity while undertaking this mentoring role. ADVANCE professors often used
funds to pay for graduate students or postdocs to support their research.

Each ADVANCE professor developed and nurtured mentoring networks
for the women faculty in her college. The focus of the mentoring activities
varied among the colleges, depending on the numbers, ranks, and needs of the
women. In the College of Engineering, a large college with about 42 women
out of 400 tenure-track faculty, isolation constituted a primary issue in many
departments. The lunches arranged by the ADVANCE professor with women
faculty from the college provided an opportunity for them to meet women in
other departments and develop social and professional networks. A popular
professional networking opportunity included evaluation of the curriculum
vitae of junior faculty by senior colleagues to assess their readiness for promotion and tenure or gaps that must be addressed for successful promotion to
the higher rank.

The ADVANCE professor often helps to explain and mediate problematic
issues in some schools with the chair and dean. In the smaller College of Computing, with eight of sixty women as tenure-track faculty, many of the women
had young children, so many of the lunches and activities focused on explica-
tion of family-friendly policies and strategies to balance career and family.
In the College of Science, lunches and activities centered on grant-writing
workshops and other means to establish successful laboratory research. In
Ivan Allen College, where 40 percent of the tenure-track faculty are women,
the ADVANCE professor chose luncheon themes on publication and scholarly productivity. Although all four ADVANCE professors held luncheons
and mentored individual women faculty, each focused the initial activities
on those issues she perceived as most problematic or critical for achieving
tenure, promotion, and advancement to career success for the women in her
particular college. By the fourth year of the grant, the professors evolved more
cross-college activities, expanding programs and initiatives particularly successful in one college to women from all colleges on campus.

2. Collection of MIT-Report-like data indicators:
To assess whether advancement of women really occurs during and after the
institutional transformation undertaken through ADVANCE, data must be

collected on indicators for comparison with baseline data on grant initiation for several indicators. Georgia Tech proposed in its grant to collect data on eleven of the following twelve indicators that NSF eventually required all ADVANCE institutions to collect by gender: faculty appointment type; rank; tenure; promotion; years in rank; time at institution; administrative positions; professorships and chairs; tenure and promotion committee members; salaries; space; and start-up packages. At the time of the Clayman Institute for Gender Research conference, data from only the initial three years of the five-year grant were available. These preliminary results suggest positive although modest gains in all indicator measures.

3. Family-friendly policies and practices:
Recent studies document that balancing career and family constitutes the major difficulty for tenure-track women faculty in general (Mason and Goulden 2004) and women science and engineering faculty in particular (Xie and Shauman 2003; Rosser 2004). Competition between the biological clock and the tenure clock becomes a significant obstacle for women faculty who have delayed childbearing until they receive a tenure-track position. For women faculty in science and engineering, significant time away from their research makes it less likely they can successfully achieve tenure in a research institution. The dual-career situation becomes an additional complicating factor for women scientists and engineers, 62 percent of whom are married to men scientists and engineers (Sonnert and Holton 1995). Given the dearth of women scientists and engineers, the reverse situation does not hold since that would mean few men scientists and engineers would be married. To facilitate the balancing of career and family, perceived overwhelmingly by women scientists and engineers (Rosser 2004), particularly those of younger ages, as the major issues, Georgia Tech instituted the following family-friendly policies and practices: stop the tenure clock, active service, modified duties, lactation stations, and day care. The specific details of these policies can be accessed under Family and Work Policies at http://www.advance.gatech.edu (accessed August 20, 2007).

4. Mini-retreats to facilitate access to decision makers and provide informal conversations and discussion on topics important to women faculty:
Research has demonstrated that women faculty tend to have less access and opportunities than their male colleagues to speak with the decision makers and institutional leaders (Rosser 2004). Often this unintended discrimination and lack of access result from women's absence from informal and social

gatherings. To ensure access of tenure-track women faculty to the senior leadership of chairs, deans, provost, vice presidents, and president, the Georgia Tech ADVANCE grant organized two-day mini-retreats during each year of the grant. Focused on topics of interest and concern to all faculty, such as case studies of promotion and tenure, training to remove subtle gender and racial bias in promotion and tenure decisions, and effective strategies in hiring dual-career couples, these retreats have provided opportunities for the tenure-track women faculty to interact with the institutional leadership and express their opinions and views on matters of mutual interest.

5. Removal of subtle gender, racial, and other biases in promotion and tenure: In my role as dean, my close involvement with the promotion and tenure process provided insight into subtle ways in which unintended subtle biases might influence decisions on promotion and tenure. For example, I observed that in some cases when the tenure clock had stopped for a year for a valid reason such as childbirth, the clock appeared not to stop in the heads of colleagues, as they considered the individual for promotion and tenure. They seemed simply to expect an additional year's worth of papers, talks, and productivity to be added.

To address this issue, the principal investigator who was the provost appointed a Promotion and Tenure ADVANCE Committee (PTAC) to assess existing promotion and tenure processes, explore potential forms of bias, provide recommendations to mitigate against them, and to elevate awareness of both candidates and committees for expectations and best practices in tenure and promotion. After one year of studying the research documenting possible biases due to gender, race/ethnicity, ability status, as well as interdisciplinarity, the committee developed nine case studies with accompanying sample curriculum vitae. Each illustrated one or more issues or areas where possible bias might impact the promotion and tenure decision. After discussion of these case studies at a mini-retreat, the refined versions served as the basis for an interactive web-based instrument, Awareness of Decision in Evaluation of Promotion and Tenure (ADEPT), designed by colleagues in the College of Computing. Individuals can use ADEPT to participate in a virtual promotion and tenure meeting, where depending on their response, the meeting takes different directions and generates different outcomes in promotion and tenure. The web-based instrument, along with best practices from PTAC, and resources on bias can be accessed at http://www.adept.gatech.edu/index.htm (accessed August 20, 2007).

Each ADVANCE institution has evolved programs and policies to address similar issues on its campus. Most have at least one program that is unique, which if successful, might serve as a model for other institutions. Virginia Tech hosts the ADVANCE portal website for all ADVANCE institutional transformation awardees; it can be accessed at http://www.advance.vt.edu (accessed August 20, 2007).

As this volume goes to press, the first round of ADVANCE awardee institutions complete their funding from NSF. Now the test of whether the project can be sustained by the institution in the absence of NSF resources and prestige begins. As the substantial literature on institutionalization of reforms in higher education documents, effective institutionalization must include both the top leadership (Heifetz and Laurie 1997; Eckel and Kezar 2003), middle administrators (Meyerson 2003), and the faculty (Woodbury and Gess-Newsome 2002; Merton et al. 2004). Changes diffuse throughout the organization (Strang and Soule 1998; Rogers 2003) at different rates but must ultimately penetrate the structure, procedures, and cultural levels (Braxton et al. 2002) of the university for genuine institutionalization. If the institution, and particularly the upper levels of institutional leadership, have not been informed, do not understand, or have not committed to sustaining the trajectory and impacts of advancing women to senior faculty and leadership positions after the grant funding ends, then the project will not succeed in sustaining this institutional transformation in the long run. Institutional transformation remains difficult, even when the environment is ripe (Seel 2000) for change and both the institutional leaders (Eckel and Kezar 2003) and grass-roots support (Woodbury and Gess-Newsome 2002) for the transformation exist. In the absence of such environments, leadership and support, and in situations where the goals of the project do not mesh with the objectives of the institution (Tierney 1988), the transformation will certainly fail.

Conclusion

As the brief summary of the history of women's programs at NSF suggests, NSF has years of success in providing support to individual women scientists to support their research, thereby retaining them in science (level 1). Beginning with VPW and especially now with ADVANCE, NSF has poured considerable resources into initiatives to transform institutional structures (level 2). Except for the Research on Gender in Science and Engineering (GSE), focused mostly at the K–12 level, NSF has not focused on reconceptualizing research to center on women and girls (level 3).

In contrast, NIH has also focused on level 1, but since the 2000 Government Accountability Office (GAO) Report concluding that NIH had "made less progress in implementing the requirement that certain clinical trials be designated and carried out to permit valid analysis by sex, which could reveal whether intervention affects women differently from men" (U.S. Department of Health and Human Services and National Institutes of Health 2000), NIH put into effect new guidelines for Phase III clinical trials covering both the inclusion of women and sex-based analysis for reviewers and scientific review administrators. In April 2001, the Institute of Medicine published *Exploring the Biological Contributions to Human Health: Does Sex Matter?* (Wizemann and Pardue 2001). The agenda validated the study of basic biologic and molecular bases for sex and gender differences in disease, including "sex-based biology as an integral part" of research conducted by the institutes (level 3).

The evident policy recommendation that emerges suggests that NIH and NSF might learn from each other. Based on NSF's experience, NIH must not interpret the increase in women medical students and entry-level physicians, particularly in the clinical track, as necessarily translating to women in decision-making positions impacting research. Level 2 institutional transformation will be necessary to ensure this impact. Simultaneously, NSF must begin to focus on level 3, to reconceptualize research in science to focus on women and gender. This reconceptualization constitutes a more difficult proposition in basic research than it does in the applications of clinical medicine where gender is obvious. However, sharing best practices and cross-talk between the agencies should facilitate the mutual learning and evolution beneficial for both agencies as they strive for women's full participation at all three levels.

12 Projects of the National Academies on Women in Science and Engineering

France A. Córdova

T HE NATIONAL RESEARCH COUNCIL (NRC) is the operating arm of the National Academy of Sciences, the National Academy of Engineering, and the Institute of Medicine. As a member of the NRC's Committee on Policy and Global Affairs (PGA, the overseer of many of the NRC's policy boards and commissions), I was recently asked to chair a review of the activities and plans of CWSE, the Committee on Women in Science and Engineering. Also recently, another of the PGA's boards called COSEPUP (Committee on Science, Engineering, and Public Policy) asked me and several other women scientists to speak on the subject of women's participation in academic science and engineering, and to consider what COSEPUP could do that would be of value to institutions and individuals concerned about the dearth of women in STEM (science, technology, math, and engineering) fields.

My participation in these projects gave me the opportunity to examine what NRC is doing on issues related to women in science, and to offer, with others, some recommendations for future work. I share some of our results below.

Thanks to Richard Bissell, Judy Harrington, and Charlotte Kuh, senior staff of the NRC, for providing NAS data and a preview of the COSEPUP proposal, quoted in this chapter, on Women in Science and Engineering: A Guide to Maximizing Their Potential; and to Michael Clegg, Lillian Wu, and Jong-On Hahm for their work with me on the review of CWSE. Several of the graphs shown here were derived from the American Council on Education's Office of Women in Higher Education publication, *An Agenda for Excellence: Creating Flexibility in Tenure-Track Faculty Careers* (ACE 2005) and the University of California website for work-family policies and programs for faculty, http://ucfamilyedge.berkeley.edu. My particular thanks go to Marc Goulden for his leadership in both of the latter efforts.

1. Is the National Academy (Still) Gender Imbalanced?

The short answer is yes, but there is momentum in the academy to address this imbalance. The proportion of women is increasing with time, especially recently, as a result of internal discussions and focus on this issue by academy members.

The current membership of the National Academy of Science (NAS) is 1899. About 10 percent, or 189, are women. Figure 12.1 shows how the number of women has increased with time since 1994. It is encouraging that the percentage of women elected in the three most recent elections (2003–2005) was more than 20 percent per year (Figure 12.2). Sixty members were elected each year from 1994 to 2000, and seventy-two members were elected each year thereafter.

Of course, a significant factor in achieving parity in the ranks of the NAS is achieving parity in the ranks of academic faculty, especially faculty in research institutions where women represent just 28 percent of the total faculty. This number is even lower in the most prestigious universities. It is the dearth of women in STEM careers in academe (and to some extent also in industry) that two policy committees of the NRC, CWSE and COSEPUP, are addressing with considerable energies. Hopefully some of this new work will be useful for studies of gendered innovation in S&E. And if it isn't, these NRC committees may welcome external input since these newly proposed projects are still in the formative stages.

2. CWSE

The Committee on Women in Science and Engineering (CWSE) was established in 1991 as a standing committee of the National Research Council. Its mandate is to coordinate, monitor, and advocate action to increase the participation of women in science and engineering.

The accomplishments of CWSE are many:

1. CWSE has produced publications that address workforce and related issues. These are listed in Appendix 1, some with brief summaries. These are a rich source of data, stories, and other information. "From Scarcity to Visibility" describes gender differences in the careers of doctoral scientists and engineers, and is an excellent resource for social scientists (Long 2001).

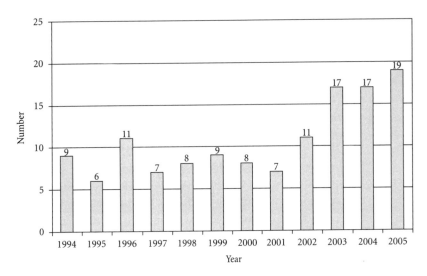

FIGURE 12.1 Number of women elected to the National Academy of Sciences.

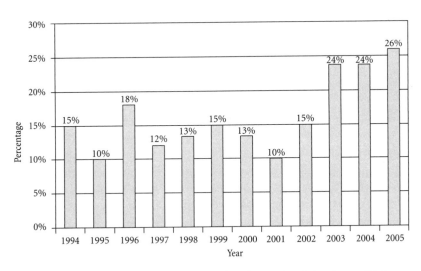

FIGURE 12.2 Percentage of women elected to the National Academy of Sciences.

2. CWSE has provided important support to the academies as they seek to address gender inequities in their membership. It is on hand to give advice to other policy groups of the NRC.

3. CWSE, with its emphasis on data collection, has proven to be a help-ful conduit to Congress and has been mandated by Congress to par-ticipate in or lead selected studies.

4. The goal of providing objective data at a national level on inequalities in pay and working conditions (for example, laboratory space) similar to the well-known MIT study is commendable. CWSE's website links to over 600 websites of organizations encouraging women in science and engineering. This is the most comprehensive set of links on this topic currently available on the Web.

5. The CWSE website is a helpful resource to researchers and policy makers, as well as those simply wishing to become more informed about issues and university responses to equity issues. For more infor-mation about CWSE and its resources, see http://www7.nationalacad-emies.org/cwse/index.html.

6. CWSE has two useful current studies:

   a. One project assesses gender differences in the careers of science, engineering, and mathematics faculty, focusing on four-year in-stitutions of higher education that award bachelor's and graduate degrees. The study will examine issues such as faculty hiring, pro-motion, tenure, and allocation of institutional resources including laboratory space.

   b. CWSE has prepared a guide on best practices in recruiting, retain-ing, and advancing women scientists and engineers in academia. The project provides guidelines and practices that institutions and individuals can use to increase the participation of women in science and engineering, by stressing successful efforts at top research universities in the United States. The guidebook is titled *To Recruit and Advance Women Students and Faculty in U.S. Sci-ence and Engineering* (CWSE 2006), and is available through the National Academies Press.

The review I chaired and the discussion surrounding it emphasized that this is the right time for CWSE to expand its portfolio of activities. There is nationwide momentum and CWSE has already established itself as a leader. Our review recommended that CWSE develop further studies to include:

1. Understanding the causes of the substantial differences in the representation of women in the physical sciences and engineering versus the biological sciences and medicine.

2. Understanding the implications of the July 2004 U.S. Government Accountability Office report on gender issues (more about this below) and perhaps hosting a conference on this subject.

3. Understanding the underlying causes of inequity. For example, the differential impacts of child rearing, the impact of extramural funding agencies, and the impact of the tenure system all deserve more careful study to point the way toward creative solutions to contemporary problems.

4. Developing a handbook on best practices perhaps based on the experience of institutions that are most effective in advancing women scientists and engineers would be a valuable contribution. For example, a manual might provide guidelines on the successful implementation of mentoring systems, and on how to protect young women faculty from being overused in minor administrative assignments.

5. Articulating how CWSE might provide a unique contribution in the national effort to address pipeline, recruitment, and retention goals. To this end the NRC might request that staff (or a task force) be deployed to compile a list of current efforts being undertaken elsewhere in the NRC (for example, COSEPUP), by federal agencies (NSF, NIH, etc.), industry, scientific and educational societies (for example, ACE, NASULGC, AACU), and individual universities (for example, NSF's ADVANCE program.).

6. Expanding its web portal to include a list of policy and issues papers and references to best practices conducted around the country (for example, in NSF's ADVANCE program).

3. COSEPUP

The Committee on Science, Engineering, and Public Policy (COSEPUP) is a joint unit of the National Academy of Sciences, National Academy of Engineering, and the Institute of Medicine. Most of its members are current or former members of the councils of the three institutions.

COSEPUP mainly conducts studies on cross-cutting issues in science and technology policy. COSEPUP was chartered by the academies to address "the concerns and requests of the President's Science Advisor, the Director of the National Science Foundation, the Chair of the National Science Board, and heads of other federal research and development departments and agencies, and the Chairs of key science and technology-related committees of the Congress." Its recent studies range from a workshop on the White House Office of Management and Budget's program rating assessment tool to a discussion of setting priorities for NSF large research facilities to a monograph on human reproductive cloning.

COSEPUP recently invited several women scientists (three of them chancellors of UC campuses, including myself) to speak on the subject of women faculty in science and engineering. A few things I would share with you from this stimulating panel discussion, which was moderated by Nancy Hopkins (MIT):

Anneila Sargent (Caltech) offered that what is not working for women is often not working for men either. She emphasized that guide books are not enough; what is critical is mass—hiring more women means getting commitment not just from the university chancellor or president but from the departments.

Alice Huang (Caltech) stressed the importance of hiring staff at universities to manage programs, assist with evaluation and status of programs, promote new policies, obtain funds, in short, help the faculty and administrators with implementation and sustainability of new programs. Huang noted that getting women as chairs of departments and deans may be even more important than getting a woman president because they have more impact on faculty hiring. She noted the importance of developing a culture that doesn't diminish women's accomplishments, and paying attention to spousal hiring and daycare.

Marye Anne Fox (chancellor, UCSD) talked about the July 2004 GAO report on Title IX, which isn't just about athletics. The Government Accountability Office said, with respect to women's participation in the sciences, that federal agencies need to do more to ensure that their grantees comply with Title IX. "The report documented salary and resource allocation inequity, sometimes hostile institutional culture, inequitable expectations, accumulated disadvantage, barriers to re-entry, a lack of faculty mentoring, and a dearth of family-friendly policies."

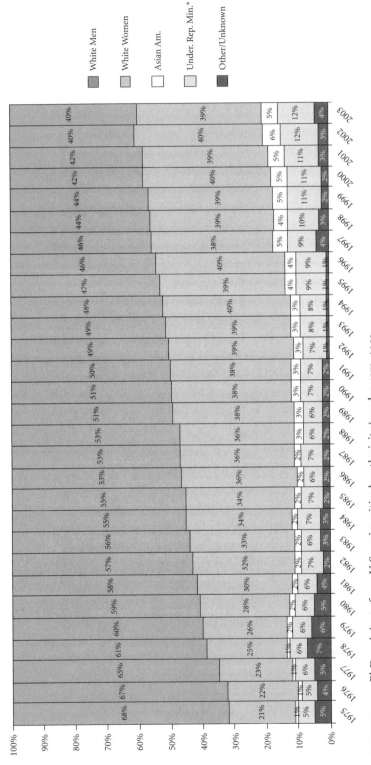

FIGURE 12.3 PhD recipients from U.S. universities by ethnicity/gender, 1975–2003.

* Under. Rep. Min. (underrepresented minorities) includes African Americans, Hispanic Americans, and Native Americans.

SOURCE: NSF, Survey of Earned Doctorates, taken from Webcaspar.

The late Denise Denton (former chancellor, UCSC) showed an example from the University of Washington, where she was dean of engineering, of how a college can hire many more women engineers while simultaneously increasing quality.

I presented a web-based sample of agency, association, consortium, academy, and university websites focused on diversity initiatives and best practices in recruitment and retention of women and minorities (see Appendix 2 of this chapter). I said that some entity should provide a web portal where all of these sites are listed, as a community resource for policy, illustrative programs, and best practices.

Charlotte Kuh of the NRC said that the new NRC rankings will list the proportion of women on every department's faculty!

As a result of this discussion, at which CWSE chair Lilian Wu also presented CWSE's plans, COSEPUP has submitted a proposal, the statement of work for which is:

> To guide faculty, department chairs and deans, academic leaders, funding organizations, and government officials on how to maximize the potential of women science and engineering researchers, an ad hoc COSEPUP committee will integrate the wealth of data available on gender issues across all fields of science and engineering. The committee will focus on academe, but will examine other research sectors to determine effective practices and develop findings and recommendations for recruiting, hiring, promotion, and retention of women science and engineering researchers. Throughout the report, profiles of effective practices, scenarios, and summary boxes will be used to reinforce the key concepts.

This study is extremely promising as an eventual resource for social scientists as well as university and industry leaders committed to effecting institutional change.

In its proposal, COSEPUP, like many other groups, notes that leaks in the pipeline are at all stages, with women leaving academe at higher rates than men. The number of women obtaining undergraduate degrees, graduate degrees, and postdoctoral positions in STEM careers has increased tremendously in the last few decades (see Figure 12.3), but the proportion of women with faculty appointments in these areas, especially at the most prestigious research universities, is disproportionately low. Cited is an outstanding example of multiple leaks along the mathematics pipeline: about one-half of undergraduate mathematics degrees are awarded to women, but women comprise only 8.3 percent of the faculty ranks in mathematics. The COSEPUP proposal notes that, "In S&E departments at top 50 universities the proportion of full professorships held by women ranges from 3–15 percent."

In the CWSE book *From Scarcity to Visibility* (2001), J. Scott Long, a sociologist at Indiana and editor of the volume, includes a study (from 1995) that shows the percentage of PhDs who *remain* in science and engineering, by gender. This is illustrated in Table 12.1.

These data show that women drop out after receiving the PhD at a much higher rate than men. The population effect of this is shown in Figure 12.4.

As cited in the COSEPUP proposal,

> In 2001, [then] University of California at Santa Cruz Chancellor M. R. C. Greenwood reported that the percentage of women hired UC-wide in S&E often falls short of the postdoctoral pool. In the life sciences in 2000, women comprised 39.3 percent of the national PhD pool and 36 percent of postdoctoral scholars, but only 29 percent of University of California hires. In chemistry, women held 31 percent of the PhDs, 20 percent of postdoctoral positions, but only 13 percent of new hires. In mathematics, the disparity was especially marked, where women comprise 22.1 percent of PhDs and 13.2 percent of postdoctoral positions, but only 5.4 percent of faculty appointments.

These are the statistics that the National Research Council, through CWSE and COSEPUP among other groups, is committed to address.

TABLE 12.1 Percent of doctoral scientists and engineers with full-time employment in science and engineering, 1995.

Field	Men	Women
All S&E	85.8	73.5
Engineering	90.6	81.3
Mathematics	90.8	79.5
Physical Sciences	87.2	77.4
Life Sciences	85.3	75.9
Social and Behavioral Sciences	79.6	69.4

SOURCE: Data extracted from Table 4-7, p. 75, J. Scott Long (ed), *From Scarcity to Visibility: Gender Differences in the Careers of Doctoral Scientists and Engineers* (National Academies Press, 2001).

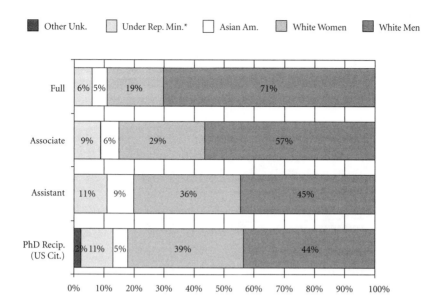

FIGURE 12.4 Faculty and PhD-recipient diversity in the United States, 1999.
* Under. Rep. Min. (underrepresented minorities) includes African Americans, Hispanic Americans, and Native Americans.
SOURCE: NCES, National Study of Post-Secondary Faculty, for faculty 1999, and NSF, Survey of Earned Doctorates, for PhD Recipients 1999.

It may be noteworthy that Greenwood is the first woman to be the provost and senior vice president for Academic Affairs of the UC; in addition, she chairs the PGA board. Both the CWSE and COSEPUP committees are chaired by women, Lilian Wu and Maxine Singer, respectively. These women and many others are providing leadership in tackling these important issues.

Summary

I have provided an overview of some of the work that the National Academies are doing to promote increased numbers of women in science and engineering careers. It is by no means an exhaustive list, but I hope it illustrates that the academy takes this issue seriously and is determined to provide both new data for analysis and new insights that may lead to more focused efforts nationwide to effect change in the culture of science.

At the end of this chapter (Appendix 1) I list the recent reports and other projects of the NRC related to this issue; I hope this will be a resource for readers. In Appendix 2, I list websites, culled from universities and agencies and organizations around the country, dealing with policy and best practices concerning women in science and engineering.

Appendix 1: Related Publications of the NRC

The following publications represent the work of the Committee on Women in Science and Education from 2000 to the present. To order any of these publications or other documents from the National Academy of Sciences, National Academy of Engineering, Institute of Medicine, or National Research Council, please contact the National Academy Press at (800) 624-6242 or (202) 334-3313; or you may visit the Academy bookstore on 500 Fifth Street, NW, Washington, DC 20001; (202) 334-3980. Please note, many of our publications can be read online free of charge.

New Release

To Recruit and Advance: Women Students and Faculty in Science and Engineering. CWSE has produced a guide to help universities recruit more women into science and engineering at all stages. This guide identifies and discusses best practices in recruitment, retention, and promotion for women scientists and engineers in academia.

Highlighted CWSE Publications:

AXXS 2002: Achieving XXcellence in Science: The Role of Professional Societies in Advancing Women's Careers in Science and Clinical Research. CWSE held a one-and-a-half-day workshop, which gathered representatives of clinical societies to discuss ways for the societies to enhance the participation of women scientists in the clinical research workforce. The workshop was a follow-up to AXXS 1999, in which representatives of science societies gathered to identify ways to improve the advancement of women in their respective fields. The workshop proceedings are available online on the NAP website: http://books.nap.edu/catalog .php?record_id=10008.

From Scarcity to Visibility: Gender Differences in the Career Outcomes of Doctoral Scientists and Engineers. This report compares the career outcomes of women and men scientists and engineers, matched by the same characteristics, across five broad fields: engineering, life sciences, mathematics, physical sciences, and social and behavioral sciences. The outcomes examined include employment status, salary, rank and tenure status, publications, amount of federal research support, employment sector, and the likelihood of remaining in science or engineering. In addition, regression analyses look at the differential effects of numerous antecedent conditions, including race/ethnicity, level of parents' education, citizenship, type of undergraduate institution, marriage, having children, quality of graduate department, and time to the PhD (http://www.nap .edu/catalog/5363.html).

Female Engineering Faculty in the U.S.: A Data Profile. This report provides information on the education and employment of approximately 1,300 female engineering faculty members in the United States, based on a survey conducted in 1996. Information is included on race/ethnicity, degrees held, employment history, tenure status, experiences with mentoring, reasons for career decisions, and employment satisfaction. The report is available for downloading at http://www.nap.edu/catalog/6130.html.

NAS Symposium on Women in Science. On April 25, 1999, the National Academy of Sciences held its first-ever symposium on women in science. Entitled "Who Will Do the Science of the Future? A Symposium on Careers of Women in Science," the event was organized by CWSE and held at the NAS annual meeting. The symposium was well attended by NAS members and the general public and received considerable attention in the scientific press. The symposium proceedings are available online on the NAP website: http://books.nap.edu/catalog.php?record_id=10008.

Other publications from NAS:

Women Scientists and Engineers Employed in Industry: Why So Few? This report addresses issues facing women entering the profession, working as bench scientists and engineers and as managers of a technological work group. (1994, 130 pp.)

Science and Engineering Programs: On Target for Women? Describes and analyzes a sample of postsecondary programs for recruiting and retaining potential and practicing scientists and engineers. Major chapters focus on undergraduate education, graduate education, and employment in academe, industry, and the federal government. (Marsha Lakes Matyas and Linda C. Skidmore, eds., 1992, 216 pp.)

Women in Science and Engineering: Increasing Their Numbers in the 1990s. In addition to providing statistics on the participation of women in the education/employment pipeline, the report summarizes the committee's deliberations relating to its role in increasing the participation and improving the status of women in science and engineering. The report further offers an ambitious strategic plan of both short- and long-term activities. (1991, 152 pp.)

Additional selected publications of the NRC:

Adviser, Teacher, Role Model, Friend: On Being a Mentor to Students in Science and Engineering (COSEPUP, 1997)

Science and Technology in the Academic Enterprise: Status, Trends, and Issues (GUIRR, 1989)

Engineering Employment Characteristics (CETS, 1985)

Personnel Needs and Training for Biomedical and Behavioral Research (IOM, 1977)

AXXS 2002: A Workshop for Clinical Societies to Enhance Women's Contributions to Science and their Profession (CWSE, 2002)

A Guide for Recruiting and Advancing Women in Science and Engineering Careers in Academia (CWSE, 2005): http://www7.nationalacademies.org/cwse/Guide.html

Gender Differences in Careers of Science, Engineering, and Mathematics Faculty (CWSE, 2006): http://www7.nationalacademies.org/cwse/Gender_differences.html

Appendix 2: Examples of Agency, Association, Consortium, Academy, and University Websites

This list, composed by Drs. France Córdova and Yolanda Moses at University of California, Riverside, focuses on diversity initiatives and best practices in recruitment and retention of women and minorities.

BEST (Building Engineering and Science Talent) report on Promoting Diversity in Higher Education: http://www.aip.org/fyi/2004/060.html

The Quiet Crisis: Falling Short in Producing American Scientific and Technical Talent: http://www.bestworkforce.org/ppt/NCTM2004.ppt

University of Washington engineering diversity programs: http://www.engr.washington.edu/advance/

National Academy of Engineering: http://www.nae.edu/nae/diversity-com.nsf?OpenDatabase

AAAS Minority Science Network: http://sciencecareers.sciencemag .org/career_development/miscinet

Faculty for the Future: http://www.engr.psu.edu/fff/

National Science Foundation, ADVANCE Program: increasing the participation and advancement of women in academic science and engineering careers: http://www.nsf.gov/funding/pgm_summ.jsp? pims_id=5383&from=fund

National Physical Science Consortium: http://www.npsc.org/

Committee on the Status of Women in Computing Research: http:// www.cra.org/Activities/craw/

Women's International Science Collaboration Program: http://www.aaas .org/international/wisc/

NSF–Alliance for Graduate Education and the Professoriate Program: http://ehrweb.aaas.org/mge/

University of California Faculty Family Friendly Edge (shows leaks in pipeline for women): http://UCfamilyedge.berkeley.edu

American Council on Education's "An Agenda for Excellence: Creating Flexibility in Tenure-Track Careers": http://www.acenet.edu/bookstore/ pdf/2005_tenure_flex_summary.pdf

Bibliography

Acharya, M., and Bennett, L. 1981. *The Status of Women in Nepal.* Volume II Part 9. Kathmandu, Nepal: Tribhuvan University.

Adovasio, J. M., Soffer, O., and Klima, B. 1996. "Upper Paleolithic Fibre Technology: Interlaced Woven Finds from Pavlov I, Czech Republic." *Antiquity* 70(269): 526–534.

Agarwal, A. 1995. "Dismantling the Divide between Indigenous and Scientific Knowledge." *Development and Change* 26:413–439.

Agarwal, B. 1986. *Cold Hearths and Barren Slopes: The Woodfuel Crisis in the Third World.* London: Zed.

Alemseged, Z., Spoor, F., Kimbel, W. H., Bobe, R., Geraads, R., Reed, D. and Wynn, J. 2006. "A Juvenile Early Hominin from Dikika, Ethiopia." *Nature* 443: 296–301.

Alibrandi, M., Thompson, A., and Hagevik, R. 2000. "Documenting a Culture." *Arc-News* 22: 27.

Alic, M. 1986. *Hypatia's Heritage.* Boston: Beacon.

Andrews, L., and Nelkin, D. 2001. *Body Bazaar: The Market for Human Tissue in the Biotechnology Age.* New York: Crown.

Angier, N. 1990. "Scientists Say Gene on Y Chromosome Makes a Man a Man." *New York Times.* July 19: 1.

Annenberg Foundation and Oregon Public Broadcasting. 2004. "Expert Interview Transcripts: Holly Ingraham, David Page, Eric Vilain." In *Rediscovering Biology: Molecular to Global Perspectives.* Electronic media: http://www.learner.org/channel/courses/biology/units/gender/experts/index.html. Accessed August 20, 2007.

Apodaca, A. 1952. "Corn and Custom: Introduction of Hybrid Corn to Spanish American Farmers in New Mexico." In *Human Problems in Technological Change: A Casebook,* ed. E. H. Spicer, 35–39. New York: Russell Sage Foundation.

Bagemihl, B. 1999. *Biological Exuberance: Animal Homosexuality and Natural Diversity*. New York: St. Martin's.

Ballard, H. L. 2004. "Impacts of Harvesting Salal (*Gaultheria shallon*) on the Olympic Peninsula, Washington: Harvester Knowledge, Science and Participation." PhD Dissertation. University of California at Berkeley.

Ballard, H., and Fortmann, L. 2007. "Collaborating Experts: Integrating Civil and Conventional Science to Inform Management of Salal (*Gaultheria shallon*)." In *Integrated Resource Management*, eds. K. Hanna and D. S. Slocombe, 164–180. Oxford: Oxford University Press.

Ballard, H. L., and Huntsinger, L. 2006. "Salal Harvester Local Ecological Knowledge, Harvest Practices and Understory Management on the Olympic Peninsula, Washington." *Human Ecology: An Interdisciplinary Journal* 34(4): 529–547.

Barry, A. 1999. "Invention and Inertia." *Cambridge Anthropology* 21(3): 62–70.

Bassey, E. J., and Ramsdale, S. J. 1994. "Increase in Femoral Bone Density in Young Women Following High-Impact Exercise." *Osteoporosis International* 4: 72–75.

Baxter, J. E. 2005. *Gender and the Archaeology of Childhood: Children, Gender and Material Culture*. Walnut Creek, CA: AltaMira.

Beale, B. 2001. "The Sexes: New Insights into the X and Y Chromosomes." *The Scientist* 15: 18.

Berta, P., Hawkins, J. B., Sinclair, A. H., Taylor, A., Griffiths, B. L., Goodfellow, P. N., and Fellous, M. 1990. "Genetic Evidence Equating SRY and the Testis-Determining Factor." *Nature* 348: 448–450.

Bertelsen, R., Lillehammer, A., and Naess, J-R. eds. 1987. *Were They All Men? An Examination of Sex Roles in Prehistoric Society*. Stavanger, Norway: Arkeologisk Museum i Stavanger.

Blondin, P. 1990. "1990 Survey of the Membership of the American Physical Society." Unpublished final report, 19, 23–24.

Blunt, A. 1994. *Travel, Gender, and Imperialism: Mary Kingsley and West Africa*. New York: Guilford.

Bocking, S. 2004. *Nature's Experts: Science, Politics and the Environment*. New Brunswick, NJ: Rutgers University Press.

Bondi, L., and Domosh, M. 1992. "Other Figures in Other Places: On Feminism, Postmodernism, and Geography." *Environment and Planning D* 10: 199–213.

Bone, K. E. 1993. "Bias in Skeletal Sexing." *American Journal of Physical Anthropology* 16(supplement): 59.

Boserup, E. 1970. *Woman's Role in Economic Development*. New York: St. Martin's.

Bradbury, H., and Reason, P. 2003. "Issues and Choice Points for Improving the Quality of Action Research." In *Community-Based Participatory Research for Health*, eds. M. Minkler and N. Wallerstein, 201–220. San Francisco: Jossey-Bass.

Brandt, S., Weedman, K., and Hundie, G. 1996. "Gurage Hide-Working, Stone Tool Use and Social Identity: An Ethnoarchaeological Perspective." In *Essays on the Gurage Language and Culture: Dedicated to Wolf Lesau on the Occasion of his 90th Birthday*, November 14, 1996, ed. G. Hudson, 35–51. Wiesbaden: Harrassowitz.

Braxton, J. M., Luckey, W., and Helland, P. 2002. *Institutionalizing a Broader View of Scholarship Through Boyer's Four Domains.* Hoboken, NJ: Jossey-Bass.

Brokensha, D., Warren, D. M., and Werner, O. 1980. *Indigenous Knowledge Systems and Development.* Washington, DC: University Press of America.

Broude, N., and Garrard, M. D. eds. 1994. *The Power of Feminist Art: The American Movement of the 1970s, History and Impact.* New York: Harry N. Abrams.

Brown, K. 2000. "Ancient DNA Applications in Human Osteoarchaeology: Achievements, Problems, and Potential." In *Human Osteology in Archaeology and Forensic Sciences,* eds. M. Cox and S. Mays, 455–474. London: Greenwich Medical Media.

Brumfiel, E. 1991. "Weaving and Cooking: Women's Production in Aztec Mexico." In *Engendering Archaeology: Women and Prehistory,* eds. J. Gero and M. Conkey, 224–251. Oxford: Basil Blackwell.

Brumfiel, E. 1992. "Breaking and Entering the Ecosystem: Gender, Class, and Faction Steal the Show." *American Anthropologist* 94(3): 551–567.

Bug, A. 2003. "Has Feminism Changed Physics?" *Signs: Journal of Women in Culture and Society* 28(3): 881–899.

Bush, V. 1945. "Science—The Endless Frontier: A Report to the President on a Program for Postwar Scientific Research." Reprinted 1990. Washington, DC: National Science Foundation.

Byrne, D. R. 2003. "Nervous Landscapes: Race and Space in Australia." *Journal of Social Archaeology* 3(2): 169–193.

Campbell, B. ed. 1996. *The Miombo in Transition: Woodlands and Welfare in Africa.* Bogor, Indonesia: Center for International Forestry Research.

Caniago, I., and Siebert, S. F. 1998. "Medicinal Plant Ecology, Knowledge and Conservation in Kalimantan, Indonesia." *Economic Botany* 52: 229–250.

Chambers, R. 1983. *Rural Development: Putting the Last First.* London: Longman.

Clayman Institute for Gender Research, Stanford University. 2006. "Dual-Career Academic Couple Study." Unpublished results.

Clutter, M. 1998. "Background Programs to POWRE." In *Final Report on Professional Opportunities for Women in Research and Education (POWRE) Workshop,* eds. S. V. Rosser and M. L. Zieseniss, Appendix B. Gainesville, FL: Center for Women's Studies and Gender Research.

Colfer, C. 1981. "Women and Men and Time in the Forests of East Kalimantan." *Borneo Research Bulletin* 13(2): 75–85.

Committee on Maximizing the Potential of Women in Academic Science and Engineering, National Academy of Sciences, National Academy of Engineering, and Institute of Medicine. 2006. *Beyond Bias and Barriers: Fulfilling the Potential of Women in Academic Science and Engineering.* Washington, DC: National Academies Press.

Committee on Women in Science and Engineering (CSWE). 2006. *To Recruit and Advance Women Students and Faculty in U.S. Science and Engineering.* Washington, DC: National Academies Press.

Conkey, M. W. 1997. "Mobilizing Ideologies: Paleolithic 'Art,' Gender Trouble, and Thinking About Alternatives." In *Women in Human Evolution*, ed. L. D. Hager, 172–207. London: Routledge.

Conkey, M. W. 2003. "Has Feminism Changed Archeology?" *Signs: Journal of Women in Culture and Society* 28: 867–880.

Conkey, M. W. 2005. "Dwelling at the Margins, Action at the Intersection? Feminist and Indigenous Archaeologies." *Archaeologies* 1(1): 9–59.

Conkey, M. W., and Gero, J. M. 1997. "From Programme to Practice: Gender and Feminism in Archaeology." *Annual Review of Anthropology* 26: 411–437.

Conkey, M. W., and Spector, J. D. 1984. "Archaeology and the Study of Gender." In *Advances in Archaeological Method and Theory*, vol. 7, ed. M. B. Schiffer, 1–38. New York: Academic Press.

Conkey, M., and Tringham, R. 1996. "Cultivating Thinking/Challenging Authority: Some Experiments in Feminist Pedagogy in Archaeology." In *Gender and Archaeology*, ed. R. Wright, 224–250. Philadelphia: University of Pennsylvania Press.

Conkey, M., and Williams, S. 1991. "Original Narratives: The Political Economy of Gender in Archaeology." In *Gender at the Crossroads of Knowledge: Feminist Anthropology in the Post-Modern Era*, ed. M. diLeonardo, 102–139. Berkeley: University of California Press.

Cooke, B., and Kothari, U. eds. 2001. *Participation: The New Tyranny?* London: Zed.

Cosgrove, L. 2000. "Speaking for Ourselves: Feminist Methods and Community Psychology." *American Journal of Community Psychology* 28(6): 815–838.

Costin, C. L. 1996. "Exploring the Relationship between Gender and Craft in Complex Societies: Methodological and Theoretical Issues of Gender Attribution." In *Gender and Archaeology*, ed. R. P. Wright, 111–142. Philadelphia: University of Pennsylvania Press.

Cowen, R. S. 1983. *More Work for Mother: The Ironies of Household Technology from the Open Hearth to the Microwave*. New York: Basic Books.

Creager, A., Lunbeck, E., and Schiebinger, L. eds. 2001. *Feminism in Twentieth-Century Science, Technology, and Medicine*. Chicago: University of Chicago Press.

Croll, E. 1985. *Women and Rural Development in China: Production and Reproduction*. Women, Work and Development, No. 11. Geneva: International Labor Office.

Crown, P. L. ed. 2000. *Women and Men in the Prehispanic Southwest*. Santa Fe, NM: School of American Research Press.

Darwin, C. 1871 (1936 edition). *The Descent of Man and Selection in Relation to Sex*. New York: Modern Library.

Davis, D. 1995. "Gender-Based Differences in the Ethnoveterinary Knowledge of Afghan Nomadic Pastoralists." *Indigenous Knowledge and Development Monitor* 3(1): 3–5.

Davison, J. ed. 1988. *Agriculture, Women and the Land: The African Experience*. Boulder: Westview.

Day, M. H., Leakey, M. D., and Olson, T. R. 1980. "On the Status of *Australopithecus afarensis*." *Science* 207: 1102–1103.

Deere, C. D. 1982. "The Division of Labor by Sex in Agriculture: A Peruvian Case Study." *Economic and Development and Cultural Change* 30(4): 795–811.

Deutsch, N. L. 2004. "Positionality and the Pen: Reflections on the Process of Becoming a Feminist Researcher and Writer." *Qualitative Inquiry* 10(6):885–902.

Dixon, R. 1978. *Rural Women at Work: Strategies for Development in South Asia*. Baltimore, MD: Johns Hopkins University Press.

Doane, M. A. 1982. "Film and the Masquerade: Theorizing the Female Spectator." *Screen* 23: 74–87.

Dobres, M.-A. 1992. "Re-Considering Venus Figurines: A Feminist-Inspired Re-Analysis." In *Ancient Images, Ancient Thought: The Archaeology of Ideology*, eds. A. S. Goldsmith, S. Garvie, D. Selin, and J. Smith, 245–262. Calgary: Archaeological Association, University of Calgary.

Dobres, M.-A. 1995. "Beyond Gender Attribution: Some Methodological Issues for Engendering the Past." In *Gendered Archaeology: The Second Australian Women in Archaeology Conference*, eds. J. Balme and W. Beck, 51–66. Canberra: Australian National University.

Dobres, M.-A. 2000. *Technology and Social Agency*. Oxford: Basil Blackwell.

Dobres, M.-A. 2004. "Digging Up Gender in the Earliest Human Societies." In *Companion to Gender History*, eds. M. Weisner-Hanks and T. Meade, 211–226. Oxford: Basil Blackwell.

Domosh, M. 1991. "Towards a Feminist Historiography of Geography." *Transactions of the Institute of British Geographers* NS 16: 95–104.

Donlon, D. 1993. "Imbalance in the Sex Ratio in Collections of Australian Aboriginal Skeletal Remains." In *Women in Archaeology: A Feminist Critique*, eds. H. DuCros and L. Smith, 98–103. Occasional Papers in Prehistory, No. 23. Canberra: Australian National University.

DuCros, H., and Smith, L. eds. 1993. *Women in Archaeology: A Feminist Critique*. Occasional Papers in Prehistory, No. 23. Canberra: Australian National University.

Duhard, J. 1989. *La Réalisme Physiologique des Figurations Féminines Sculptées du Paléolithique Supérieur en France*. Bordeaux: Université de Bordeaux I.

Eagly, A., and Karau, S. 2002. "Role Congruity Theory of Prejudice Towards Female Leaders." *Psychological Review* 109: 573–598.

Eckel, P., and Kezar, A. 2003. *Taking the Reins: Institutional Transformation in Higher Education*. Westport, CT: Praeger.

Edsall, T. 1995. "Pollsters View Gender Gap as Political Fixture: White Men Heed GOP Call; Women Lean to Democrats." *Washington Post*. August 15: A-1.

Eicher, E. M., and Washburn, L. L. 1986. "Genetic Control of Primary Sex Determination in Mice." *Annual Review of Genetics* 20: 327–360.

Engelstad, E. 1992. "Images of Power and Contradiction: Feminist Theory and Post-Processual Archaeology." *Antiquity* 65(248): 502–514.

Etzkowitz, H., Kemelgor, C., and Uzzi, B. 2000. *Athena Unbound: The Advancement of Women in Science and Technology*. New York: Cambridge University Press.

European Commission. 2006. "Annex 4: Integrating the Gender Dimension in FP6

Projects." *Guide for Proposers, Research and Innovation: Structuring the European Research Area*: 52.

Falk, D. 1997. "Brain Evolution in Females: An Answer to Mr. Lovejoy." In *Women in Human Evolution*, ed. L. D. Hager, 114–136. London: Routledge.

Fausto-Sterling, A. 1989. "Life in the XY Corral." *Women's Studies International Forum* 12: 319–331.

Fausto-Sterling, A. 2005. "The Bare Bones of Sex: Part 1—Sex and Gender." *Signs: Journal of Women in Culture and Society* 30: 1491–1527.

Fedigan, L. M. 1986. "The Changing Role of Women in Models of Human Origins." *Annual Review of Anthropology* 15: 25–66.

Ford, C. E., Miller, O. J., Polani, P. E., de Almeida, J. C., and Briggs, J. H. 1959. "A Sex-Chromosome Anomaly in a Case of Gonadal Dysgenesis (Turner's Syndrome)." *Lancet* 1: 711–713.

Fortmann, L. 1981. "The Plight of the Invisible Farmer: The Effect of National Agricultural Policy on Women in Africa." In *Women and Technological Change in Developing Countries. AAAS Selected Symposium* 53, eds. R. Dauber and M. L. Cain, 205–214. Boulder: Westview.

Fortmann, L. 1984. "Economic Status and Women's Participation in Agriculture: A Botswana Case Study." *Rural Sociology* 49(3): 452–464.

Fortmann, L., and Rocheleau, D. 1985. "Women and Agroforestry: Four Myths and Three Case Studies." *Agroforestry Systems* 2(4): 253–272.

Franklin, M. 2001. "A Black Feminist-Inspired Archaeology?" *Journal of Social Archaeology* 1(1): 108–125.

Franklin, S., and Roberts, C. 2006. *Born and Made: An Ethnography of Pre-implantation Genetic Diagnosis*. Princeton, NJ: Princeton University Press.

Frickel, S., and Vincent, M. B. 2007. "Katrina, Contamination and the Unintended Organization of Ignorance." *Technology in Society* 29: 181–188.

Gamble, C. 1982. "Interaction and Alliance in Palaeolithic Society." *Man* (n.s.) 17(1): 92–107.

Gero, J. 1991. "Genderlithics: Women's Roles in Stone Tool Production." In *Engendering Archaeology: Women and Prehistory*, eds. J. Gero and M. Conkey, 163–193. Oxford: Basil Blackwell.

Gero, J., and Conkey, M. W. eds. 1991. *Engendering Archaeology: Women and Prehistory*. Oxford: Basil Blackwell.

Gifford-Gonzalez, D. 1992. "Gaps in Zooarchaeological Analyses of Butchery: Is Gender an Issue?" In *Bones to Behavior*, ed. J. Hudson, 181–199. Carbondale, IL: Southern Illinois University Center for Archaeological Investigations.

Gilchrist, R. 1999. *Gender and Archaeology: Contesting the Past*. London: Routledge.

Goldberg, P. 1968. "Are Women Prejudiced Against Women?" *Transaction* 5: 28–30.

Goodfellow, P. N., Craig, I. W., Smith, J. C., and Wolfe, J. 1987. *The Mammalian Y Chromosome: Molecular Search for the Sex-Determining Factor*. Cambridge, UK: Company of Biologists Ltd.

Graves, J. A. 2000. "Human Y Chromosome, Sex Determination, and Spermatogenesis: A Feminist View." *Biology of Reproduction* 63: 667–676.

Graves, J. A. 2006. "Sex Chromosome Specialization and Degeneration in Mammals." *Cell* 124: 901–914.

Graves, J. A., and Short, R. V. 1990. "Y or X—Which Determines Sex?" *Reproductive Fertility Development* 2: 729–735.

Grosz, E. 1992. "Voyeurism/Exhibitionism/The Gaze." In *Feminism and Psychoanalysis: A Critical Dictionary*, ed. E. Wright, 447–450. Oxford: Blackwell.

Grove, R. H. 1995. *Green Imperialism: Colonial Expansion, Tropical Island Edens, and the Origins of Environmentalism, 1600–1860*. Cambridge, UK: Cambridge University Press.

Gura, T. 1995. "Estrogen: Key Player in Heart Disease Among Women." *Science* 269: 771–773.

Guthrie, R. 1984. "Ethological Observations from Palaeolithic Art." In *La Contribution de la zoologie et de l'éthologie à l'interprétation de l'art des peuples chasseurs préhistoriques*, eds. H.-G. Bandi, W. Huber, M.-R. Sauter, and B. Sitter, 35–74. Fribourg, Switzerland: Editions Univérsitaires.

Hager, L. D. 1991. "The Evidence for Sex Differences in the Hominid Fossil Record." In *The Archaeology of Gender*, eds. D. Walde and N. Willows, 46–49. Calgary: Archaeological Association, University of Calgary.

Hager, L. D. 1996. "Sex Differences in the Sciatic Notch of Great Apes and Modern Humans." *American Journal of Physical Anthropology* 99: 287–300.

Hager, L. D. ed. 1997. *Women in Human Evolution*. New York: Routledge.

Hanson, S. 2002. "Connections." *Gender, Place and Culture* 9(3): 301–303.

Hanson, S., Kominiak, T., and Carlin, S. 1997. "Assessing the Impact of Location on Women's Labor Market Outcomes: A Methodological Exploration." *Geographical Analysis* 29(4): 282–297.

Haraway, D. 1991. *Simians, Cyborgs, and Women: The Reinvention of Nature*. New York: Routledge.

Haraway, D. 1999. "Situated Knowledges: The Science Question in Feminism and the Privilege of Partial Perspective." In *The Science Studies Reader*, ed. M. Biagioli, 172–188. New York: Routledge.

Harding, S. 1991. *Whose Science? Whose Knowledge*. Ithaca, NY: Cornell University Press.

Harley, J. B. 1992. "Deconstructing the Map." In *Writing Worlds: Discourse, Text and Metaphor in the Representation of Landscape*, eds. T. J. Barnes and J. S. Duncan, 231–247. New York: Routledge.

Haseltine, F., and Jacobson, B. eds. 1997. *Women's Health Research: A Medical and Policy Primer*. Washington, DC: Health.

Hecht, S. 1999. *Client-Orientation in the Management of Participatory Plant Breeding*. Draft prepared for the Systemwide Program on Participatory Research and Gender Analysis, CIAT: Cali Colombia.

Heifetz, R., and Laurie, D. 1997. "The Work of Leadership." *Harvard Business Review* 75: 124–134.

Heilman, M. E., Wallen, A. S., Fuchs, D., and Tamkins, M. M. 2004. "Penalties for Success: Reactions to Women Who Succeed at Male Gender-Typed Tasks." *Journal of Applied Psychology* 89: 416–427.

Hochschild, A. 1989. *The Second Shift.* New York: Avon.

Hopkins, N. 2006. "Diversification of a University Faculty: Observations on Hiring Women Faculty in the Schools of Science and Engineering at MIT." *MIT Faculty Newsletter* 18(4): 1, 16–23.

Horn, S. P., and R. L. Sanford, Jr. 1992. "Holocene Fires in Costa Rica." *Biotropica* 24(3): 354–361.

Hrdy, S. B. 1981. "Lucy's Husband: What Did He Stand For?" *Science Watch*, July–August.

Hrdy, S. B. 1999. *The Woman that Never Evolved.* Cambridge, Mass.: Harvard University Press.

Hubbard, R. 1979. "Have Only Men Evolved?" In *Discovering Reality*, eds. S. Harding and M. Hintikka, 45–69. Cambridge, MA: Schenkman.

Huffman, N. H. 1997. "Charting the Other Maps: Cartography and Visual Methods in Feminist Research." In *Thresholds in Feminist Geography: Difference, Methodology, Representation*, eds. J. P. Jones III, H. J. Nast, and S. M. Roberts, 255–283. Lanham, MD: Rowman and Littlefield.

Hulme, D., and Murphree, M. eds. 2001. *African Wildlife and Livelihoods: The Promise and Performance of Community Conservation.* Oxford: James Currey.

Isaac, G. L. 1978. "The Food Sharing Behavior of Protohuman Hominids." *Scientific American* 238: 90–108.

İşcan, M. Y., and Kennedy, K. A. R. eds. 1989. *Reconstruction of Life from the Skeleton.* New York: Alan R. Liss.

Ivie, R., and Ray, K. N. 2005. *Women in Physics and Astronomy, 2005.* AIP Publication No. R-430.02.

Johanson, D. C., and Edey, M. 1981. *Lucy: The Beginnings of Humankind.* New York: Simon and Schuster.

Johanson, D. C., Lovejoy, C. O., Kimbel, W. H., White, T. D., Ward, R. C., Asfaw, B., and Coppens, Y. 1982. "Morphology of the Pliocene Partial Hominid Skeleton (A.L. 288-1) from the Hadar Formation, Ethiopia." *American Journal of Physical Anthropology* 57: 403–451.

Johnson, M. 1999. *Archaeological Theory: An Introduction.* Oxford: Blackwell.

Jones, S. 2002. *Y: The Descent of Men.* London: Little Brown.

Jost, A., Gonse-Danysz, P., and Jacquot, R. 1953. "Studies on Physiology of Fetal Hypophysis in Rabbits and Its Relation to Testicular Function." *Journal of Physiology (Paris)* 45: 134–136.

Joyce, R. 1993. "Women's Work: Images of Production and Reproduction in Pre-Hispanic Southern Central America." *Current Anthropology* 34(3): 255–274.

Joyce, R. 1998. "Performing the Body in Prehispanic Central America." *Res: Anthropology and Aesthetics* 33: 147–165.

Joyce, R. 2000. "Girling the Girl and Boying the Boy: The Production of Adulthood in Ancient Mesoamerica." *World Archaeology* 31(3): 473–483.

Joyce, R. 2001. *Gender and Power in Prehispanic Mesoamerica.* Austin: University of Texas Press.

Joyce, R. 2004. "Embodied Subjectivity: Gender, Femininity, Masculinity, Sexuality." In *A Companion to Social Archaeology,* eds. L. Meskell and R. Preucel, 82–95. Oxford: Blackwell.

Joyce, R. 2005. "Archaeology of the Body." *Annual Review of Anthropology* 34: 139–158.

Joyce, R., and Gillespie, S. eds. 2000. *Beyond Kinship: Social and Material Reproduction in House Societies.* Philadelphia: University of Pennsylvania Press.

Jurmain, R., Kilgore, L., and Trevathan, W. 2005. *Introduction to Physical Anthropology.* Tenth edition. Belmont, CA: Thomson Wadsworth.

Just, W., Rau, W., Vogel, W., Akhverdian, M., Fredga, K., Marshall Graves, J. A., and Lyapunova, E. 1995. "Absence of SRY in Species of the Vole Ellobius." *Natural Genetics* 11: 117–118.

Kaestle, F., and Horsburgh, K. A. 2002. "Ancient DNA in Anthropology: Methods, Applications and Ethics." *Yearbook of Physical Anthropology* 45: 92–130.

Kahle, J. 1987. "Images of Science: The Physicist and the Cowboy." In *Gender Issues in Science Education,* eds. B. Fraser and G. Giddings, 1–11. Perth: Curtin University of Technology.

Katz, C. 1994. "Playing the Field: Questions of Fieldwork in Geography." *Professional Geographer* 46(1): 67–72.

Kealhofer, L. 2002. "Changing Perceptions of Risk: The Development of Agro-Ecosystems in SE Asia." *American Anthropologist* 104: 178–194.

Keller, E. F. 1992. *Secrets of Life, Secrets of Death: Essays on Language, Gender and Science.* New York: Routledge.

Keller, E. F. 2000. *The Century of the Gene.* Cambridge, MA: Harvard University Press.

Keller, E. F., and Longino, H. 1996. *Feminism and Science (Oxford Readings in Feminism).* Oxford: Oxford University Press.

Kerns, B. K., Pilz, D., Ballard, H., and Alexander, S. J. 2003. "Compatible Management of Understory Forest Resources and Timber." In *Compatible Forest Management,* eds. R. A. Monserud, R. W. Haynes, and A. C. Johnson. Boston: Kluwer Academic Publishers, 337–381.

Kimbel, W. H., and White, T. D. 1988. "Variation, Sexual Dimorphism and the Taxonomy of *Australopithecus.*" In *The Evolutionary History of the Robust Australopithecines,* ed. F. Grine, 175–192. New York: Aldine.

Kirch, P., and Sharp, W. 2005. "Coral 230-Th Dating of the Imposition of a Ritual Control Hierarchy in Precontact Hawai'i." *Science* 307: 102–104.

Kirkby, R. A. 1981. "The Study of Agronomic Practices and Maize Varieties Appropriate to the Circumstances of Small Farmers in Highland Ecuador." PhD Dissertation. Cornell University.

Kjellström, A. "Evaluations of Sex Assessment Using Weighted Traits on Incomplete Skeletal Remains." *International Journal of Osteoarchaeology* 14: 360–373.

Koblitz, A. H. 1983. *A Convergence of Lives: Sofia Kovalevskaia, Scientist, Writer, Revolutionary.* Cambridge, MA: Birkhäuser Boston.

Kole, A. 1995, August 3. *Highlights of the Affirmative Action Review—Report to the President by the Office of the General Counsel.* Department of Education. Washington, DC: GPO.

Konrad, M. 2005. *Nameless Relations: Anonymity, Melanesia, and Reproductive Gift Exchange between British Ova Donors and Recipients.* Oxford: Berghahn.

Koopman, P., Gubbay, J., Vivian, N., Goodfellow, P., and Lovell-Badge, R. 1991. "Male Development of Chromosomally Female Mice Transgenic for SRY." *Nature* 351: 117–121.

Krogman, W. M., and İşcan, M. Y. 1986. *The Human Skeleton in Forensic Medicine.* Second edition. Springfield, IL: C.C. Thomas.

Kuhnlein, H. V., and Receveur, O. 1996. "Dietary Change and Traditional Food Systems of Indigenous Peoples." *Annual Review of Nutrition* 16: 417–442.

Kwan, M-P. 2000. "Interactive Geovisualization of Activity-Travel Patterns Using 3D GIS: A Methodological Exploration with a Large Data Set." *Transportation Research C* 8: 185–203.

Kwan, M-P. 2002a. "Is GIS for Women? Reflections on the Critical Discourse in the 1990s." *Gender, Place and Culture* 9: 271–279.

Kwan, M-P. 2002b. "Feminist Visualization: Re-envisioning GIS as a Method in Feminist Geographic Research." *Annals of the Association of American Geographers* 92: 645–661.

Kwan, M-P. 2004. "Beyond Difference: From Canonical Geography to Hybrid Geographies." *Annals of the Association of American Geographers* 94: 756–763.

Kwan, M-P. 2007a. "Affecting Geospatial Technologies: Toward a Feminist Politics of Emotion." *Professional Geographer* 59(1): 22–34.

Kwan, M-P. 2007b. "Beyond Master Narrative: Re-presenting the Experience of American Muslims After 9/11 Through Oral Histories and Visual Narratives." Manuscript.

Kwan, M-P., and Lee, J. 2004. "Geovisualization of Human Activity Patterns Using 3D GIS." In *Spatially Integrated Social Science: Examples in Best Practice*, eds. M. F. Goodchild and D. G. Janelle, 48–66. Oxford: Oxford University Press.

Lancaster, J. B. 1975. *Primate Behavior and the Emergence of Human Culture.* New York: Holt, Rinehart and Winston.

Landecker, H. 2000. "Immortality, in Vitro: A History of the HeLa Cell Line." In *Biotechnology and Culture*, ed. P. Brodwin, 53–72. Bloomington: Indiana University Press.

Laws, G. 1997. "Women's Life Courses, Spatial Mobility, and State Policies." In *Thresholds in Feminist Geography: Difference, Methodology, Representation*, eds. J. P. Jones III, H. J. Nast, and S. M. Roberts, 47–64. New York: Rowman and Littlefield.

Lauer, N. C. 2000, July 18. "Judge Upholds Bush's Anti-Affirmative Action Plan." Accessed August 20, 2007 from http://www.womensenews.org.

Leach, M. 1994. *Rainforest Relations: Gender and Resource Use Among the Mende of Gola, Sierra Leone.* Washington, DC: Smithsonian.

Leakey, M. D. 1984. *Disclosing the Past: An Autobiography.* New York: Doubleday.

Lederman, M., and Bartsch, I. eds. 2001. *The Gender and Science Reader.* New York: Routledge.

Lee, R. B. 1968. "What Hunters Do for a Living." In *Man the Hunter*, eds. R. B. Lee and I. DeVore, 30–48. Chicago: Aldine.

Lesure, R. 1997. "Figurines and Social Identities in Early Sedentary Societies of Coastal Chiapas, Mexico, 1550–800 B.C." In *Women in Prehistory: North America and Mesoamerica*, eds. C. Claassen and R. Joyce, 227–248. Philadelphia: University of Pennsylvania Press.

Lewis, W., and Lewis, M. E. 1990. "Obstetrical Use of Parasitic Fungus *Balansia cyperi* by Amazonian Jivaro Women." *Economic Botany* 44: 131–133.

Light, J. 1995. "The Digital Landscape: New Space for Women?" *Gender, Place and Culture* 2: 133–146.

Lock, M. 2001. *Twice Dead: Organ Transplants and the Reinvention of Death.* Berkeley: University of California Press.

Long, J. S. 2001. *From Scarcity to Visibility: Gender Differences in the Careers of Doctoral Scientists and Engineers.* Washington, DC: National Academies Press.

Longino, H. 1990. *Science as Social Knowledge.* Princeton, NJ: Princeton University Press.

Longino, H. 1994. "In Search of Feminist Epistemology." *Monist* 77(4): 472–485.

Longino, H. 2002. *The Fate of Knowledge.* Princeton, NJ: Princeton University Press.

Lovejoy, C. O. 1981. "The Origin of Man." *Science* 211: 341–350.

MacCormack, C. P. 1982. "Control of Land, Labor, and Capital in Rural Southern Sierra Leone." In *Women and Work in Africa*, ed. E. Bay, 35–53. Boulder: Westview.

Mack, R. T. 1992. "Gendered Site: Archaeology, Representation, and the Female Body." In *Ancient Images, Ancient Thought: The Archaeology of Ideology*, eds. A. S. Goldsmith, S. Garvie, D. Selin, and J. Smith, 235–244. Calgary: University of Calgary Archaeological Association.

Marvel, K. Forthcoming. "The Ongoing Demographic Shift in the AAS." In *Women in Astronomy II: Why So Few Women in Science and What Can Be Done About It*, ed. C. M. Urry.

Mason, M. A., and Goulden, M. 2002. "Do Babies Matter (Part I)? The Effect of Family Formation on the Lifelong Careers of Academic Men and Women." *Academe* 88(6): 21–27.

Mason, M. A., and Goulden, M. 2004. "Do Babies Matter (Part II)? Closing the Baby Gap." *Academe* 90(6): 10–15.

Mason, S. R., Hather, J. G., and Hillman, G. 1994. "Preliminary Investigation of the Plant Macro-Remains from Dolní Vestonice II, and Its Implications for the Role of Plant Foods in Palaeolithic and Mesolithic Europe." *Antiquity* 68(258): 48–56.

Matson, P. 1996. "The Atmosphere and You." Talk presented in the Department of Environmental Science, Policy and Management. University of California, Berkeley. April 10.

Matthews, S., Burton, L., and Detwiler, J. 2001. "Viewing People and Places: Conceptual and Methodological Issues in Coupling Geographic Information Analysis and Ethnographic Research." Paper presented at conference on GIS and Critical Geographic Research, Hunter College, New York, February 25.

Mattingly, D., and Falconer-Al-Hindi, K. 1995. "Should Women Count? A Context for the Debate." *Professional Geographer* 47: 427–435.

Mauer, R. 1996. *Beyond the Wall of Resistance: Unconventional Strategies that Build Support for Change.* New York: Bard.

Mayberry, M., Subramaniam, B., and Weasel, L. eds. 2001. *Feminist Science Studies: A New Generation.* New York: Routledge.

Mays, S., and Cox, M. 2000. "Sex Determination in Skeletal Remains." *In Human Osteology in Archaeology and Forensic Sciences*, eds. M. Cox and S. Mays, 117–130. London: Greenwich Medical Media.

McDermott, L. 1996. "Self-Representation in Upper Paleolithic Figurines." *Current Anthropology* 37: 227–276.

McDowell, L. 1992. "Doing Feminism, Feminists, and Research Methods in Human Geography." *Transactions of the Institute of British Geographers* New Series 17(4): 399–416.

McElreavey, K., Vilain. E., Abbas, N., Herskowitz, I., and Fellous, M. 1993. "A Regulatory Cascade Hypothesis for Mammalian Sex Determination: SRY Represses a Negative Regulator of Male Development." *Proceedings of the National Academy of Science USA* 90: 3368–3372.

McHenry, H. M. 1991. "Sexual Dimorphism in *Australopithecus afarensis.*" *Journal of Human Evolution* 20: 21–32.

McLafferty, S. 1995. "Counting for Women." *Professional Geographer* 47: 436–442.

McLafferty, S. 2002. "Mapping Women's Worlds: Knowledge, Power and the Bounds of GIS." *Gender, Place and Culture* 9: 263–269.

McNeil, L., and Sher, M. 1998. *Dual Science Career Study.* Electronic media: http://www.physics.wm.edu/~sher/survey.html. Accessed August 20, 2007.

Merton, P., Froyd, J., Clark, M. C., and Richardson, J. 2004. "Challenging the Norm in Engineering Education: Understanding Organizational Culture and Curricular Change." *Proceedings, ASEE Annual Conference*, June 20–23, 2004.

Meskell, L. 1998. "Intimate Archaeologies: The Case of Kha and Merit." *World Archaeology* 29: 363–379.

Meyerson, D. E. 2003. *Tempered Radicals: How Everyday Leaders Inspire Change at Work.* Boston: Harvard Business School Press.

Minkler, M., and Wallerstein, N. eds. 2003. *Community-Based Participatory Research for Health.* San Francisco: Jossey-Bass.

Monyo, E. S., Ipinge, S. A., Heinrich, G. M., and Lechner, W. R. 1977. *Farmer Participatory Research in Practice: Experiences with Pearl Millet Farmers in Namibia.*

Paper presented at SADC/ICRISAT Regional Workshop on Farmer Participatory Research Approaches, Harare, Zimbabwe, July 7–11, 1977.

Moore, H. 1995. "The Problems of Origins: Poststructuralism and Beyond." In *Interpreting Archaeology, Finding Meaning in the Past*, eds. I. Hodder, M. Shanks, A. Alexandri, V. Buchli, J. Carman, J. Last, and G. Lucas, 51–53. London: Routledge.

Moser, S. 1998. *Ancestral Images: The Iconography of Human Evolution*. Ithaca, NY: Cornell University Press.

Muntemba, S. 1982. "Women as Food Producers and Suppliers in the Twentieth Century: The Case of Zambia." *Development Dialogue* 1–2: 29–50.

Murail, P., Bruzek, J., and Braga, J. 1999. "A New Approach to Sexual Diagnosis in Past Populations: Practical Adjustments from Van Vark's Procedure." *International Journal of Osteoarchaeology* 9:39–53.

Murphy, J. S. 1989. "The Look in Sartre and Rich." In *The Thinking Muse: Feminism and Modern French Philosophy*, eds. J. Allen and I. M. Young, 101–112. Bloomington: Indiana University Press.

Nash, C. 1994. "Remapping the Body/Land: New Cartographies of Identity, Gender, and Landscape in Ireland." In *Writing Women and Space: Colonial and Postcolonial Geographies*, eds. A. Blunt and G. Rose, 227–250. New York: Guilford.

Nash, C. 1996. "Reclaiming Vision: Looking at Landscape and the Body." *Gender, Place and Culture* 3: 149–169.

National Science Foundation (NSF). 1993. *Education and Human Resources Program for Women and Girls Program Announcement* (NSF 93-126). Arlington, VA: National Science Foundation.

National Science Foundation (NSF). 1997. *Professional Opportunities for Women in Research and Education Program Announcement*. Arlington, VA.: National Science Foundation.

National Science Foundation (NSF). 2000. *Women, Minorities, and Persons with Disabilities in Science and Engineering* (NSF 00-327). Arlington, VA: National Science Foundation.

National Science Foundation (NSF). 2001a. *ADVANCE Program Solicitation*. Arlington, VA: National Science Foundation.

National Science Foundation (NSF). 2001b. *ADVANCE Institutional Transformation Awards*. Electronic media: http://www.nsf.gov/advance. Accessed October 1, 2001.

Nead, L. 1997. "Mapping the Self: Gender, Space, and Modernity in Mid-Victorian London." *Environment and Planning A* 29: 659–672.

Nelson, M., Nelson, S., and Wylie, A. eds. 1994. *Equity Issues for Women in Archaeology*. Archaeological Papers of the American Anthropological Association. Washington, DC: American Anthropological Association.

Nelson, S. 1990. "Diversity of the Upper Paleolithic 'Venus' Figurines and Archaeological Mythology." In *Powers of Observation*, eds. S. Nelson and A. Kehoe, 11–22. Archaeological Papers of the American Anthropological Association, 2(1). Washington, DC: American Anthropological Association.

Neumaier, D. ed. 1995. *Reframings: New American Feminist Photographies*. Philadelphia: Temple University Press.

Norsigian, J., Diskin, V., Doress-Worters, P., Pincus, J., Sanford, W., and Swenson, N. 1999. "The Boston Women's Health Book Collective and Our Bodies, Ourselves: A Brief History and Reflection." *Journal of the American Medical Women's Association* 54(1): 35–39.

Novartis Foundation. 2002. *The Genetics and Biology of Sex Determination.* Novartis Foundation Symposium no. 244. New York: John Wiley.

Ohmagari, K., and Berkes, F. 1997. "Transmission of Indigenous Knowledge and Bush Skills Among the Western James Bay Cree Women of Subarctic Canada." *Human Ecology* 25(2): 197–222.

Osborne, W. 1994. *"You Sound Like a Ladies Orchestra": A Case History of Sexism Against Abbie Conant in the Munich Philharmonic.* Electronic media: http://www.osborne-conant.org/ladies.htm. Accessed August 20, 2007.

Owen, L. 2005. *Distorting the Past: Gender and the Division of Labor in the European Upper Paleolithic.* Tübingen: Kerns.

Page, D., Mosher, R., Simpson, E., Fisher, E., Mardon, G., Pollack, J., McGillivray, B., de la Chapelle, A., and Brown, L. 1987. "The Sex-Determining Region of the Human Y Chromosome Encodes a Finger Protein." *Cell* 51(6): 1091–1104.

Paludi, M., and Strayer, L. 1985. "What's in an Author's Name? Differential Evaluations of Performance as a Function of Author's Name." *Sex Roles* 12: 353–360.

Pavlovskaya, M. E. 2002. "Mapping Urban Change and Changing GIS: Other Views of Economic Restructuring." *Gender, Place and Culture* 9(3): 281–289.

Peterson, J. 2002. *Sexual Revolutions: Gender and Labor at the Dawn of Agriculture.* Walnut Creek, CA: AltaMira.

Pickford, M., and Senut, B. 2001. "Millennium Ancestor, a 6-Million Years-Old Bipedal Hominid from Kenya: Recent Discoveries Push Back Human Origins by 1.5 Million Years." *South African Journal of Science* 97: 2–22.

Pile, S., and Thrift, N. 1995. "Mapping the Subject." In *Mapping the Subject: Geographies of Cultural Transformation,* eds. S. Pile and N. Thrift, 13–51. London: Routledge.

Podolsky, S., and Tauber, A. 1997. *The Generation of Diversity: Clonal Selection Theory and the Rise of Molecular Immunology.* Cambridge, MA: Harvard University Press.

Pollock, G. 1988. *Vision and Difference: Femininity, Feminism and Histories of Art.* London: Routledge.

Posey, D. A., and Dutfield, G. 1996. *Beyond Intellectual Property: Toward Traditional Resource Rights for Indigenous People and Local Communities.* Ottawa: IDRC.

Puffer, J. C. 2002. "Gender Verification of Female Olympic Athletes." *Medicine and Science in Sports and Exercise* 34: 1543.

Pyburn, K. A. ed. 2004. *Ungendering Civilization.* London: Routledge.

Rahm, J., and Charbonneau, P. 1997. "Probing Stereotypes through Students' Drawings of Scientists." *American Journal of Physics* 65: 774–778.

Rapp, R. 1999. *Testing Women, Testing the Fetus: The Social Impact of Amniocentesis in America.* New York: Routledge.

Reardon, J. 2004. *Race to the Finish: Identity and Governance in an Age of Genomics.* Princeton, NJ: Princeton University Press.

Reed, K., and Graves, J. A. M. 1993. *Sex Chromosomes and Sex-Determining Genes.* Langhorne, PA: Harwood Academic Publishers.

Reiter, R. R. 1975. *Towards an Anthropology of Women.* New York: Monthly Review.

Roberts, D. 2003. *Shattered Bonds: The Color of Child Welfare.* New York: Basic Books.

Rocheleau, D. 1988. "Women, Trees and Tenure: Implications for Agroforestry." In *Whose Trees: Proprietary Dimensions of Forestry*, eds. L. Fortmann and J. W. Bruce, 254–272. Boulder: Westview.

Rocheleau, D. 1991. "Gender, Ecology, and the Science of Survival: Stories and Lessons from Kenya." *Agriculture and Human Values* 8(1–2): 156–165.

Rocheleau, D. 1995. "Maps, Numbers, Text, and Context: Mixing Methods in Feminist Political Ecology." *Professional Geographer* 47: 458–466.

Rogers, E. 2003. *Diffusion of Innovation.* Fifth edition. New York: Free Press.

Rosaldo, M. Z., and Lamphere, L. 1974. *Women, Culture and Society*, Stanford: Stanford University Press.

Rose, G. 1995. "Making Space for the Female Subject of Feminism: The Spatial Subversions of Holzer, Kruger and Sherman." In *Mapping the Subject: Geographies of Cultural Transformation*, eds. S. Pile and N. Thrift, 332–354. London: Routledge.

Rose, G. 2001. *Visual Methodologies: An Introduction to the Interpretation of Visual Materials.* London: Sage.

Rosenberg, K. R. 1992. "The Evolution of Modern Human Childbirth." *Yearbook of Physical Anthropology* 35: 89–124.

Rosser, S. V. 1994. *Women's Health: Missing from U.S. Medicine.* Bloomington: Indiana University Press.

Rosser, S. V. 2004. *The Science Glass Ceiling: Academic Women Scientists and the Struggle to Succeed.* New York: Routledge.

Rosser, S. V. 2005. "Through the Lenses of Feminist Theory: Focus on Women and Information Technology." *Frontiers: A Journal of Women Studies* 26: 1–23.

Rosser, S. V., and Chameau, J. L. 2006. "Institutionalization, Sustainability, and Repeatability of ADVANCE for Institutional Transformation." *Journal of Technology Transfer* 31: 335–344.

Rosser, S. V., and Lane, E. O. 2002. "A History of Funding for Women's Programs at the National Science Foundation: From Individual POWRE Approaches to the ADVANCE of Institutional Approaches." *Journal of Women and Minorities in Science and Engineering* 8(3–4): 327–346.

Rosser, S. V., and Zieseniss, M. 1998. *Final Report on Professional Opportunities for Women in Research and Education (POWRE) Workshop.* Gainesville, FL: Center for Women's Studies and Gender Research.

Rossiter, M. 1982. *Women Scientists in America: Struggles and Strategies to 1940.* Baltimore, MD: Johns Hopkins Press.

Roughgarden, J. 2004. *Evolution's Rainbow: Diversity, Gender, and Sexuality in Nature and People.* Berkeley: University of California Press.

Russell, P. 1991. "Men Only? The Myths about European Paleolithic Artists." In *The Archaeology of Gender,* eds. D. Walde and N. Willows, 346–351. Calgary: Archaeological Association, University of Calgary.

Ruzek, S., Clarke, A., and Olesen, V. 1997. "Social, Biomedical, and Feminist Models of Women's Health." In *Women's Health: Complexities and Differences,* eds. S. Ruzek, V. Olesen, and A. Clarke, 11–28. Columbus: Ohio State University Press.

Sanford Jr., R. L., Saldarriaga, J., Clark, K., Uhl, C., and Herrera, R. 1985. "Amazon Rain-Forest Fires." *Science* 227: 53–55.

Sarkar, S. 2006. "From Genes as Determinants to DNA as Resource: Historical Notes on Development and Genetics." *Genes in Development: Re-Reading the Molecular Paradigm,* eds. E. Neumann-Held and C. Rehmann-Sutter, 77–97. Durham, NC: Duke University Press.

Satterthwait, L. 1987. "Socioeconomic Implications of Australian Aboriginal Net Hunting." *Man* (n.s.) 22(4): 613–636.

Scheper-Hughes, N., and Wacquant, L. eds. 2002. *Commodifying Bodies.* Thousand Oaks, CA: Sage.

Schiebinger, L. 1987. "Skeletons in the Closet: The First Illustrations of the Female Skeleton in Eighteenth Century Anatomy." In *The Making of the Modern Body,* eds. C. Gallagher and T. Laqueur, 42–82. Berkeley: University of California Press.

Schiebinger, L. 1989. *The Mind Has No Sex? Women and the Origins of Modern Science.* Cambridge, MA: Harvard University Press.

Schiebinger, L. 1993. *Nature's Body: Gender in the Making of Modern Science.* Boston: Beacon.

Schiebinger, L. 1999. *Has Feminism Changed Science?* Cambridge, MA: Harvard University Press.

Schiebinger, L., ed. 2003. "Feminism Inside the Sciences." *Signs: Journal of Women in Culture and Society* 28: 859–922.

Schiebinger, L. 2004. *Plants and Empire: Colonial Bioprospecting in the Atlantic World.* Cambridge, MA: Harvard University Press.

Schmidt, R., and Voss, B. eds. 2000. *Archaeologies of Sexuality.* London: Routledge.

Schuurman, N. 2002. "Women and Technology in Geography: A Cyborg Manifesto for GIS." *Canadian Geographer* 46: 262–265.

Seel, R. 2000. "Culture and Complexity: New Insights on Organisational Change." *Organisations & People* 7(2): 2–9.

Sinclair, A. H., Foster, J. W., Spencer, J. A., Page, D. C., Palmer, M., Goodfellow, P., and Marshall-Graves, J. A. 1988. "Sequences Homologous to ZFY, a Candidate Human Sex-Determining Gene, Are Autosomal in Marsupials." *Nature* 336: 780–783.

Slocum, S. 1975. "Woman the Gatherer: Male Bias in Anthropology." In *Towards an Anthropology of Women,* ed. R. R. Reiter, 36–50. New York: Monthly Review.

Soderman, K., Bergstrom, E., Lorentson, R., and Alfredson, H. 2000. "Bone Mass and

Muscle Strength in Young Female Soccer Players." *Calcified Tissue International* 67(4): 297–303.

Soffer, O. 1985a. *The Upper Palaeolithic on the Central Russian Plain.* New York: Academic Press.

Soffer, O. 1985b. "Patterns of Intensification as Seen from the Upper Paleolithic of the Central Russian Plain." In *Prehistoric Hunter-Gatherers: The Emergence of Cultural Complexity,* eds. T. D. Price and J. A. Brown, 235–270. New York: Academic Press.

Soffer, O. 2004. "Recovering Perishable Technologies Through Use Wear on Tools: Preliminary Evidence for Upper Paleolithic Weaving and Net Making." *Current Anthropology* 45(3): 407–413.

Soffer, O., Adovasio, J. M., and Hyland, D. 2000. "The 'Venus' Figurines: Textiles, Basketry and Gender in the Upper Paleolithic." *Current Anthropology* 41(4): 511–537.

Soffer, O., Adovasio, J. M., and Hyland, D. 2002. "Perishable Technologies and Invisible People: Nets, Baskets and 'Venus' Wear ca. 26,000 BP." In *Enduring Records: The Environmental and Cultural Heritage of Wetlands,* ed. B. Purdy, 233–245. Oxford: Oxbow.

Sonnert, G., and Holton, G. 1995. *Who Succeeds in Science? The Gender Dimension.* New Brunswick, NJ: Rutgers University Press.

Spain, D. 1992. *Gendered Space.* Chapel Hill, NC: University of North Carolina Press.

Spanier, B. 1995. *Im/partial Science: Gender Ideology in Molecular Biology.* Bloomington: Indiana University Press.

Spar, D. 2006. *The Baby Business: How Money, Science, and Politics Drive the Commerce of Conception.* Cambridge, MA: Harvard Business School Press.

Sparke, M. 1998. "Mapped Bodies and Disembodied Maps: (Dis)placing Cartographic Struggle in Colonial Canada." In *Places Through the Body,* eds. H. J. Nast and S. Pile, 305–337. New York: Routledge.

Sperling, L. 1992. "Farmer Participation and the Development of Bean Varieties in Rwanda." In *Diversity, Farmer Knowledge, and Sustainability,* eds. J. Moock and R. Rhoades. Ithaca, NY: Cornell University Press.

Sperling, L. 2001. "The Effect of the Civil War on Rwanda's Beans Seed System and Unusual Bean Diversity." *Biodiversity and Conservation* 10: 989–1009.

Sperling, L., Ashby, J. A., Smith, M. E., Weltzien, E., and McGuire, S. 2001. "A Framework for Analyzing Participatory Plant Breeding Approaches and Results." *Euphytica* 122: 439–450.

Sperling, L., and Berkowitz, P. 1994. *Partners in Selection: Bean Breeders and Women Bean Experts.* Washington, DC: Consultative Group on International Agricultural Research Gender Program.

Sperling, L., Loevinsohn, M., and Ntambomvura, B. 1993. "Rethinking the Farmer's Role in Plant Breeding: Local Bean Experts and On-Station Selection in Rwanda." *Experimental Agriculture* 29: 509–519.

Sperling, L., and Muyaneza, S. 1995. "Intensifying Production Among Smallholder Farmers: The Impact of Improved Climbing Beans in Rwanda." *African Crop Science Journal* 3(1): 117–125.

Sperling, L., and Scheidegger, U. 1995. *Participatory Selection of Beans in Rwanda: Results, Methods and Institutional Issues*. Gatekeeper Series No. 51. London: International Institute for Environment and Development.

Spoor, F., Leakey, M. G., Gathogo, P. N., Brown, F. H., Anton, S. C., McDougall, I., Kiarie, C., Manthi, F. K., and Leakey, L. N. 2007. "Implications of New Early *Homo* Fossils from Ileret, East of Lake Turkjana, Kenya." *Nature* 448: 688–691.

SRI International. 1994. *The Visiting Professorships for Women Program: Lowering the Hurdles for Women in Science and Engineering. NSF Summary and Comments. (NSF 93-159)*. Arlington, VA: SRI International.

Stacey, J. 1988. "Desperately Seeking Difference." In *The Female Gaze*, eds. L. Gamman and M. Marshment, 112–200. London: Woman's Press.

Steinpreis, R., Anders, K., and Ritzke, D. 1999. "The Impact of Gender on the Review of the Curricula Vitae of Job Applicants and Tenure Candidates: A National Empirical Study." *Sex Roles* 41: 509–528.

Stewart, A. J., LaVaque-Manty, D., and Malley, J. E. 2004. "Recruiting Women Faculty in Science and Engineering: Preliminary Evaluation of One Intervention Model." *Journal of Women and Minorities in Science and Engineering* 10: 361–375.

Stewart, A. J., Malley, J. E., and LaVaque-Manty, D. 2007. "Faculty Recruitment: Mobilizing Science and Engineering Faculty." In *Transforming Science and Engineering: Advancing Academic Women*, eds. A. Stewart et al., 133–151. Ann Arbor: University of Michigan Press.

Strang, D., and Soule, S. A. 1998. "Diffusion in Organizations and Social Movements: From Hybrid Corn to Poison Pills." *Annual Review of Sociology* 2: 265–290.

Strathern, M. 2005. *Kinship, Law and the Unexpected: Relatives Are Always a Surprise*. Cambridge, UK: Cambridge University Press.

Sturm, S. Forthcoming a. "Gender Equity as Institutional Transformation: The Pivotal Role of 'Organizational Catalysts.'" In *Advancing Women in Science and Engineering: Lessons for Institutional Transformation*, eds. A. Stewart et al. Ann Arbor: University of Michigan Press.

Sturm, S. Forthcoming b. "Advancing Gender Equality in the Workplace: A New Public Approach." *Harvard Journal of Law & Gender*.

Sturm, S. 2006. "The Architecture of Inclusion: Advancing Workplace Equity in Higher Education." *Harvard Journal of Law & Gender* 29(2): 247–334.

Suchman, L. 2005. "Agency in Technology Design: Feminist Reconfigurations." Presented at Gendered Innovations in Science and Engineering Conference, Clayman Institute for Gender Research, April 15–16.

Swoboda, F. 1995. "Glass Ceiling Firmly in Place, Panel Finds." *The Washington Post*. March 16: A1, A18.

Sykes, B. 2003. *Adam's Curse: A Future without Men*. New York: Bantam.

Tague, R., and Lovejoy, C. O. 1986. "The Obstetric Pelvis of A.L.288-1 (Lucy)." *Journal of Human Evolution* 15: 237–255.

Tanner, N., and Zihlman, A. 1976. "Women in Evolution. Part I. Innovation and Selection in Human Origins." *Signs: Journal of Women in Culture and Society* 1(3): 585–608.

Thompson, C. 2005. *Making Parents: The Ontological Choreography of Reproductive Technologies.* Cambridge, MA: MIT Press.

Thompson, C. 2007. "Why We Should, in Fact, Pay for Egg Donation." *Regenerative Medicine* 2(2): 203–209.

Tierney, W. 1988. "Organizational Culture in Higher Education." *Journal of Higher Education* 59(1): 2–21.

Tinker, I. 2004. "Challenging Wisdom, Changing Policies: The Women in Development Movement." In *Developing Power: How Women Transformed International Development,* eds. A. S. Fraser and I. Tinker, 65–77. New York: Feminist Press.

Tobias, P. 1965. "*Australopithecus, Homo habilis,* Tool-Using and Tool-Making." *Nature* 209: 953–960.

Tringham, R. 1991. "Households with Faces: The Challenge of Gender in Prehistoric Architectural Remains." In *Engendering Archaeology: Women and Prehistory,* eds. J. Gero and M. Conkey, 93–131. Oxford: Basil Blackwell.

Trinkaus, E. 2005. "The Adiposity Paradox in the Middle Danubian Gravettian." *Anthropologie* XLIII/2: 101–109.

Trix, F., and Psenka, C. 2003. "Exploring the Color of Glass: Letters of Recommendation for Female and Male Medical Faculty." *Discourse and Society* 14: 191–220.

"University Leaders Pledge to Lift Barriers for Women Faculty." 2005. *The Stanford Report.* December 7: 13.

Urry, M. 2000. "The Status of Women in Astronomy." *STATUS:* 1-4, 7. Electronic media: www.aas.org/cswa/status/status_jun00.pdf. Accessed August 20, 2007.

Urry, M. 2005. "Diminished by Discrimination." *Washington Post.* February 6: B04.

Urry, M., Danly, L., and Schreier, E. 1993. *Baltimore Charter for Women in Astronomy.* Electronic media: http://www.stsci.edu/stsci/meetings/WiA/BaltoCharter.html. Accessed August 20, 2007.

U.S. Department of Health and Human Services. National Institutes of Health. 2000. *Implementation of the NIH Guidelines on the Inclusion of Women and Minorities as Subjects in Clinical Research. Comprehensive Report (Fiscal Year 1997 Tracking Data) Second Revision May 2000.*

U.S. Government Accountability Office. 2004. *Gender Issues: Women's Participation in the Sciences Has Increased, But Agencies Need to Do More to Ensure Compliance with Title IX.* Electronic media: http://www.gao.gov/htext/d04639.html. Accessed August 20, 2007.

Valian, V. 1998. *Why So Slow? The Advancement of Women.* Cambridge, MA: MIT Press.

Valian, V. 2001. *The Advancement of Women in Science and Engineering: Why So Slow?* Rice University webcast: http://webcast.rice.edu/speeches/20010329valian.html. Accessed August 20, 2007.

Vandiver, P., Soffer, O., Klíma, B., and Svoboda, J. 1989. "The Origins of Ceramic Technology at Dolní Vestonice, Czechoslovakia." *Science* 246: 1002–1008.

Vandiver, P., Soffer, O., Klíma, B., and Svoboda, J. 1990. "Venuses and Wolverines: The Origins of Ceramic Technology at Dolní Vestonice, ca. 26,000 BP." In *Ceram-*

ics and Civilization, Volume 5, ed. D. Kingery, 13–81. Westville, OH: American Ceramics Society.

Vitousek, P. M., Mooney, H. A., Lubchenco, J., and Melillo, J. M. 1997. "Human Domination of Earth's Ecosystems." *Science* 277(5325): 494–499.

Vollrath, D., Foote, S., Hilton, A., Brown, L. G., Beer-Romero, P., Bogan, J. S., and Page, D. C. 1992. "The Human Y Chromosome: A 43-Interval Map Based on Naturally Occurring Deletions." *Science* 258: 52–59.

Wadley, L. ed. 1997. *Our Gendered Past: Archaeological Studies of Gender in Southern Africa.* Johannesburg: University of Witwatersrand Press.

Waldby, C., and Mitchell, R. 2006. *Tissue Economies: Blood, Organs, and Cell Lines in Late Capitalism.* Durham, NC: Duke University Press.

Walker, A., and Leakey, R. 1978. "The Hominids of East Turkana." *Scientific American* 239: 54–66.

Walker, P. 1995. "Problems of Preservation and Sexism in Sexing: Some Lessons from Historical Collections for Paleodemographers." In *Grave Reflections: Portraying the Past Through Cemetery Studies*, eds. I. Saunders and A. Herring, 31–47. Toronto: Canadian Scholar's Press.

Walker, P. 2005. "Greater Sciatic Notch Morphology: Sex, Age, and Population Differences." *American Journal of Physical Anthropology* 127: 385–391.

Walker, P., Johnson, J., and Lambert, P. 1988. "Age and Sex Biases in the Preservation of Human Skeletal Remains." *American Journal of Physical Anthropology* 76: 183–188.

Walrath, D. E., Turner, P., and Bruzek, J. 2004. "Reliability Test of the Visual Assessment of Cranial Traits for Sex Determination." *American Journal of Physical Anthropology* 125: 132–137.

Walsh, E. 1995. *Divided Lives.* New York: Simon and Schuster.

Washburn, S. L., and Lancaster, C. S. 1968. "The Evolution of Hunting." In *Man the Hunter*, eds. R. B. Lee and I. DeVore, 293–303. Chicago: Aldine.

Watkins, J. K., Pyburn, A., and Cressey, P. 2000. "Community Relations: What the Practicing Archaeologist Needs to Know to Work Effectively with Local and/or Descendant Communities." In *Teaching Archaeology in the Twenty-First Century*, eds. S. Bender and G. S. Smith, 73–82. Washington, DC: Society for American Archaeology.

Watson, P. J., and Kennedy, M. 1991. "The Development of Horticulture in the Eastern Woodlands of North America: Women's Role." In *Engendering Archaeology: Women and Prehistory*, eds. J. Gero and M. Conkey, 255–275. Oxford: Basil Blackwell.

Weber, R. 1997. "Manufacturing Gender in Commercial and Military Cockpit Design." *Science, Technology, and Human Values* 22: 235–253.

Weiss, K. W. 1972. "On the Systematic Bias in Skeletal Sexing." *American Journal of Physical Anthropology* 37: 239–250.

Wennerås, C., and Wold, A. 1997. "Nepotism and Sexism in Peer Review." *Nature* 387: 341–343.

Westoby, J. 1989. *Introduction to World Forestry.* Oxford: Basil Blackwell.

White, R. 2001. "Professor Jennifer A.M. Graves, FAA." *Women in Science Network Journal* 58 (November 2001): 12–13. Electronic media: http://wisenet-australia .org/. Accessed August 20, 2007.

Wilkie, L. A. 2003. *The Archaeology of Mothering: An African-American Midwife's Tale.* London: Routledge.

Wilkie, T. 1991. "At the Flick of a Genetic Switch." *London Independent.* May 13: 18.

Williams, J. 2000. *Unbending Gender: Why Family and Work Conflict and What to Do About It.* New York: Oxford University Press.

Williams, N. 1990. "So That's What Little Boys Are Made Of." *Guardian.* July 20.

Wilmsen, C. 2005. "Perils on the Road to Participatory Research." In *Urban and Community Forestry: Working Together to Facilitate Change,* eds. Z. H. Ning and K. K. Abdollahi, 49–56. Baton Rouge, LA: Southern University.

Witcombe, J. R., Joshi, K. D., Gyawali, S., Musa, A. M., Johansen, C., Virk, D. S., and Sthapit, B. R. 2005. "Participatory Plant Breeding Is Better Described as Highly Client-Oriented Plant Breeding." *Experimental Agriculture* 41: 299–319.

Wizemann, T. M., and Pardue, M. eds. 2001. *Exploring the Biological Contributions to Human Health: Does Sex Matter?* Institute of Medicine. Washington, DC: National Academies Press.

Wolf, D. L. 1996. *Feminist Dilemmas in Fieldwork.* Boulder: Westview.

Wolf-Wendel, L., Twombly, S., and Rice, S. 2003. *The Two-Body Problem: Dual-Career Couple Hiring Policies in Higher Education.* Baltimore, MD: Johns Hopkins University Press.

Wolpoff, M. 1971. "Competitive Exclusion among Lower Pleistocene Hominids: The Single Species Hypothesis." *Man* 6: 601–614.

Wood, B. A. 1985. "Sexual Dimorphism in the Hominid Fossil Record." In *Human Sexual Dimorphism,* eds. J. Ghesquiere, R. D. Martin, and F. Newcombe, 105–123. London: Taylor and Francis.

Woodbury, S., and Gess-Newsome, J. 2002. "Overcoming the Paradox of Change without Difference: A Model of Change in the Arena of Fundamental School Reform." *Educational Policy* 16(5): 763–782.

Woolf, V. 1929. *A Room of One's Own.* New York: Harcourt, Brace.

Wyer, M. ed. 2001. *Women, Science, and Technology: A Feminist Reader.* New York: Routledge.

Wylie, A. 1992. "The Interplay of Evidential Constraints and Political Interests: Recent Archaeological Research on Gender." *American Antiquity* 57(1): 15–35.

Wylie, A. 1995. "Doing Philosophy as a Feminist: Longino on the Search for a Feminist Epistemology." *Philosophical Topics* 23(2): 345–358.

Wylie, A. 1997. "The Engendering of Archaeology: Refiguring Feminist Science Studies." *Osiris* 12: 80–99.

Wylie, A. 2001. "Doing Social Science as a Feminist: The Engendering of Archaeology." In *Science, Medicine, Technology: The Difference Feminism Has Made,* eds. A. N. H. Creager, E. Lunbeck, and L. Schiebinger, 23–45. Chicago: University of Chicago Press.

Xie, Y., and Shauman, K. 2003. *Women in Science: Career Processes and Outcomes.* Cambridge, MA: Harvard University Press.

Zihlman, A. L. 1985. "*Australopithecus afarensis*: Two Sexes or Two Species?" In *Hominid Evolution: Past, Present, and Future*, ed. P. V. Tobias, 213–220. New York: Alan R. Liss.

Zihlman, A. L. 1997. "The Paleolithic Glass Ceiling: Women in Human Evolution." In *Women in Human Evolution*, ed. L. D. Hager, 91–113. London: Routledge.

Zinsser, J. P., and Hayes, J. C. 2006. *Emilie Du Châtelet: Rewriting Enlightenment Philosophy and Science.* Oxford: Voltaire Foundation.

Zuckerman, H., Cole, J., and Bruer, J. eds. 1991. *The Outer Circle: Women in the Scientific Community.* New Haven: Yale University Press.

Index